AF478084

Souls Grown Deep like the Rivers

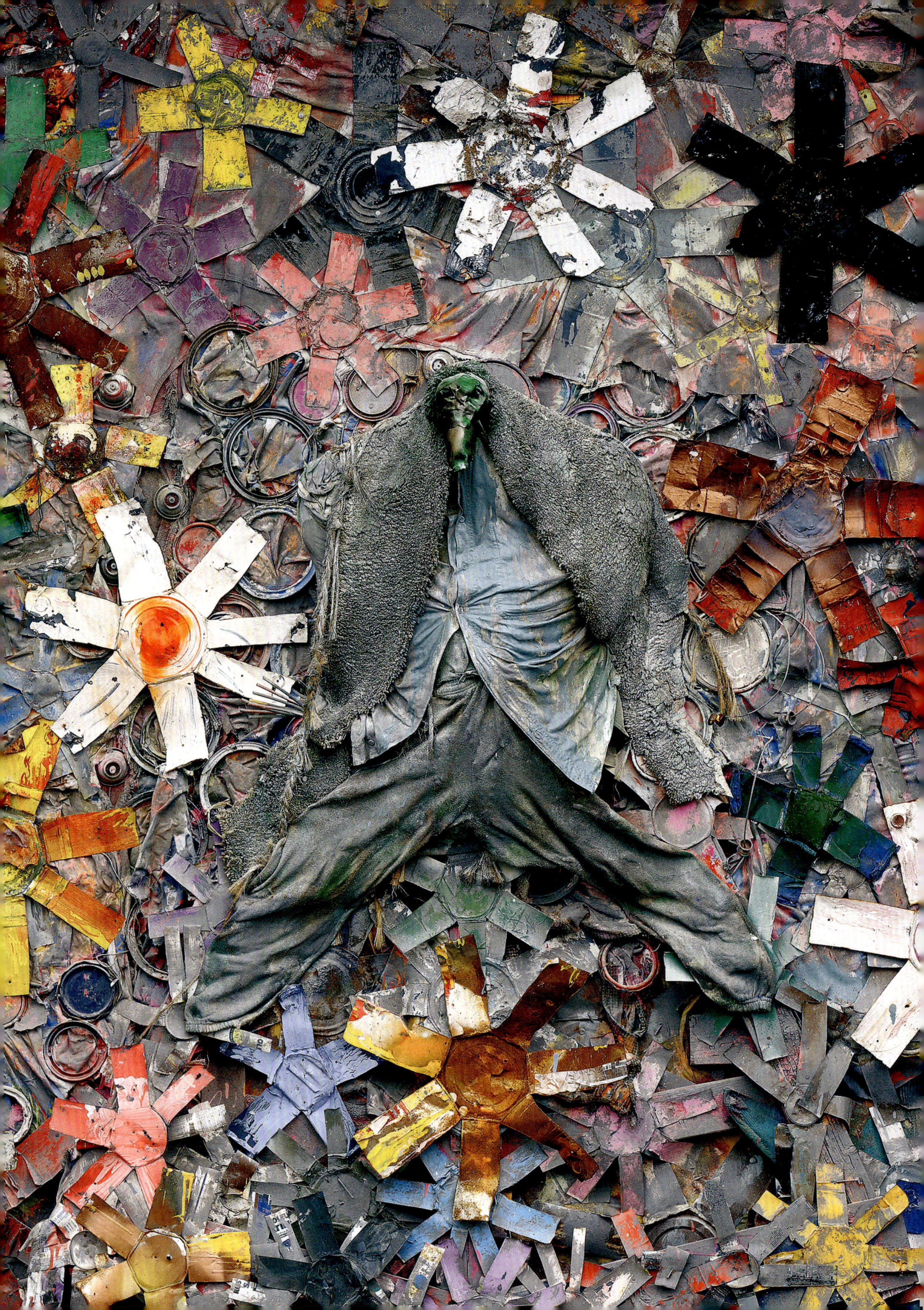

Souls Grown Deep like the Rivers

Black Artists from the American South

Royal Academy of Arts

First published on the occasion of the exhibition 'Souls Grown Deep like the Rivers: Black Artists from the American South'

Royal Academy of Arts
17 March – 18 June 2023

Sponsored by

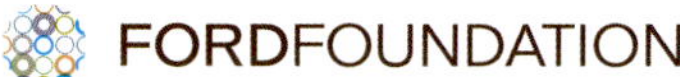

Brooke Brown Barzun and
Matthew Barzun

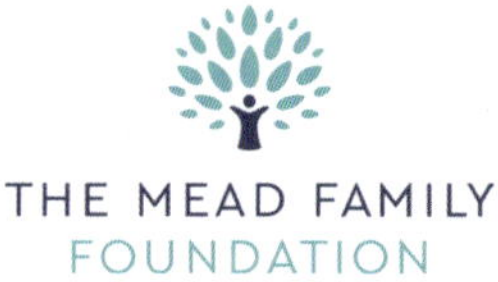

THE MEAD FAMILY
FOUNDATION

This exhibition has been made possible as a result of the Government Indemnity Scheme. The Royal Academy of Arts would like to thank HM Government for providing indemnity and the Department for Digital, Culture, Media & Sport and Arts Council England for arranging the indemnity.

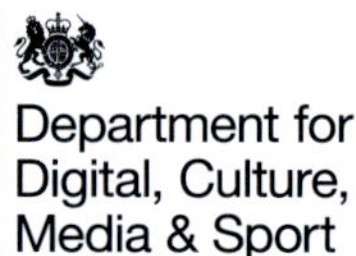

Department for
Digital, Culture,
Media & Sport

Director of Exhibitions
Andrea Tarsia

Exhibition Curators
Raina Lampkins-Fielder
with Emma Yau
Axel Rüger
with Rebecca Bray

Exhibition Organisation
Flora Fricker
with Abbie Latham

**Photographic and Copyright
Co-ordination**
Caroline Arno

Exhibition Catalogue
Royal Academy Publications
Florence Dassonville, Production
    and Distribution Co-ordinator
Carola Krueger, Production
    and Distribution Manager
Peter Sawbridge, Head of Publishing
    and Editorial Director

Design: Patrick Morrissey / Unlimited
Colour origination and print:
Gomer Press, Wales

British Library Cataloguing-in-Publication Data
A catalogue record for this book is available from the British Library

ISBN 978-1-912520-95-4

Distributed outside the United States and Canada by ACC Art Books Ltd, Riverside House, Dock Lane, Melton, Woodbridge, IP12 1PE

Distributed in the United States and Canada by ARTBOOK | D.A.P., 75 Broad Street, Suite 630, New York, NY 10004

Editorial Note
Dimensions of all works of art are given in centimetres, height before width before depth.

Illustrations
Page 3: detail of cat. 1
Page 5: detail of cat. 13
Page 6: detail of cat. 54
Page 10: detail of cat. 29
Page 32: detail of cat. 49
Page 120: detail of cat. 23

Acknowledgements
The Royal Academy of Arts acknowledges the assistance of the following individuals in the making of this exhibition and its catalogue: Matt Arnett, Ronni Baer, Loretta Pettway Bennett, Laura Bickford, Rebecca Bissonnet, Giselle Blanco-Santana, Polly Chiapetta, Debra Collis, Edwina Dunn, Kaywin Feldman, Jayquan Franklin, Yanique Hall, Danny Horner, Isabel Horovitz, Amy Horst, Clive Humby, Katherine Jentleson, Jay Johnson, Ammiel Lewis, Charlie Lucas, Joe Minter, Anastasia Papaonisiforou, Amanda Paulley, Mark Pennell, Kaiyanna Price, Mathew Rausch, Cleo Roberts-Komireddi, Amy Simon, Caroline Snowberger, Darren Walker, June Wallis, and Katy Wickremesinghe.

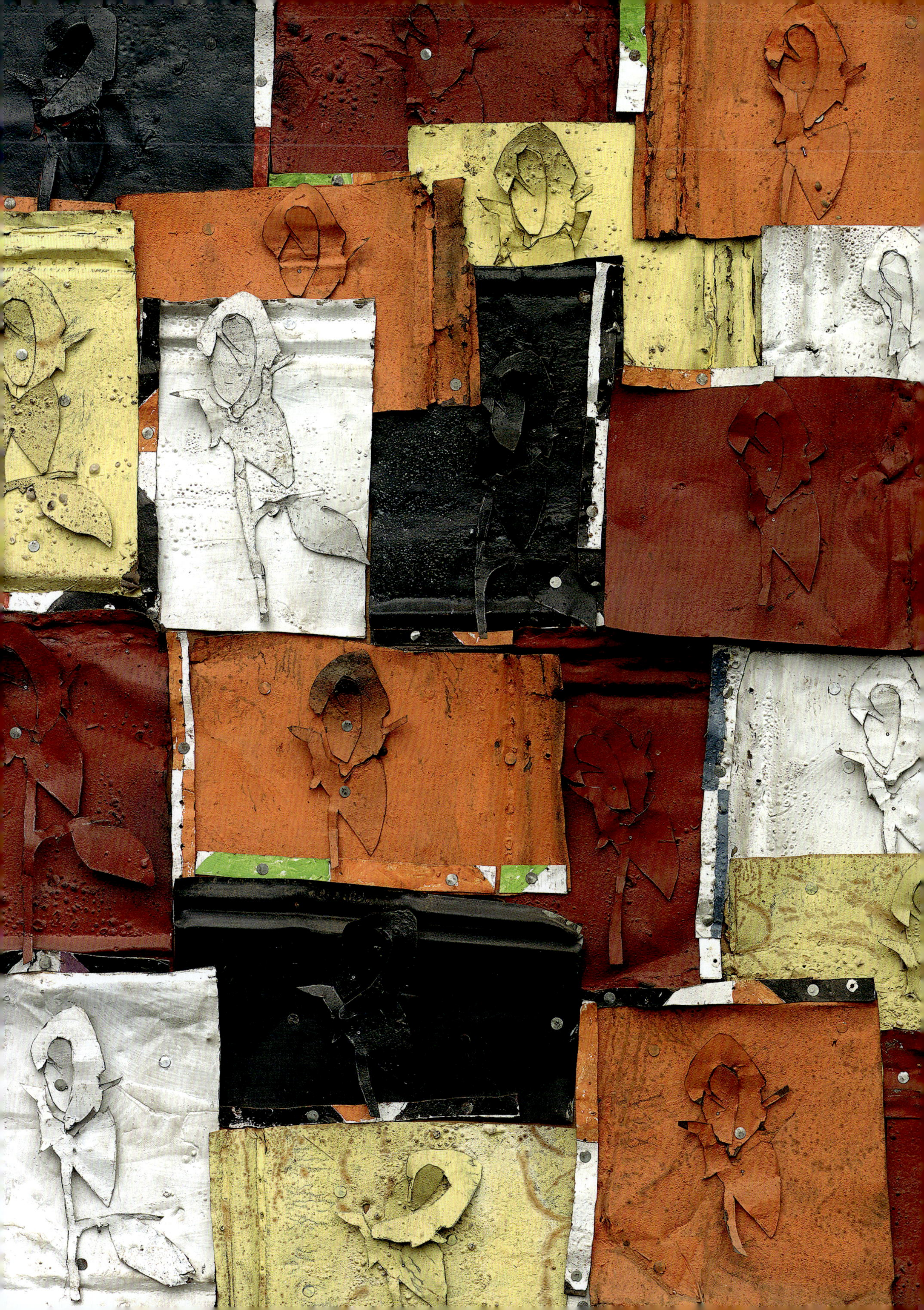

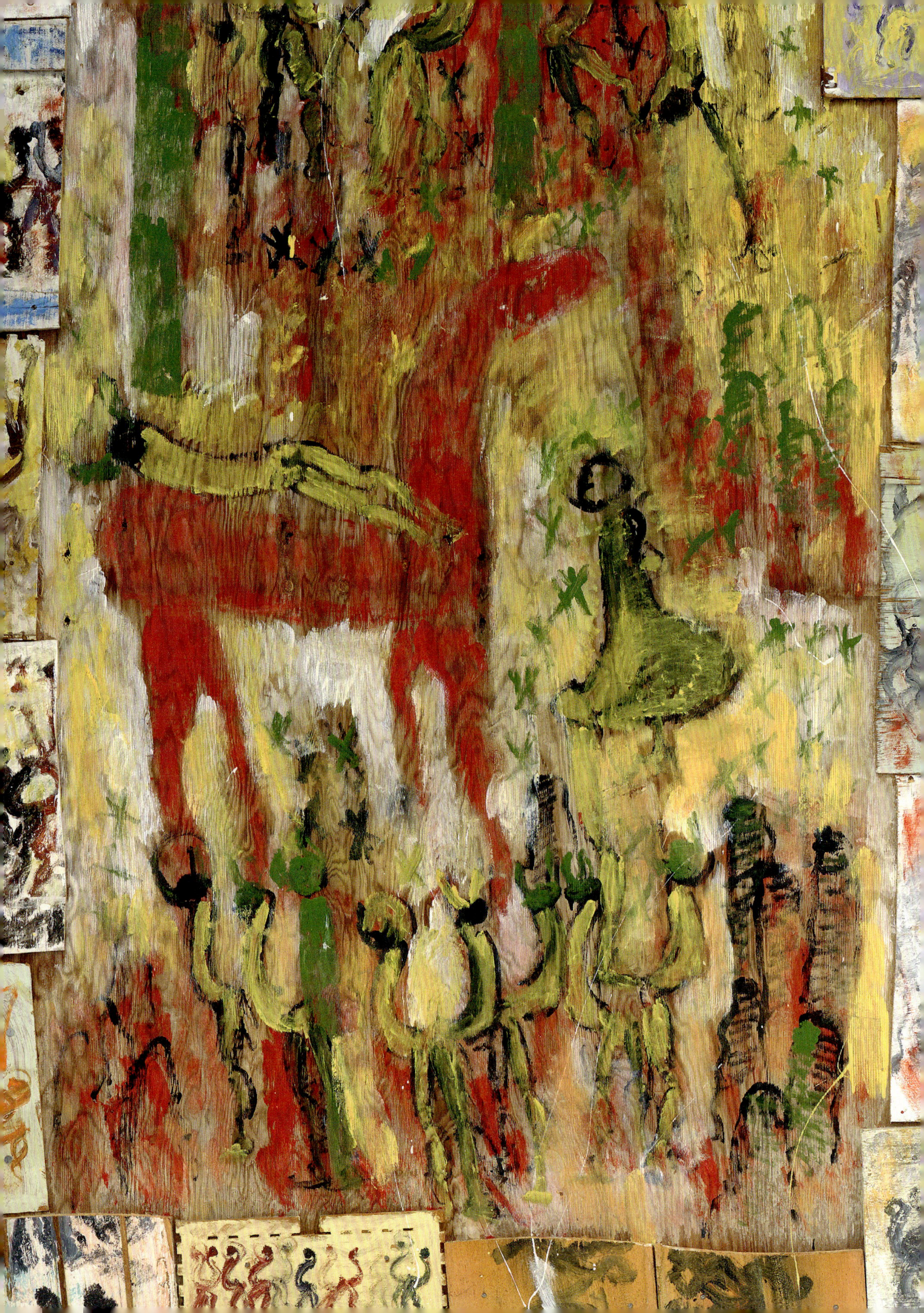

Contents

President's Foreword

This exhibition presents the work of Black artists who were born in the American South between 1887 and 1965. Instead of taking part in the Great Migration of 1910–70, during which millions of Black people moved to the Northern States with the promise of greater economic prosperity, they stayed in their native communities in the South. There they were subjected to the harrowing legacy of the region's history of enslavement. They endured poor economic conditions, legalised racism and segregation, lynchings, murder and myriad of forms of violence. In their work they confronted not only the historical background of the South but also the realities of economic and social inequalities and racial conflict. Much of their inspiration came from everyday life, historical and current events, religion and music, as well as African traditions. With limited access to traditional artists' materials they frequently turned to scrap metal, found objects, branches, roots, clay, soil and composite materials, all of which they transformed into some of the most imaginative and powerful artworks of the twentieth century.

The Royal Academy was founded by a group of artists, led by Sir Joshua Reynolds PRA, whose aim was to establish Britain's first art school, offering a formalised training for artists and architects. This aim has always remained at the heart of the institution. Few of the artists in this exhibition enjoyed an education beyond elementary level, and none had access to formal artistic training. Instead they learned their skills from more informal sources, often family members or friends. It is thus particularly poignant that the Royal Academy is showing their work and thereby stimulating discourse about different modes of learning and the teaching of artistic skills.

The exhibition was partly inspired by the Royal Academy's Summer Exhibition of 2021, co-ordinated by Yinka Shonibare CBE RA, which included many works by artists from Africa and the diaspora as well as African-American artists such as Thornton Dial and Mary Lee Bendolph, who are also featured here. This brought us into contact with the Souls Grown Deep Foundation in Atlanta, Georgia, which generously lent several works to that exhibition. The idea soon came about of organising an exhibition to introduce the British public more fully to the extraordinary collection of the Georgia-based art collector William Arnett (1939–2020), who established the Souls Grown Deep Foundation. Most works in the show are being seen in Europe for the first time.

We would like to express our deepest gratitude to the President of the Souls Grown Deep Foundation, Maxwell L. Anderson, and to its curator, Raina Lampkins-Fielder, for so readily agreeing to embark on this project and for lending us such an extraordinary number of works. Raina's expertise in the field and her knowledge of the artists and their work have been invaluable in her role as the show's principal curator, in which she has been ably assisted by Emma Yau. We would also like to thank the Foundation's Board Chair, Mary Margaret Pettway, and Scott Browning, Director of Collections, for his help with many organisational and practical matters. Max, Raina and Scott also kindly hosted our curators on a memorable trip to Alabama during which they visited Joe Minter's *African Village in America* in Birmingham, and Gee's Bend for the first Airing of the Quilts Festival.

At the Royal Academy, the exhibition has been curated by Axel Rüger with Rebecca Bray, Assistant Curator. The challenges of a relatively short planning period and the myriad details of the exhibition's organisation were skilfully managed by Flora Fricker with Abbie Latham, and photographic rights and reproduction were overseen by Caroline Arno. We would also like to thank Andrea Tarsia, Director of Exhibitions, and Idoya Beitia, Head of Exhibitions, for their support, and the Royal Academy's Exhibitions Committee, chaired by Stephen Chambers RA, for their enthusiastic endorsement of the project from the outset.

Although most loans have come from the Souls Grown Deep Foundation, we owe a debt of thanks to a few other lenders in the United States: Rand Suffolk, Director of the High Museum of Art in Atlanta; Alex Nyerges, Director of the Virginia Museum of Fine Arts, and Valerie Cassel-Oliver, who generously agreed loans at short notice; Steve Pitkin, not only for the loans but also for brilliant photography; Mary Lee Bendolph, Essie Bendolph Pettway and Rubin Bendolph Jr; Thomas Scanlin; and an anonymous private collection. In London we express our gratitude to Maciej Urbanek and Graham Fleming for sharing with us their passion for Purvis Young and lending several of his works, as well as

to the Zabludowicz Collection for their loan. The exhibition's elegant design and graphics are the work of Ian Gardner of ILK Ltd, with lighting design by Lucy Record. We hope this handsome exhibition catalogue with an essay by Raina Lampkins-Fielder and individual artist's biographies by Rebecca Bray and Emma Yau will serve as a useful introduction to these less well-known artists and their work. It was designed by Patrick Morrissey of Unlimited and the text was copy-edited by Caroline Ellerby. We would like to thank Peter Sawbridge, our Head of Publishing and Editorial Director, for steering the book to publication with the greatest sense of calm and patience.

The exhibition came late into the programme, and presented a considerable financial challenge. We are therefore especially grateful to the Ford Foundation and its President, Darren Walker, who quickly came to our aid. We would also like to thank the Souls Grown Deep Foundation for their financial support as well as Brooke Brown Barzun and Matthew Barzun, the Mead Family Foundation, and Alison Jacques and Hannah Robinson. We are grateful too to Charlie Fellows and Jeremy Epstein of Edel Assanti Gallery for their support and for helping us to bring Lonnie Holley to London to perform at the opening of the exhibition.

Rebecca Salter PRA
President, Royal Academy of Arts

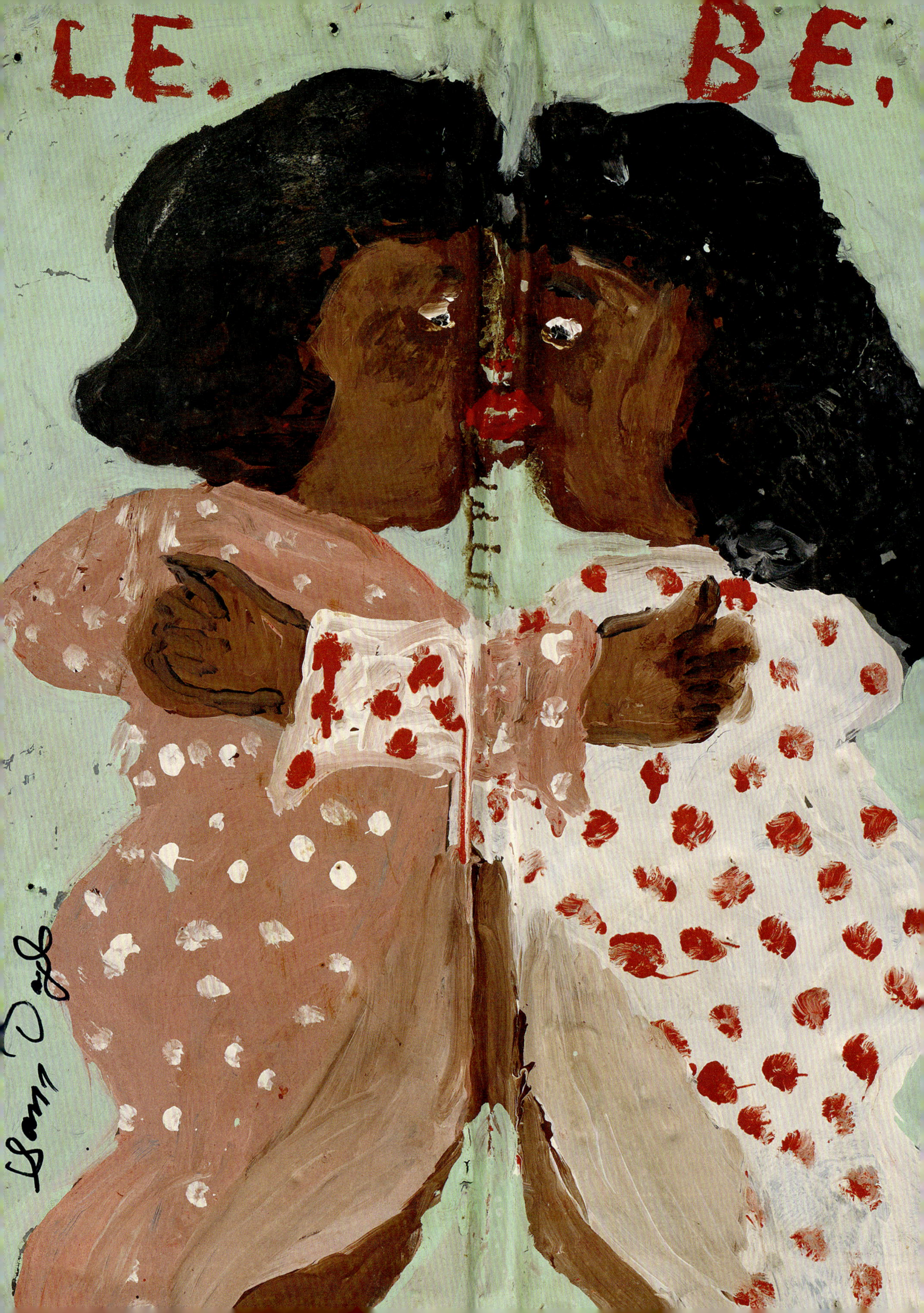
LE.
BE.

Preface

For two centuries before the American Civil War (1861–65), the American South was an agrarian region economically dependent on the enslavement of Black people. The Transatlantic trade in enslaved people was the primary factor in wealth creation in the South, but also benefited families in Britain from the time of Elizabeth I to the Slavery Abolition Act of 1833. Enslavement yielded a massive, unremunerated labour force that spawned industries in commodities ranging from sugar to tobacco, cotton, coffee and corn, enriching traders and enslavers alike.

In 2023 we find ourselves reviewing the lasting stain of racial oppression through various lenses. The murder of George Floyd on 25 May 2020 catalysed a global reassessment of the persistent legacy of racism, amplified by Covid-19's suspension of normal daily life and a coincident opportunity for reflection.

The present exhibition is one of many recent exercises to recalibrate our collective social responsibilities. The erasure of artistic achievements by Black artists from the American South was but one of an infinity of transgressions spawned by slavery. Lynchings, murders and sexual violence were the most heinous examples of the oppression of Black people. But in the cultural sphere, the achievements of Black artists who remained in the South went largely unrecognised, and when acknowledged, have been saddled with patronising epithets ranging from 'self-taught' to 'visionary'.

Twentieth- and twenty-first-century Black artists whose ancestors and families left the South during Reconstruction (1865–77) and the Great Migration (1910–70) were afforded a prospective advantage over those who remained. Life in major American cities in the North, Midwest and West included proximity, if not guaranteed access to universities, museums, galleries and a network of art-world interests. Those artists who remained in the South were effectively excluded from this network.

'Souls Grown Deep like the Rivers' serves to introduce the Royal Academy's audiences to some of the countless Black artists from the South whose creative contributions warrant assessment. And that assessment must no longer be in isolation, like curiosities from an undiscovered land. Instead, the particularities and universalities of these works in various media must be accorded the dignity of art-historical evaluation applied to every other art form throughout history – as the products of women and men whose impulses to make objects were informed by their heritage, contemporary conditions and worldview, and by their talent.

Maxwell L. Anderson
President, Souls Grown Deep Foundation
& Community Partnership

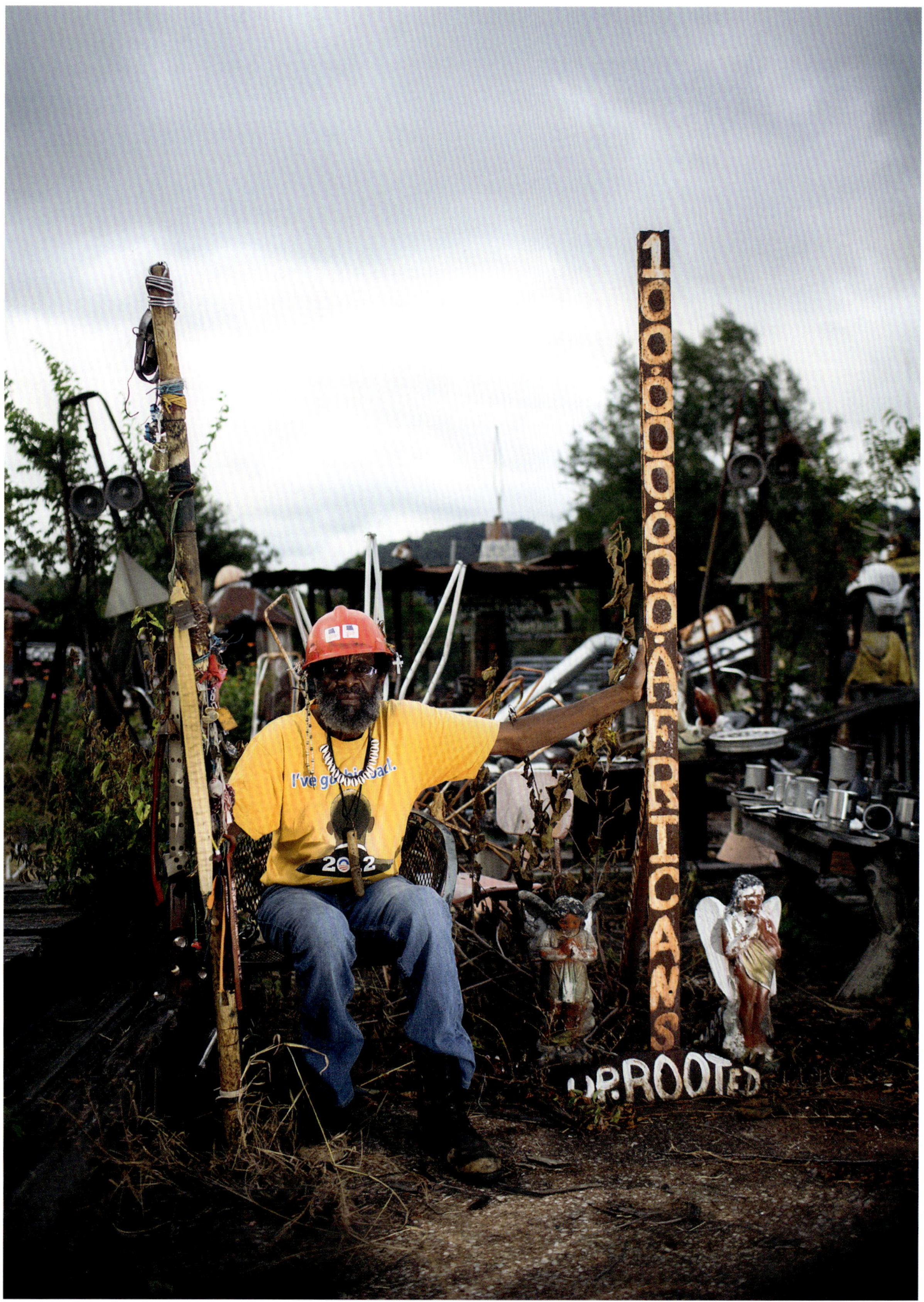

Fig.1
Joe Minter at the entrance to his *African Village in America,* Birmingham, Alabama

Stories of Reclamation

Raina Lampkins-Fielder

For generations, Black artists from the southern United States, working with little recognition, have created masterpieces whose subjects and material often resound with the harrowing history of the region – its barbaric practice of slavery and the Jim Crow laws. These cruel and divisive State and local segregation regulations effectively made Black people second-class citizens by restricting both their physical freedom and their freedom of expression.[1]

The works shown here respond to issues and themes that, though shot through the lens of the United States, are global in nature: economic inequality and oppression, social marginalisation, racial conflict, the uncertain political landscape, the environment and the influence of place, and ancestral memory. Not only are these concerns played out through their various subjects, they are also implicit in the materiality of the works themselves. Having for generations been denied access to education beyond their elementary years, let alone given entrée to tertiary education and classical art training, many southern Black artists established informal, alternative academies of sorts, in which kitchens and porches took the place of traditional lecture halls and studios, and the professor was often a cousin, an uncle, a mother, a grandmother or a family friend.

These extraordinary artists have lived and worked throughout the American South, where their deep family roots and creative connections remain. There are many diverse areas in the South: from the sandy banks of South Carolina to the Mississippi Delta, from isolated, rural areas like Gee's Bend and Marion, Alabama, to the urban centres of Atlanta, Memphis and Miami. Most of the work here was made in the region of the United States encompassing rural Georgia, Alabama and Mississippi, the so-called 'Black Belt', a term that refers to the region's rich black soil, as well as to its association with the legacies of enslaved African Americans, whose forced labour shaped the economic, social and agrarian culture of the deep South.

The resulting collective body of work is defined by the artists' use of recycled and found materials, both mass-produced and organic – from house paint, scrap metal, wooden planks, rags and textile remnants, old paint tins, rusted tools, worn clothing, toys, shoes, disused furniture and electronic appliances, to driftwood, roots, stone pieces, animal bones, soil and feathers. This 'trash' is transformed into art through their imagination. A dearth of economic resources and a lack of access to more conventional art supplies meant that the use of salvaged materials arose out of necessity, and artists had to make do with whatever was readily available. However, conceptual and aesthetic intentions do inform their selection of cast-off objects. Although spent and discarded, found objects are imbued with the energy of their past uses; their history is embedded within the materials themselves. In the hands of these artists, that which has been thrown away or ignored has been reclaimed, reformed, exalted. One may view this reclamation as a metaphor of the brutalisation and resurrection of the Black body itself, having been kidnapped, enslaved, dehumanised, beaten, worked as chattel, and summarily disposed of. The artist Thornton Dial asserted, 'It is exactly the truth that the Negro has been mistreated in the United States, that he [has] been used.'[2] His statement is made even more meaningful within this material context.

These artists are storytellers, recounting tales of hardship, oppression, poverty and racism as well as joy, creation, faith, resilience, family and triumph. Theirs is a story of transcendence, of the recuperative power of recycled – and reimagined – material. By using repurposed materials, each artist has uniquely been able to address these subjects through distinct conceptual and creative practices.

An area rich in iron ore, limestone and coal, all key components in American iron and steel production, the Alabama Black Belt contains a fertile area of artistic exchange and creation. This manifested itself in the work of a group of artists clustered around Birmingham, led by Lonnie Holley and Joe Minter, and in the adjacent town of Bessemer, led by Thornton Dial and Ronald Lockett. Beyond their geographical proximity, these artists shared thematic explorations of American history and the Black experience – the legacy of slavery, the Jim Crow laws, labour issues, the civil rights movement and inequality – as well as their use of found and discarded materials reclaimed from their environment.

Like other artists here, they also share familial and personal ties and were nourished by a profound, decades-long artistic tradition. Thornton Dial was the older cousin of Ronald Lockett, and the mentor to whom Lockett was

to credit his development as an artist. In search of like-minded Black Southern artists, Lonnie Holley met Dial through a former girlfriend, acquiring several of his handmade fishing lures (mid-1980s; cat. 2) in the process; later, in 1987, Holley brought Dial's work to the attention of his friend and collector William Arnett – the eventual founder of the Souls Grown Deep collection – who cited his first visit to Holley's home in 1986 as revelatory: '[Holley] was actually the catalyst who started me on a much deeper search.'[3] Joe Minter, like Holley at the time, created an immersive art environment in his yard. His was named *African Village in America* (see fig. 1), and was composed largely of sculptures fabricated from found objects, scrap metal and discarded materials in metropolitan Birmingham.

Thornton Dial: 'My art is the evidence of my freedom'[4]

A former steelworker, Thornton Dial was a master assembler and manipulator of metal, and skilled in sourcing both manufactured and organic materials from his environment, among them tin, wood, rope, salvaged fabric, plant life, discarded plastic objects and other non-biodegradable materials. His highly original artistic output, encompassing paintings, drawings, assemblages and sculpture – often executed on a massive scale – is diverse in both medium and form.

Dial's mixed-media work *Stars of Everything* (2004; cat. 1) explores the long history of Black creativity by finding inspiration in the symbolic energies of discarded objects and their transformation. The work's central figure – part American eagle, part buzzard in a suit of worn clothing, old carpet and strands of rope, Dial's markers of social oppression – can be understood as a surreal self-portrait: Dial saw himself as a sort of scavenger or 'pick-up bird', an acknowledgement of his practice of artistic recycling. The figure is embedded within a

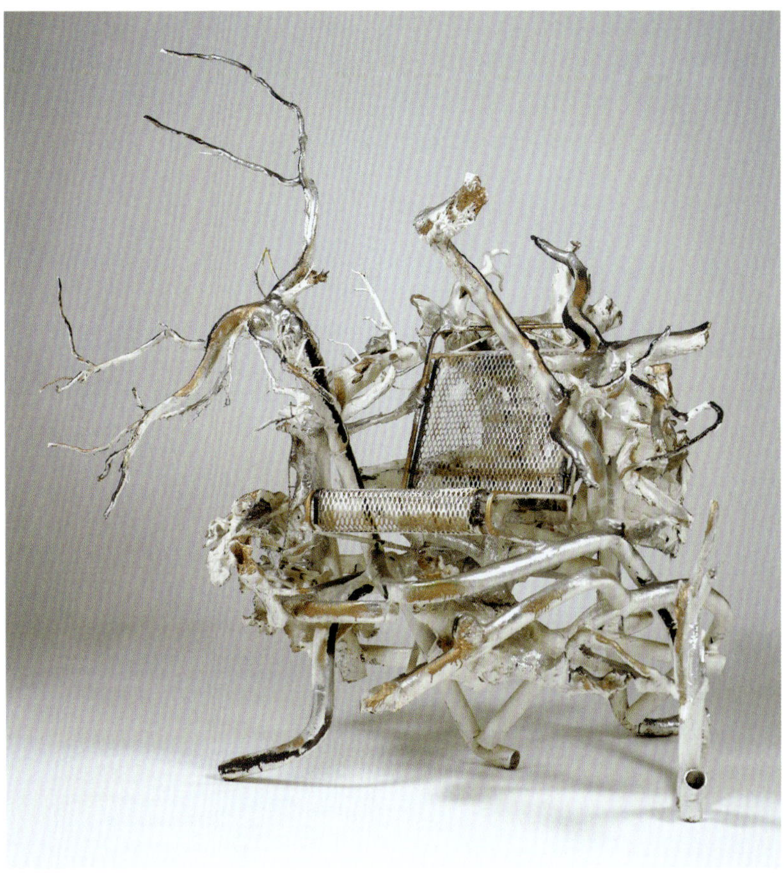

colourful cosmos of stars fabricated from cut and splayed paint cans – a satirical statement about celebrity as well as Dial's quest to find beauty in the rubble and acknowledgement in the art world. As he states, 'Art is like a bright star up ahead in the darkness of the world... Art is a guide for every person who is looking for something.'[5]

Dial was raised, in part by his great-aunt Sarah Lockett. His root sculpture *Tree of Life (In the Image of Old Things)* (1994; cat. 6) was created shortly before her death and relates both to her life and her impending passing, and to Dial's own complicated genealogy with its twisting and interconnecting branches recalling a family tree, in his painted assemblage of roots and found wood, an old car tyre, wire and fabric. An astute observer and a shrewd commentator, Dial was inspired by historical and contemporary events, often tackling these moments as they were enacted on the world stage. Turning to more conventional media – pen, pencil, pastel, watercolour – a drawing such as *Katrina* (2005; cat. 7) is a direct response to the devastation wrought by the hurricane of that name in New Orleans, Louisiana, which disproportionately affected Black and lower-income people, who found themselves displaced in their own city. *Slavery* (2009; cat. 9) and *Cotton Field* (1996; cat. 8) pay homage to those enslaved Africans in America whose forced labour was used to fuel the economy of the South.

Animals often operate as avatars in Dial's work: the oft-recurring tiger is his personal emblem and an allegory of the African-American experience, and birds represent freedom in his symbolic lexicon. In *Blue Skies: The Birds that Didn't Learn How to Fly* (2008; cat.

3), dead blackbirds, fashioned from used paint rags and old gloves, are suspended from a clothes line. Serving as a signifier of the Jim Crow laws, the hanged, flightless blackbirds, denied their liberty, suggest the lynchings and racial terror inflicted upon Black people in the South. Thornton Dial presents us with a body of work that attests to the struggles and triumphs of Black people in a changing America; at their core, these speak to the essence of our humanity.

The Dial family

With their father as creative patriarch, Dial's sons Thornton Jr and Richard inherited not only the family business[6] but their father's socio-political and artistic proclivities. Richard Dial's abstract chair sculpture *Which Prayer Ended Slavery?* (1988; cat. 11), constructed of welded steel, wire and paint, is composed of two registers perched on a metal chair seat: in the lower section he depicts a Black figure being whipped, another being hanged, and a third in chains; above this devastating scene are kneeling figures in black and white. This indictment of slavery is at once a stark visualisation of torture and an invocation. Recalling his father's furniture designs of the 1980s, Richard presages Thornton Sr's throne-like chair sculptures of the 1990s, including *Testing Chair (Remembering Bessie Harvey)* (1995; fig. 2), a homage to his fellow artist, the root sculptor Bessie Harvey.

King of the Jungle (1990; cat. 10) by Thornton Jr is a reflection upon addiction, represented here by chains wrapped around a bottle. The work is composed of a lion's head, with a chair and table completing the body. Animals figured prominently in the symbolic universe of Thornton Dial Sr, but whereas the tiger had reigned in his father's work, Thornton Jr chooses a lion. Ironically, this work was the result of a commission proposed by Absolut Vodka for potential advertisements. Thornton Jr's social critique is evident in his irreverent take on the

subject. In addition, Thornton Sr's younger brother, Arthur Dial, similarly embraced a diversity of media in his painted wall-based constructions, including tin, cinder-block pieces, wire, rope, enamel and wood.

Ronald Lockett: 'Once something has lived it can never really die'[7]

Born and raised in the Pipe Shop neighbourhood of Bessemer, Ronald Lockett (fig. 3) always knew that he wanted to be an artist. When his classmates pursued a trade after graduation from high school, Lockett followed his own creative path under the guidance of his artistic mentor and relative Thornton Dial Sr, who encouraged his use of recycled metals – sheets of which were provided to him from Dial's personal cache on his property – wood and such non-traditional media as industrial sealing compound, to realise his tableaux. Lockett recalled,

I told [Dial] I wanted to go to art school and he told me I had the best school of all just making artwork… He helped me to find out that you could take tin or barbed wire or different small little metals and make things out of them. All the pieces that I made are primarily because of him because he helped me to keep going on even when I couldn't afford to buy paint, he had paint and would pour me out blue paint, red paint… He was kind of a big driving force to where I am today.[8]

Following visits to Gee's Bend, Dial's and Lockett's admiration for the unique quilting tradition of the area proved influential upon their practices. Dial, who frequently lauded African-American women in his art, acknowledged the quilt artist Mary Lee Bendolph in his 2002 mixed-media work *Mrs Bendolph* (cat. 4). Bendolph herself returned the salutation in her intaglio print *To Honor Mr Dial* (2005; fig. 4). In *Sarah Lockett's Roses* (1997; cat. 13), Lockett honours the great-grandmother, Sarah Lockett, who years earlier had opened her home to her

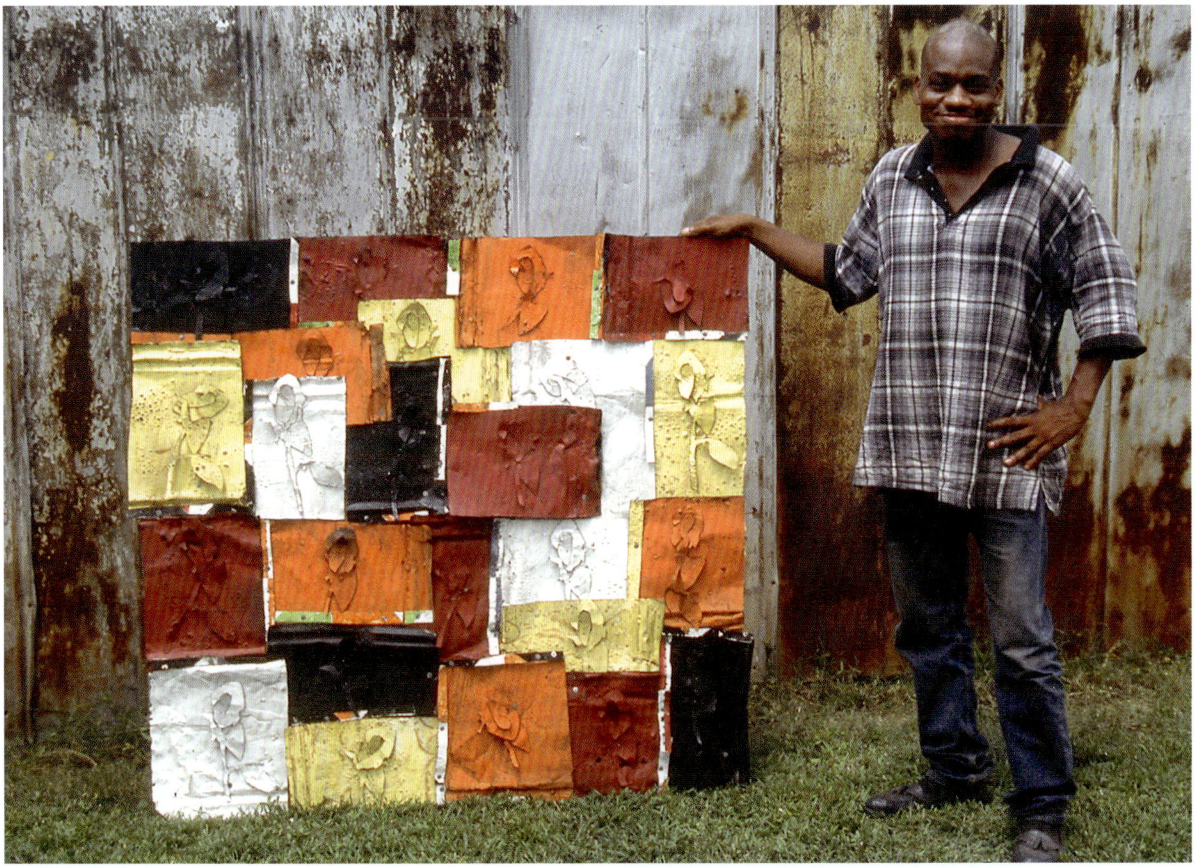

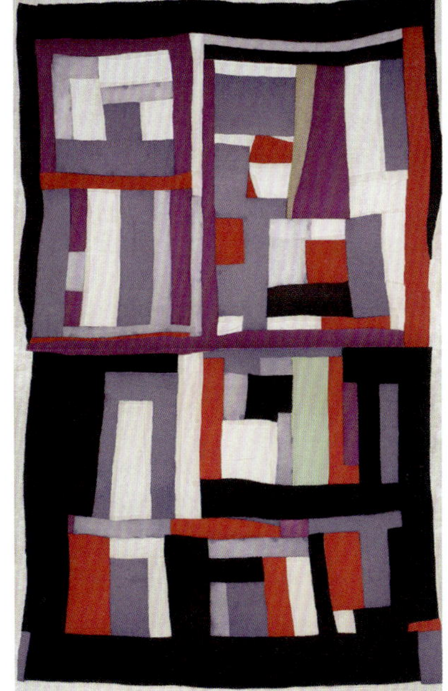

Fig. 3
Ronald Lockett with *Sarah Lockett's Roses*, 1997 (cat. 13)
Cut tin, nails and enamel on wood, 129.5 x 123.2 x 3.8 cm.
Souls Grown Deep Foundation, Atlanta

great-nephew Thornton Dial.[9] The quiltmaker Sarah Lockett was a seminal figure in his personal development who instilled in Lockett an appreciation of the beauty to be found in the everyday. His placement of painted tin tiles embossed with roses – a poignant offering of love and remembrance – assumes the form of the patchwork quilts of the region, but his use of salvaged metal instead of fabric scraps adapts the genre to his own visual practice.

In *Oklahoma* (1995; cat. 14), Lockett looks beyond familial relationships to tackle contemporary issues of the time. In April 1995 Oklahoma City was rocked by an explosion caused by two American anti-government extremists with white-nationalist allegiances that resulted in the destruction of the Alfred P.

Fig. 4
Mary Lee Bendolph, *To Honor Mr Dial*, 2005
Colour aquatint, spit-bite aquatint and soft-ground etching on paper, 116.8 x 71.1 cm. Souls Grown Deep Foundation, Atlanta

Murrah Federal Building. This act of terrorism killed 168 people, including 19 children attending a daycare programme housed in the facility. In response, Lockett created *Oklahoma* – part of a larger series – to reckon with the outrage provoked by such hateful devastation. Again, the influence of the quilt is felt, but here it is shorn of the comforting softness implicit in *Sarah Lockett's Roses*. The materials are rough-edged and rusted, the wire metal grid in the centre imagining the blasted façade of the ruined government building. Lockett's indictment is clear: destruction of that magnitude cannot be made whole again, the traces of the devastation remain.

Lonnie Holley: 'Thumbs up for Mother Universe'
It is difficult to find a more apt modern-day embodiment of the Renaissance man than the artist and musician Lonnie Holley. His multidisciplinary artistic practice includes painting, sculpture, photography, film-making, sound, song-writing and performance, and he moves fluently between all these expressive forms. Concurrently he is a teacher, philosopher, oral historian, collector and storyteller. To enter Holley's world is to recognise that the various disciplines in which he works are all interlinked in a seamless whole of consummate communication. A committed environmentalist, his appreciation for the Earth – or as Holley refers to it, 'our Mothership' – is made clear in his personal motto 'Thumbs up for Mother Universe', as well as in his lyrics and his selection of materials. Be it near his Atlanta studio or on his travels, Holley reclaims that which has been left behind. Bits of wire, fabric, disused furniture, antique objects, shoes, boxes, wood, roots, grasses, twigs all form the foundation of his visual work (fig. 5). Acknowledging the history and the power inherent in castaway objects, Holley's stated goal is to make work that encourages people to understand how we are all connected.

Holley endured a childhood rife with hardships in the Jim Crow-era South, working various jobs and living in several foster homes. In 1979 he carved tombstones for his sister's two children, who had died in a house fire, because his sister could not afford to buy proper grave-markers, and it was this that brought him to his role as a conduit for reminiscence and storytelling through art. He found the material for the tombstones – discarded piles of a soft, sandstone-like by-product of metal casting – in a foundry near his sister's home. Speaking about that catalysing moment, Holley remarked: 'I had been thrown away as a child, and here I was building something out of unwanted things in memorial of my little nephew and niece. I discovered art as service.'[10]

Keeping a Record of It (Harmful Music) (1986; cat. 16) fuses Holley's imaginative use of found objects with his work as a musician and social commentator. In the 1940s and 1950s, music made by Black people was considered 'dangerous' to the sensibilities of white America, with white parents fearful that their children would be corrupted by exposure to it. Holley uses a salvaged phonograph top, a broken record and an animal skull as material to critique this notion. Ever the archivist, he is quite literally keeping a record of the racist assumptions so often heaped upon Black self-expression.

Spirit of the Man by the Chicken House Door (1984; cat. 15) is a testament to some of Holley's principal concerns, among them preservation, recollection, transformation and eventual rejuvenation. The work's poetic visual narrative summons the memory of his grandfather, whose favourite old wooden chair still bears the physical traces of the patriarch, with a rusty metal can hanging from the side. Leaning against the empty chair is the dilapidated door of the chicken house with the silhouette of his grandfather elegantly carved along the top edge. Profiles of male and female heads recur throughout Holley's work. Carved in wood or sandstone-like by-products, emerging as spectral forms in his paintings, and sculpted in metal wire, they reorient the viewer to consider a past or a projected human presence, to recognise the humane.

The Growth of Communication (2022; cat. 20), a new work, was inspired by the history of Orford Ness on the East Anglian coast as a landscape-laboratory for technological innovation. The work utilises salvaged materials and draws upon the narratives that Holley assembled in Britain during his artist residency in Suffolk.[11] His interest in and critique of technology can be observed in other works and is informed, in part, by his roots in Birmingham, Alabama, the steel- and iron-manufacturing capital of the South, an industry propelled by Black labour. Commenting on *Copying the Rock* (1995; cat. 19), he states, 'We people have had a hard time, but we struggled through it. Now we are in a new time, computer-operated machines drive us. All of that brings us new problems, we can't just copy the past. We got to deal with the new. Sometimes it's like living in hell.'[12] In *The Growth of Communication*, a wooden milk crate contains an obsolescent rotary telephone from which a tangle of metal and electrical wires and cables emerges, forming silhouettes of faces.

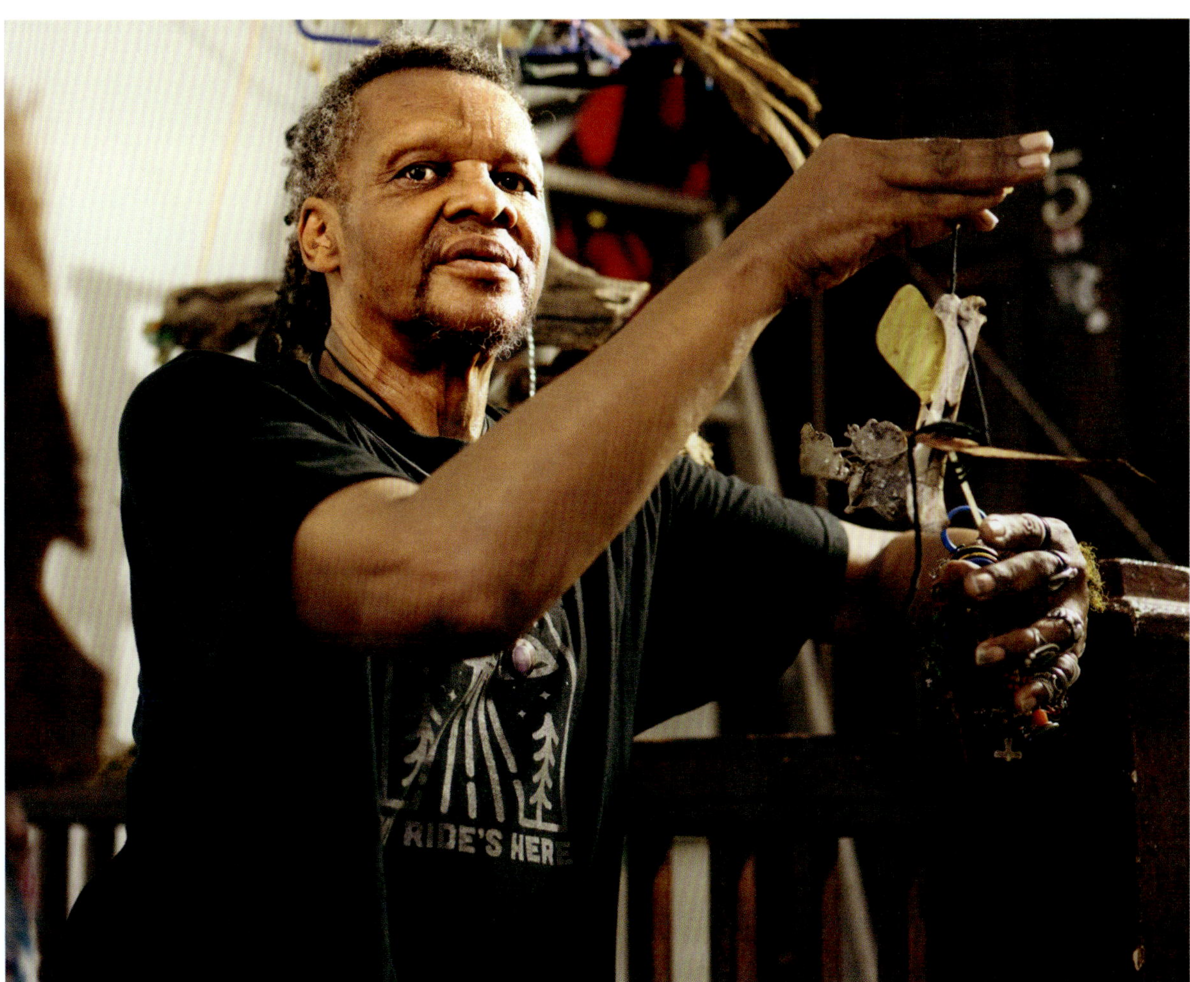

Fig. 5
Lonnie Holley in his apartment in Atlanta, Georgia, 2021

Shooting upwards, the cables liberate themselves from the confines of the box and the detritus of our electronic age, to form a cluster of faces on top of the crate. The work reminds the viewer that true communication transcends technology and, like Holley's use of roots and wood in his work, these wires, like driftwood, carry with them their own stories, possess their own histories, and yet allow us to be teleported beyond the technological cacophony to find ourselves. These ancestral tendrils connect us to our past, embrace our present, and allow us to find salvation in our shared future.

The message in the material

Their early lives shaped by segregation and living in economically deprived circumstances, most artists here had to find alternative means to obtain both education and art materials. Their ingenuity is revealed by their circumvention of this hardship and scarcity of supplies to realise significant works of art. Some turned to more conventional media and tools when these were available; when acrylics and watercolours were impossible to acquire, house paint was in large supply. Mose Tolliver frequently employed readily available house paint as his preferred medium, with repurposed supports such as Masonite, metal trays, tabletops and found pieces of wood. His propensity for invention extended to his hanging devices, which were often fashioned from metal pull-rings from tin cans. His subjects ranged from unusual animals and humorous erotic vignettes to idiosyncratic self-portraits (1987; cat. 25) and figures, both real and imagined, as in *Mary* (1986; cat. 24), whose source was a commemorative plate resting on his mantelpiece (fig. 6).

Painted enamel animated the whimsical, vibrant works of Joe Light, whose landscapes, such as *Blue River Mountain* (1988; cat. 30), portraits like *My Main Man Dan* (1988; cat. 31) and self-portraits – in which Light recasts himself as his avatars the Birdman and the

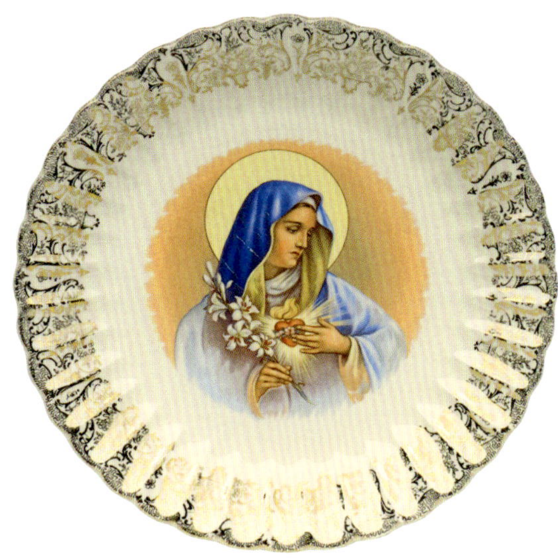

Fig. 6
Commemorative plate depicting the Virgin Mary, owned by Mose Tolliver. Souls Grown Deep Foundation, Atlanta

Hobo – are in dialogue with both comic books and Pop Art. The often audacious sensuality found in Georgia Speller's nudes, such as *Untitled* (1985; cat. 26), was rendered in watercolour and pencil. Her husband Henry Speller made use of easily acquired markers, crayons and pencils in his fanciful pictorial documentations of local life, for example *People Looking at a Man on a Motorcycle* (1987; cat. 27).

Likewise, commonly found art supplies comprised the palette for Nellie Mae Rowe's exuberant drawings and hand-coloured photographs of friends, neighbours, fantastical beasts and colourful flora displayed in her art studio, which she christened the 'playhouse'. She was herself a recurring subject in her work, both figuratively and symbolically. After a cancer diagnosis, Rowe explored her impending passing in a series of remarkably poignant, autobiographical drawings. One of her final works before her death, *Pocketbook* (1982; cat. 47) is a stark personal portrait of her eventual journey to the Promised Land. Like that of the

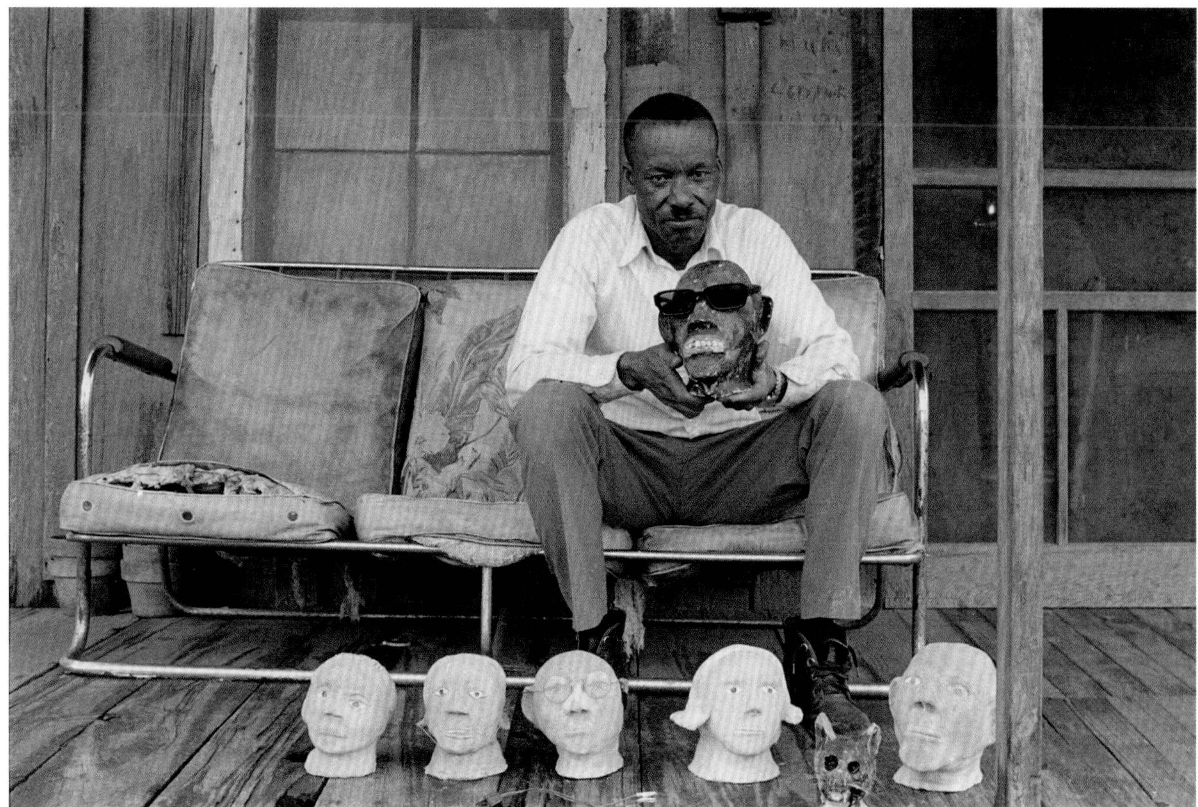

Fig. 7
James 'Son Ford' Thomas on his porch with clay heads, 1973

ancient Egyptians, who took elements from their terrestrial existence with them into the afterlife, Rowe immortalises her closest personal possession, her purse. Framed with drawings of dying flowers, her *Pocketbook* is a striking surrogate for both her spiritual presence and her physical absence.

Many artists sourced art-making materials directly from the landscape, harvesting grasses and plants, plucking berries for natural pigments, mining the soil for clay, and uncovering naturally formed tree branches, driftwood and roots collected from forests and along the banks of rivers and streams. The son of a traditional medicine woman who gathered roots, herbs and weeds for their healing properties, Jimmy Lee Sudduth was schooled from a young age in the arts of conjuring and harnessing the creative power of plants. He used blackberry juice, mud and grasses from his native Fayette, Alabama,

and his fingers as brushes to depict the local Caines Ridge Baptist Church (1986; cat. 35) and the skyscrapers of Atlanta (1988; cat. 36).

A native of Yazoo County, Mississippi, the artist and musician James 'Son Ford' Thomas (fig. 7) turned to the sediment found at the bottom of the Yazoo River, the lower hills around Greenwood, and the area around Leland and Black Bottoms – where red 'gumbo' soil could be found in abundance – for substance and inspiration. He was attracted to the high clay content in gumbo soil to create his intimate sculptures. Thick and sticky when wet, it proved an exceptionally versatile and highly malleable sculpting material. Known as 'Son Ford' – a nickname from his childhood, given his penchant for modelling Ford tractors out of clay – Thomas continued to use his moniker as a celebrated bluesman playing in the Mississippi Delta. He learned both to sculpt

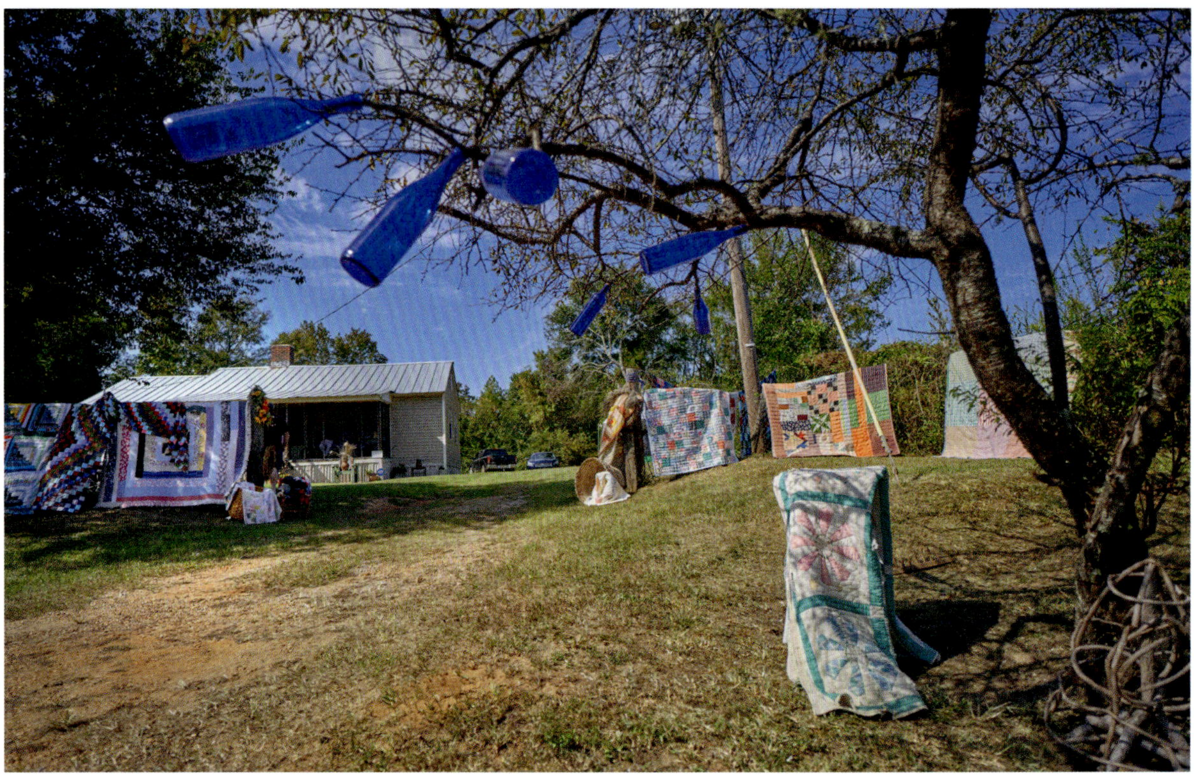

Fig. 8
Bottles in trees at the Airing of the Quilts Festival, Gee's Bend, Alabama, October 2022

and to play the guitar from his uncle, Joe Cooper, a noted blues guitarist in the Delta. These two creative pursuits supplemented Thomas's income from picking cotton and digging graves. Although he would sculpt animals from his native area as well as funerary figures, he is best known for his sculptures of skulls with open mouths lined with human teeth, and his busts adorned with human hair, wigs, costume jewellery and eyewear (cats 43–46).

Artists chose roots, tree branches and driftwood used in sculpture and works of assemblage not simply for their material qualities but also for their aesthetic form. Rather than alter the found wood, artists like Ralph Griffin and Bessie Harvey were drawn to the naturally occurring, twisted, often anthropomorphic shapes found in branches and roots, attracted to the idea of working in collaboration with nature. Harvey's manipulation of roots began

when she was a child constructing toys and dolls from twigs. A deeply spiritual artist, she acknowledged the organic creations of the Creator, maintaining that He granted her the ability to discern the personages hidden within the wood. With her application of costume jewels, marbles, modelling paste and paint to the tree root, Harvey awakens the spirits of characters previously lying dormant (cat. 39).

The yard show
Beginning in the nineteenth century, and a distinctly Southern phenomenon, yard shows – along with their cousin, yard art – are large-scale, site-specific art installations constructed in the surroundings of domestic properties. It is common to encounter articulate yards[13] in the South adorned in varying degrees of intensity: gardens twinkling as sunlight strikes glass bottles dangling from tree branches (fig. 8), hand-painted signs extolling the virtues of

forgiveness or humility, a deliberate assembly
of chairs or a stack of painted tyres. Borrowing
from this Southern vernacular tradition, yard
shows often employ found and discarded objects,
traces of human consumption, instruments of
labour and everyday life that artists salvage
from the dustbin of history to transform
their yards into extraordinary *plein-air* art
environments. Predominantly found on the
homesteads of African Americans, they arose
as a result of their creators' lack of access to
mainstream display spaces. They provided
a platform from which Black artists born in
the era of the Jim Crow laws could express
themselves freely and on their own terms.

Yard shows are an exercise of self-
determination, a grand artistic proclamation
denied to the artists' enslaved ancestors, who
had been so savagely silenced for generations.
They gave Black artists agency over their own
representation, enabling them to confront
visitors with the brutal history bound up within
the Black experience in America as well as to
acknowledge the boundless Black creativity
and historical contributions that had so often
been ignored under a racist system. In fact, the
creative inventiveness found in Southern yard
shows has influenced the work of other artists,
notably Robert Rauschenberg, a fellow Southern
artist, who revealed that seeing yard art helped
to inspire his assemblages of the 1950s and
1960s.[14] Rauschenberg has sourced materials
from junkyards in his sculptural series *Glut*,[15]
and has incorporated into his work textile pieces
that recall the 'Bricklayer' pattern (also called
'Courthouse Steps') of Gee's Bend quilts, for
example *Bed* (1955; fig. 9).

Uninhibited by art-world norms or
strictures, many Black artists used their homes
as sites of ever-evolving creation and display,
and thus as part of their expanded practice.
The sculptor Eldren M. Bailey's Atlanta-based
environment was informed by the African-
American funerary tradition; the painters Mary

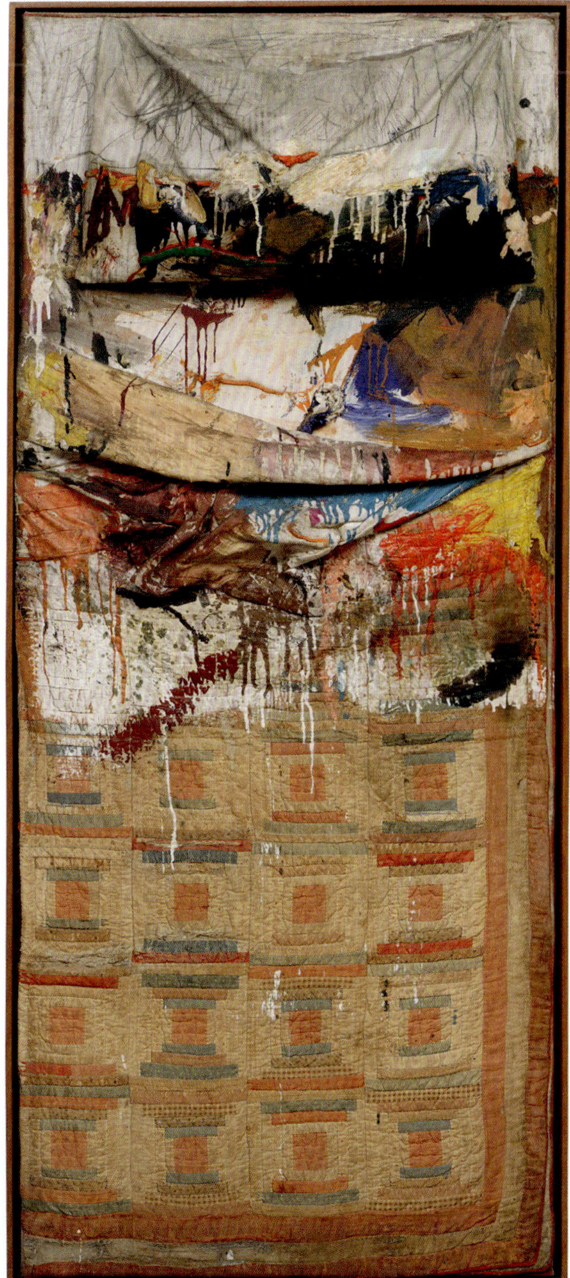

Fig. 9
Robert Rauschenberg, *Bed*, 1955
Combine painting: oil and pencil on pillow, quilt and sheet on
wood supports, 191.1 x 80 x 20.3 cm.
Gift of Leo Castelli in honour of Alfred H. Barr, Jr. Acc. n.: 79.1989
Museum of Modern Art (MoMA), New York

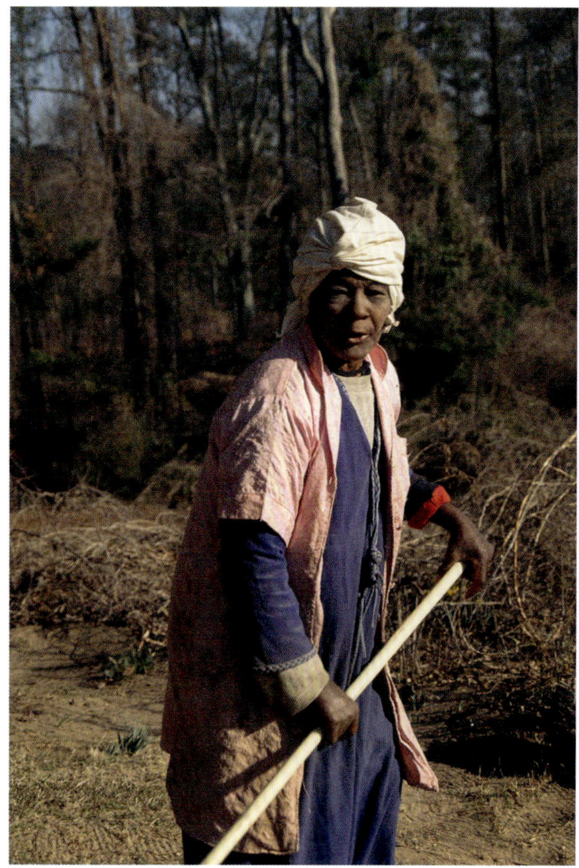
Fig. 10
Emmer Sewell in her yard in Marion, Alabama, 2001

T. Smith and Purvis Young hung their work
from fences and derelict buildings, mounting
eye-catching, in-situ solo exhibitions, while
Emmer Sewell (fig. 10), privileging found organic
materials in her outdoor assemblages, spoke
with a quieter, although no less impactful,
conceptual voice, her environment a
performance of self as she literally swept
through her shifting and manipulated grounds.
Thornton Dial Sr, Joe Minter and Lonnie Holley
all displayed their work on their homesteads.
Tragically, Holley's impressive art environment,
which consisted of thousands of artworks,
was destroyed in 1997 after the Birmingham
Airport Authority condemned the property
as part of a planned expansion that in the end
was never realised. In Gee's Bend and Alberta,
Alabama, the airing of the quilts – when
colourful, hand-sewn textile creations are
strung along clotheslines, draped over
woodpiles or laid out on porches to be aired
in the sun before the winter frost (fig. 8) –
operated, in a sense, as ad-hoc yard shows
in which quilt masterpieces could be admired
by members of the tight-knit community.

Joe Minter: 'Art is for universal understanding'
*Art is the one way man can have a common thread
that would connect the hearts of all people. Art is
for universal understanding. There is no 'insider' or
'outsider' art, because art is one. All that we know,
all that we have been, can be explained in art.*[16]

African Village in America, Joe Minter's magnum
opus, has been recognised as one of the nation's
most extraordinary sculpture gardens, and it
represents one of the last great yard shows in
the South (figs 1, 11).[17] Since 1989 Minter has
tirelessly continued the tradition, creating
a densely packed sculptural environment
extending to a half acre around his home in
Birmingham, Alabama. Referencing 400 years
of African-American history, the environment's
sculpture invokes an ancestral African village.
The grounds are transformed by thousands of
mostly found objects, reclaimed metal and
salvaged materials that Minter has collected,
painted, deconstructed, reconfigured and
reimagined as a living memorial to the 'foot
soldiers' – those ordinary citizens who combat
injustice in America.

Minter's evolving environment posits a
multi-layered sculptural narrative on the history
of Africans in America: constructed from found
materials, a slave ship envisages the forced
voyage millions of enslaved African men,
women and children endured in the Middle
Passage – the journey across the Atlantic Ocean
to the New World so named because it was one
leg of the triangular trade route plied from
about 1518 to the mid-nineteenth century.

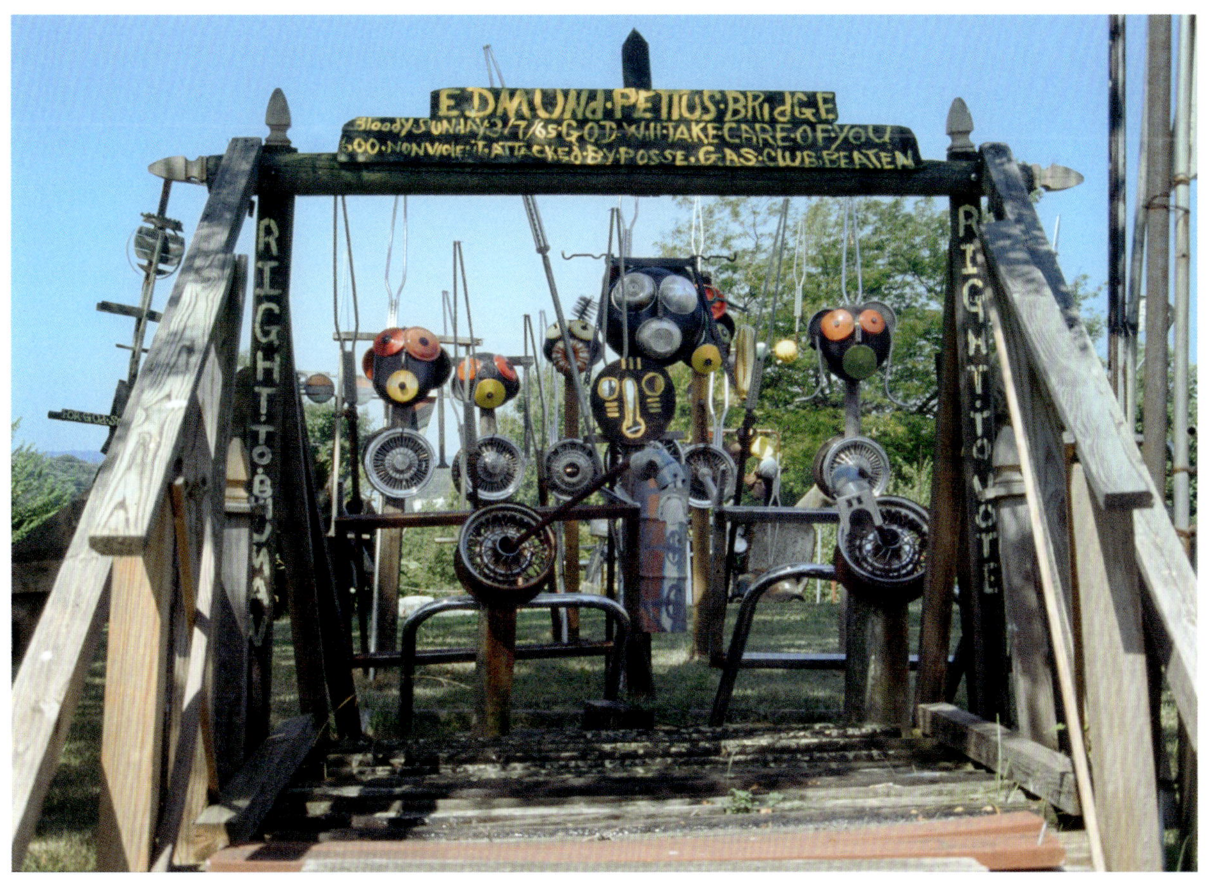

Fig. 11
Sculpture commemorating the Selma to Montgomery march for voting rights over the Edmund Pettus Bridge, the site of the Bloody Sunday attacks and the historic Martin Luther King Jr-led demonstrations, in Joe Minter's *African Village in America*, Birmingham, Alabama

Enslaved Africans had to survive deplorable conditions in overcrowded sailing ships manned by crews mostly from Great Britain, the Netherlands, Portugal and France.[18] Other works grapple with enslavement; the injustices Black people suffered under the Jim Crow laws; the civil rights movement; persistent systemic racism; and the violence and inequality that continue to plague Black and disenfranchised people in the United States.

Minter holds the dishearteningly reasonable belief that the struggles and triumphs of Black people will be lost to a history that largely excludes Black voices in its telling. To that end, he has made works that commemorate key moments in American history, such as the incarceration of Martin Luther King Jr in Birmingham, and the 1963 bombing by white racists of the 16th Street Baptist Church in the same city that took the lives of four young girls and marked a turning point in the civil rights movement, as well as addressing more contemporary issues such as the scourge of school shootings in the United States, the Iraq wars, or the lack of potable water in rural areas of Alabama. Like his yard, Minter transforms himself as he escorts visitors through his village, donning a construction hard hat and assuming the posture of a West African griot armed with a wooden staff seven feet tall and adorned with bells, ribbons, metal wire and crosses – a talking stick – as he prepares them to receive the message broadcast from within his immersive sculptural installation.

Minter's independent sculptural work, produced alongside his yard, becomes the poetry to his prose, retaining the spirit of his environment in both its formal and conceptual intention. His sculpture *And He Hung His Head and Died* (1999; cat. 51) is a testament to Minter's astute imagination and gifted eye. The title references Christ's crucifixion and the last moments before his death. The three figures on Calvary are reimagined using industrial brackets mounted on black metal crosses; the dark rust on the white brackets suggests blood spilled from the wounds inflicted on the crucified. It is an elegiac piece in which the common tools of labour are transfigured into religious objects.

Minter has told visitors to *African Village in America*: 'We are in the presence of about 100,000 African ancestors.' Although he means this metaphorically, there is truth in the assertion: abutting the grounds are two historically Black cemeteries: Shadow Lawn Memorial Gardens, the final resting place of Minter's father Lawrence, as well as the great-great-grandfather of the former First Lady, Michelle Obama; and New Grace Hill Cemetery, where Minter's cherished late wife Hilda Jo and one of his children, Alfonzo, are buried. On the other side of Minter's property stands a grid of power lines. *African Village in America* and its environs comprise a charged, dynamic landscape, the ground impregnated with palpable energy commemorating loss – both personal and universal – and promoting hope through remembrance as we gain power from those who have travailed, endured and triumphed before us.

Mary T. Smith: 'I don't need nothing. I got it all here'[19]

Although Mary T. Smith's yard show was declarative in nature – indeed, she mounted her paintings on fences and sheds around her home (fig. 12) partly in an attempt to rival a commercial billboard erected within sight of her property in Hazlehurst, Mississippi – hers was a more personal pronouncement than Minter's overtly political and social stance. From an early age, Smith was profoundly hard of hearing, making it difficult for her to communicate with others. Her paintings were a source of self-reflection and connection, serving as surrogates for her own voice. Known for her paintings on corrugated tin and wood, which she gathered from a scrapyard near her home, Smith boldly used a restrained palette of deep blues, reds, yellows, greens, blacks and whites to create a host of figures, including portraits of neighbours and saints, and to depict issues facing her community, often accompanied by words or phrases (*We All Want a Jobe* [*We All Want a Job*] [early 1980s; cat. 21]).

Smith's deep religious faith and love of Christ were present throughout her environment, with religious iconography appearing in abstracted form in her paintings as well as in her sculpture *He* (c. 1980; cat. 22), a stylised realisation of Christ on the cross. The sculpture, composed of an old wooden board scarred by rusted nails, a chrome tyre rim denoting a crown of thorns or an industrial halo, and a square piece of tin painted simply with the word 'HE', exemplifies her facility to make powerful statements with the sparest of means.

Purvis Young: 'I paint the problems of the world'[20]

Arguably one of the most significant examples of an artist transplanting the yard onto the street is found in the work of the Miami artist Purvis Young. Young had been drawing since his childhood, studying books on art in local libraries, but he began painting figures seriously in the early 1970s, in part to commemorate those fighting injustice. He witnessed the anti-war and civil-rights demonstrations in the United States during that era as well as the aggressive tactics used by local authorities to effectively isolate his predominantly Black area of Overtown in Miami, hastening its socio-economic decline.

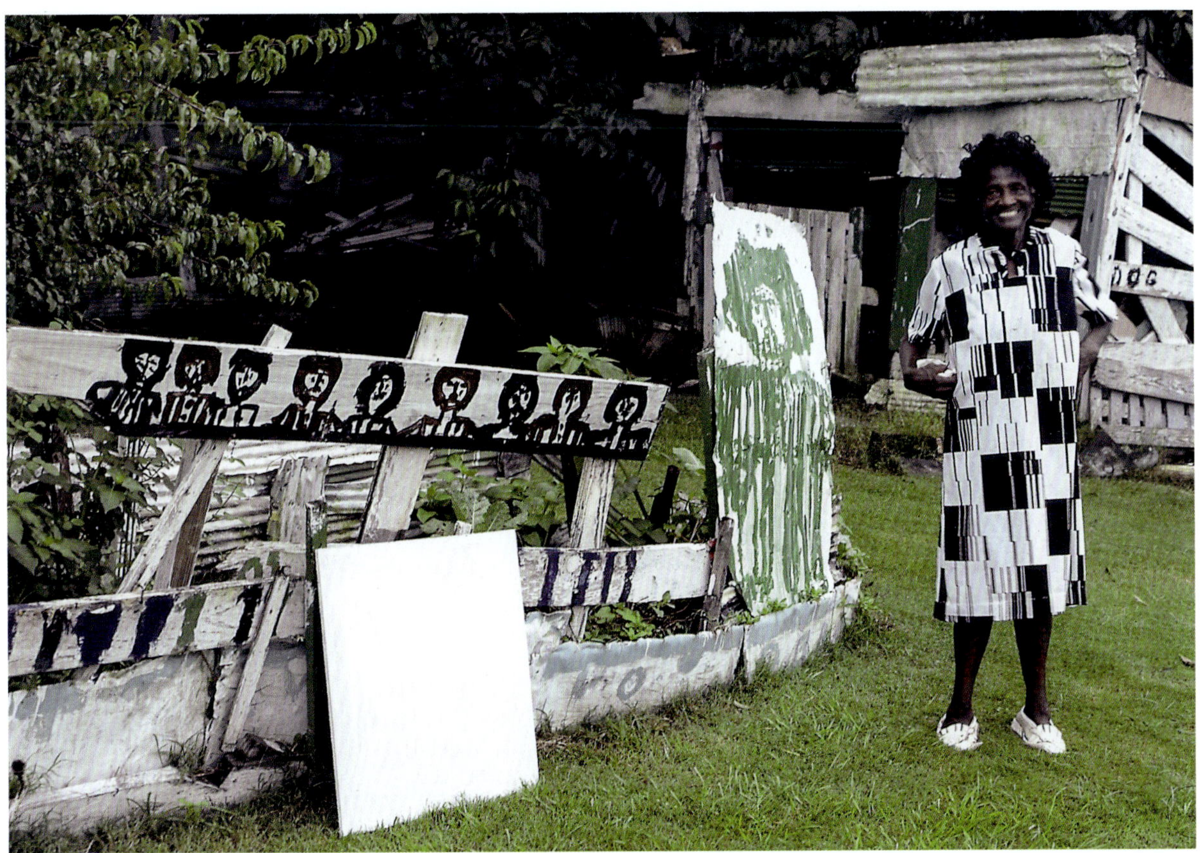

Fig. 12
Mary T. Smith in her yard in Hazlehurst, Mississippi, surrounded by examples of her work, August 1987

Young took inspiration from the African-American-led Black Arts Movement, which was active in the 1960s and 1970s, and the *Wall of Respect*, an outdoor community mural first painted in 1967 in Chicago. Comprising portraits of African-American political and cultural heroes and heroines, the *Wall of Respect* was the motivation for Young's own form of protest, which he began in 1971 in Good Bread Alley in Miami. He made a public display there of his paintings, which he nailed, in the manner of a collage, to the exterior walls of abandoned buildings (fig. 13). Like his creative counterparts in the rural Black Belt, Young scoured the streets and vacant lots of his urban landscape to gather plywood, scrap lumber, metal trays, carpet remnants, broken furniture and paper of all sorts, be it discarded piles of placemats, old business letters, magazines or financial ledgers,

as supports for his paintings and drawings. Fortified by a vast personal visual vocabulary, his creative outpouring was prodigious – wild horses, portraits, warriors, angels, pregnant women, prison bars, boats and other symbolic figures representing social and political actors all occupy his paintings. His politically engaged works visualised the struggle and concerns of Black people in America. *Carrying the Angel to the People* (1994; cat. 54) depicts dozens of figures with arms and faces directed skyward in anticipation of receiving their celestial gift. Among them are some of Young's preferred subjects: God's heavenly messengers, the red 'freedom horse' symbolising liberation, and a sole pregnant woman rendered in greens and yellows and outlined in black, who dominates the lower-right portion of the work. For Young, the fecundity of the pregnant woman represented a source of salvation and the interconnection of the divine and the mortal: 'The way I feel about it, they all giving birth to angels. They giving birth to a new nation, they gonna start us a new kingdom.'[21] Figures also populate the patchwork frame of the piece. Young generally constructed unique frames for his tableaux, often using them as another surface upon which to expand his symbolic universe.

Young's *Untitled (Narrative Scene)* (1980s; cat. 57) posits an expressionist parable about the immigrant experience in America. On one side of the painting, crowded boats bob on choppy waters, bringing to mind the perilous journeys undertaken by Haitian refugees and others fleeing political persecution, war, or economic and environmental instability. The right section visualises day labourers – a group largely drawn from undocumented immigrant workers – transported by the truckload across the American landscape to travail in minimally paid jobs with few rights and often under punishing working conditions. Overlooking these voyagers are four haloed figures in the foreground. Symbolic of 'good people', the angels' protective presence is fitting for those in search of a better life. With their backs turned to the viewer, these harbingers of hope bear witness to the migrant struggle.

Through his paintings, artist's books and his large-scale wall installations, Young wanted to 'paint the truth' and address issues of racism, poverty and social injustice to encourage Black intellectual, political and artistic liberation.[22]

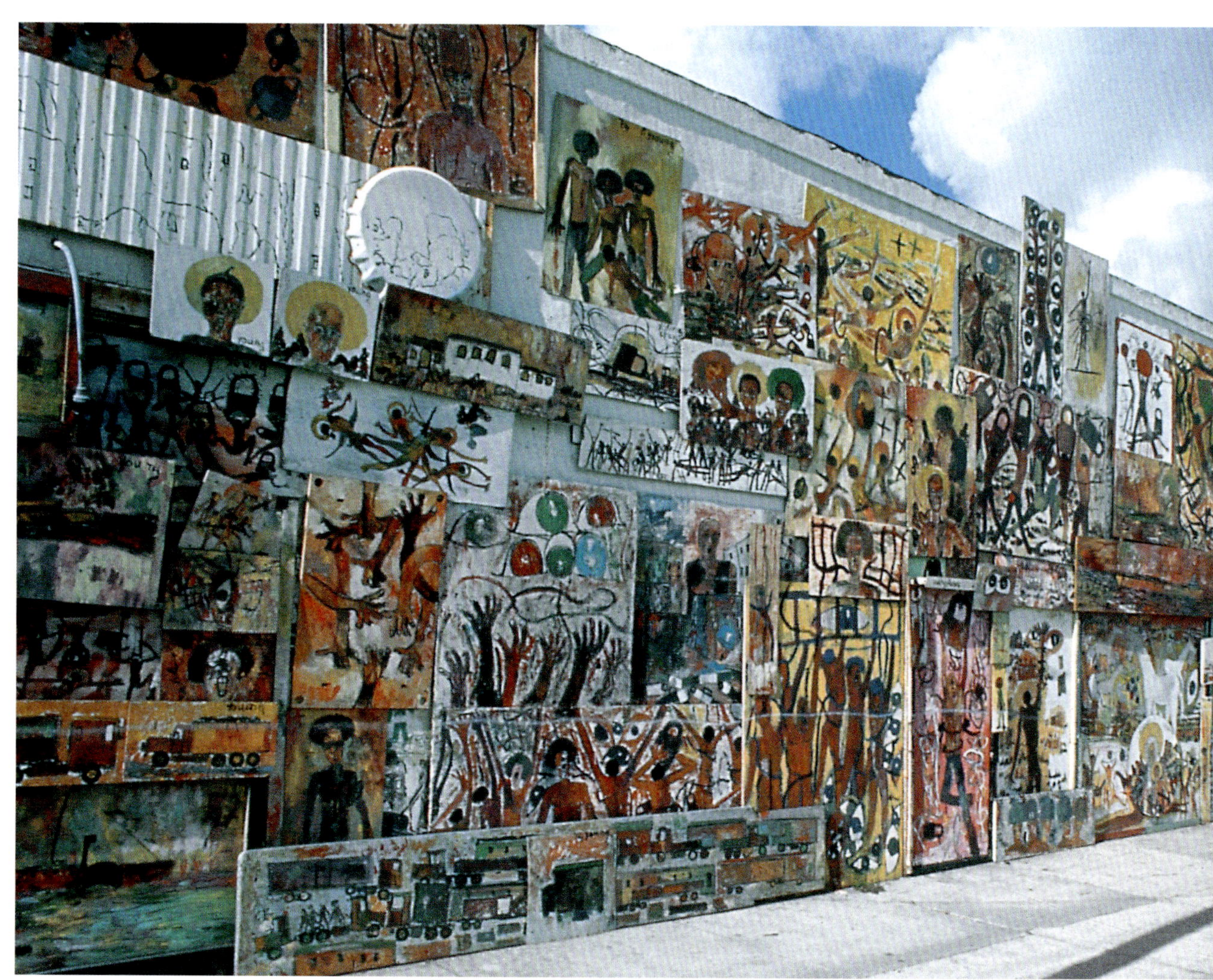

As he said, 'I make like I'm a warrior, like God sending an angel to stop war, like in my art.'[23] His is a call for harmony and hope, with his Good Bread Alley display functioning as an epic visual poem of Black experience.

The quilts of Gee's Bend

I came to realise that my mother, her mother, my aunts, and all the others from Gee's Bend had sewn the foundation, and all I had to do now was thread my own needle and piece a quilt together.
— Loretta Pettway Bennett[24]

Situated on the banks of the Alabama River, Gee's Bend, also known as Boykin, is positioned in the middle of a looping, hairpin turn – the 'bend' of the river. Since the early 1800s,

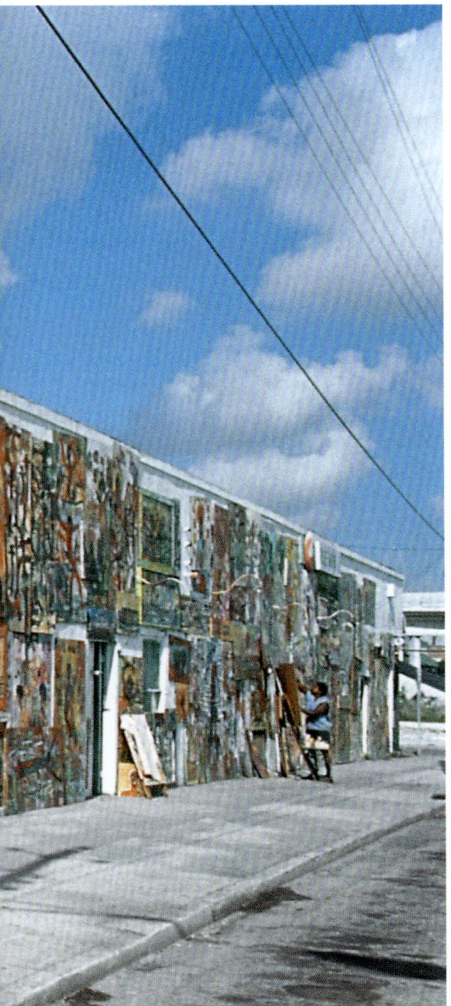

Fig. 13
Purvis Young,
Good Bread
Alley, Miami,
Florida, 1972

this geographically isolated settlement, with its nearby communities of Rehoboth and Alberta – home of the Freedom Quilting Bee – has given rise to over five generations of African-American quiltmakers possessing creative talents unparalleled in American art.

Slavery's enduring legacy in the community is recalled in the place's name. Joseph Gee was a white North Carolinian planter who bought over 6,000 acres along the Alabama River in 1816 and established a cotton plantation on the fertile land. This was purchased by Mark Pettway in 1845. Despite the American Civil War heralding emancipation in 1865, true freedom remained elusive for this small, rural area's Black community, who mostly remained as sharecroppers under white landlords; to this day, the majority of the 700 or so inhabitants are descended from those formerly enslaved, many of them bearing Pettway's name as part of their own.

The tradition of patchwork was born of a scarcity of materials coupled with the ingenuity of the quiltmakers, who would salvage fabric scraps, textile remnants – including flour and rice sacks – and worn, disused clothing for their quilts. Until the middle of the twentieth century, the majority of patchwork quilts from the area were constructed from the remains of ragged shirts, dress bottoms and worn-out denim work trousers. Given new life as part of a work-clothes quilt, they act as extended family portraits, with ancestral echoes detected in shirt tails and faded knees.

Triangles (2021; cat. 63) by Marlene Bennett Jones (fig. 14) pays homage to the work-clothes quilt tradition. Her version of a medallion quilt is animated by the triangular pieces of orange, red and gold corduroy in the centre (the medallion), around which the faded denim pockets from old jeans and coloured cotton blocks and strips produce a kaleidoscopic effect.

In the wake of the economically ruinous Great Depression, Gee's Bend became a site for President Franklin D. Roosevelt's New Deal

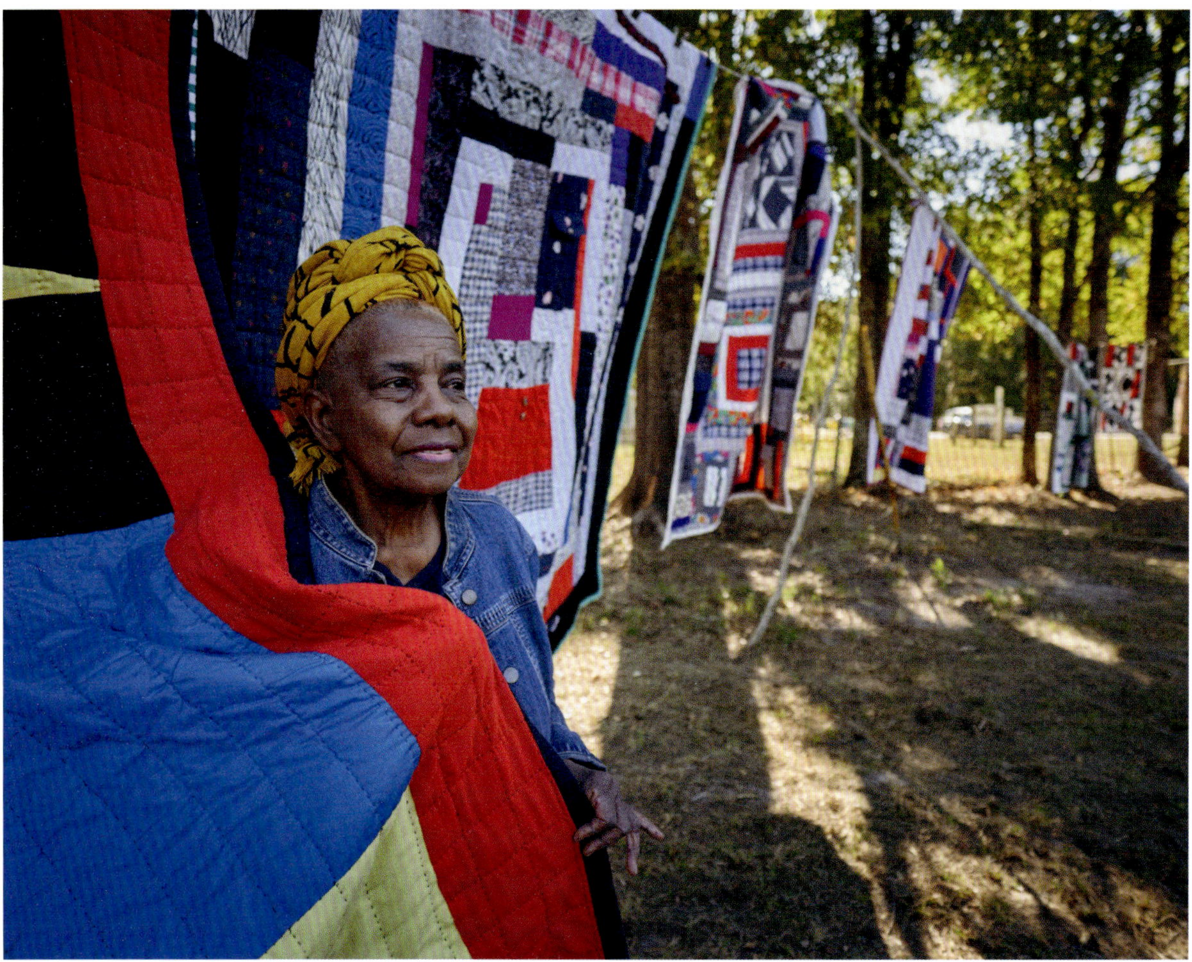

Fig. 14
Marlene Bennett Jones at the Airing of the Quilts Festival, Gee's Bend, Alabama, October 2022

programme, when the government bought and divided the land of the former Pettway plantation and constructed new houses, allowing families to own their own homes for the first time. A leader in the community at the time, Martha Jane Pettway (*'Housetop'* – *nine-block 'Half-Log Cabin' variation, c.* 1945; cat. 59) was among the first to purchase a government-built 'Roosevelt house'. Although living conditions generally improved with this development, the new houses lacked indoor plumbing and electricity; in unheated houses, quiltmaking was not merely a creative pastime but an essential skill for survival.

With the advent of the civil rights movement two decades later, private ownership of property in Gee's Bend was to prove invaluable to the community. Many Black families elsewhere in the county found themselves evicted by their white landlords for attending civil rights demonstrations. Community members were inspired by a visit to the area by Martin Luther King Jr in February 1965. Empowered by his speech at the Pleasant Grove Baptist Church – a focal point for the community, with some quiltmakers contributing their singing voices to the church choir – many of the women marched for voting rights in Camden, the nearby white-majority town and county seat, and in Selma, the site of the Bloody Sunday massacre the following month. In 1966 more than sixty quilters came together to establish the Freedom

Quilting Bee, a cooperative managed by the quiltmaker and community activist Estelle Witherspoon to champion the work of local quilters to a national market; within three years, it had altered the local economy and quiltmaking had become one of the few Black-owned businesses in the county.

In 1972 the Freedom Quilting Bee received an important commercial commission from Sears, Roebuck and Co., an American retailer, to fabricate corduroy pillow shams to be sold nationwide. A material rarely used by quilters at the time, corduroy leftovers from these pillow shams were recycled by the resourceful women and shared among the community to be used for quiltmaking. A member of the Freedom Quilting Bee, Flora Moore grew up in the nearby hamlet of Rehoboth; her *'Log Cabin' variation* quilt (*c.* 1975; cat. 61) gave new life and form to corduroy scraps destined for the dustbin.

The women in the Bend bring an idiosyncratic swagger, almost an eccentricity, to their pattern creation, aesthetics and fabric selection. Whereas the 'Housetop' quilt – a small centre square bordered by larger and larger squares, echoing the right-angles of the quilt's borders – reigns as a preferred pattern in the Bend (see cats 58 and 59), most Gee's Bend quilts can be called improvisational or 'my way' quilts, in which quiltmakers start with basic forms and then follow their own individual artistic paths ('their way') to stitch unexpected patterns and colours.

Transference of aesthetic knowledge and skills from generation to generation is the defining ethos of the area, where artists are nurtured both by family and the surrounding quiltmaking community. That familial relationship can be seen in the work of Mary Lee Bendolph and her daughter Essie Bendolph Pettway (2018; cat. 64), who experiment with Housetop and 'Blocks and Strips' quilts that embody the themes of utility and frugality seen in many works from Gee's Bend. The 'Strips and Strings' pattern was reserved for the smallest scraps of irregular shapes and sizes of prints and solids.

Mary Lee Bendolph's *Burgle Boys* (2007; cat. 12) demonstrates her mastery of generating complex geometric abstractions. As she blends Blocks and Strips and the structural framework of the Housetop pattern, her willingness to break pattern conventions – a hallmark of the quiltmakers in the area – and her haptic skill create a rhythmic improvisational work.

If Mary Lee Bendolph's work bristles with the dynamism of geometric form, Loretta Pettway Bennett creates an almost minimalist textile tableau in *Medallion* (2005; cat. 62) with a pared-down colour palette of red, black and white, and a spare piecing of undulating strips of black and red forming the medallion where, at opposite corners of the diagonal, single lines of red and black boldly escape from the confines of the centre, both contributing to the stark visual impact of the piece.

Even the town's name can tell a story. In 1949 Gee's Bend was officially renamed Boykin, after Frank Boykin, a white congressman and segregationist who as far as anyone knows had never visited the place. Residents of Gee's Bend petitioned the state of Alabama in 1968 to incorporate the community and name it the 'Town of King' in honour of Martin Luther King Jr, but the petition was denied by the courts.[25] In resisting the official change of name by continuing to call the area Gee's Bend, the community have refused to let it be removed from the map; indeed, the quiltmakers alone have now ensured that it is on the map for good. Creators of both functional objects and of masterful works of art, they have adhered to a unique artistic tradition nurtured and upheld for centuries. Reclaiming the scraps and tattered remnants of lives lived, they have transformed these relics into some of the most visually compelling and contextually profound works of abstract art in any tradition.

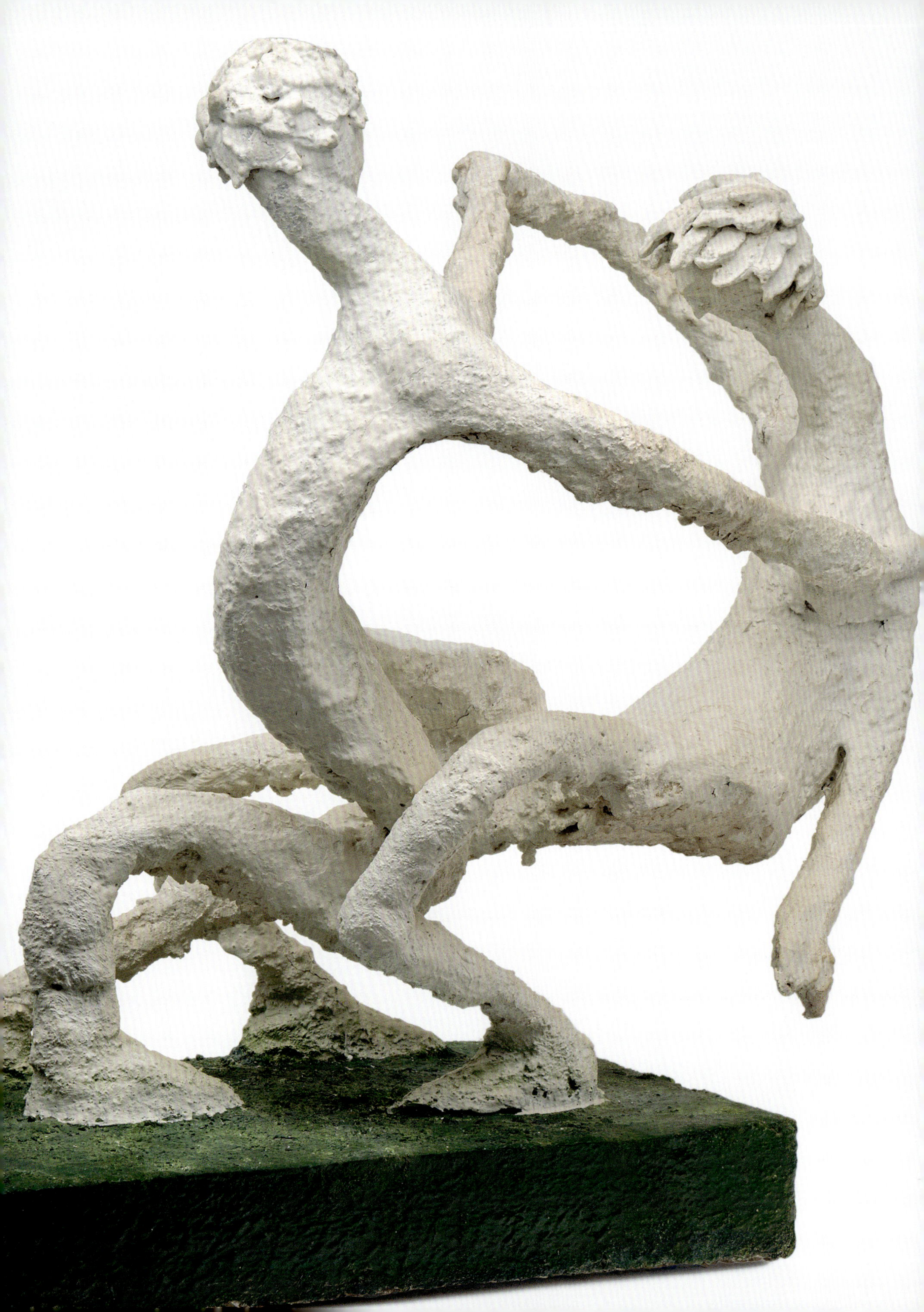

Catalogue plates

1
Thornton Dial
Stars of Everything, 2004
Paint cans, plastic cans, spray-paint cans, clothing, wood, steel, carpet,
plastic straws, rope, oil, enamel, spray paint and Splash Zone
compound on canvas on wood, 248.9 x 257.8 x 52.1 cm
Souls Grown Deep Foundation, Atlanta

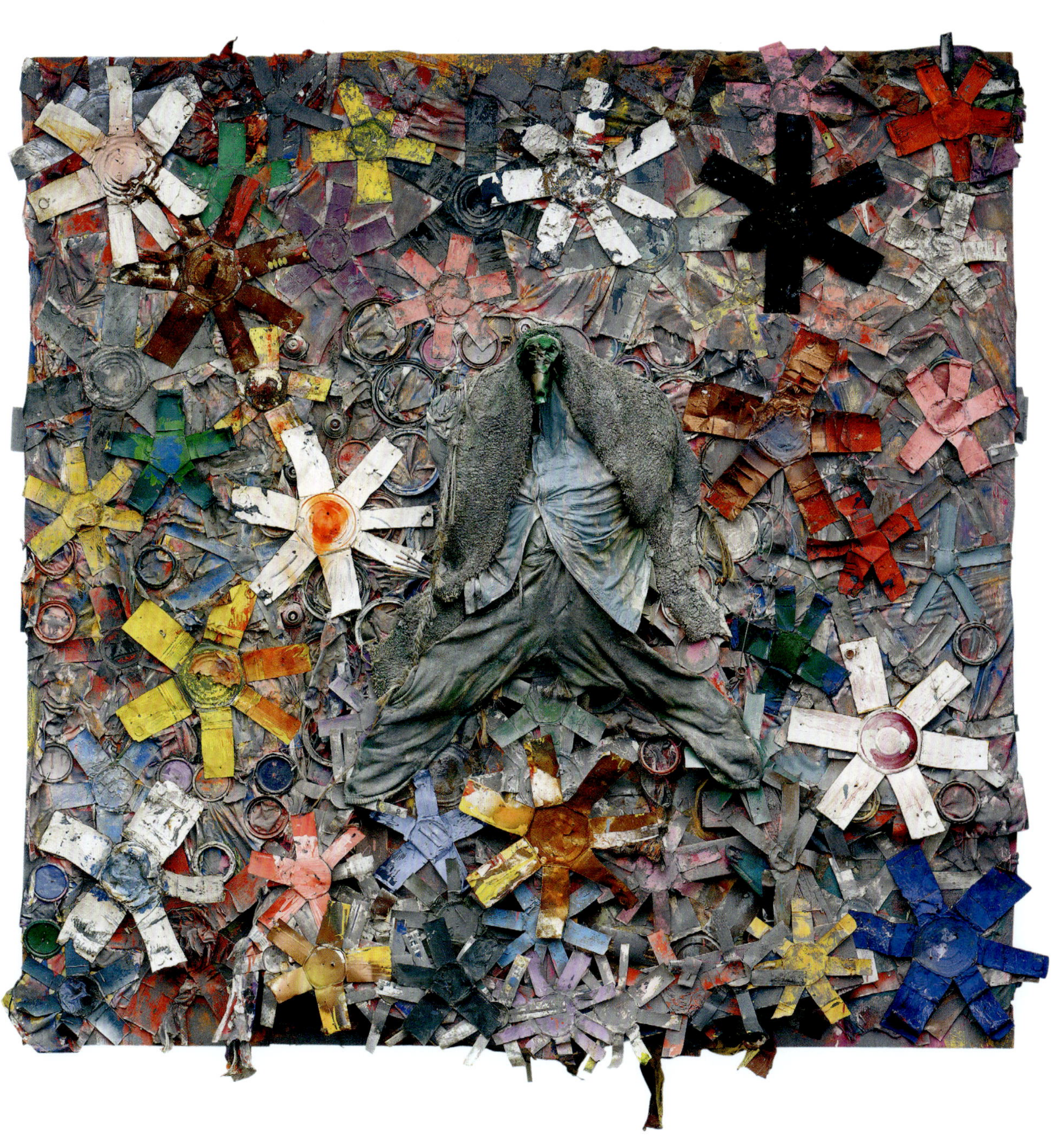

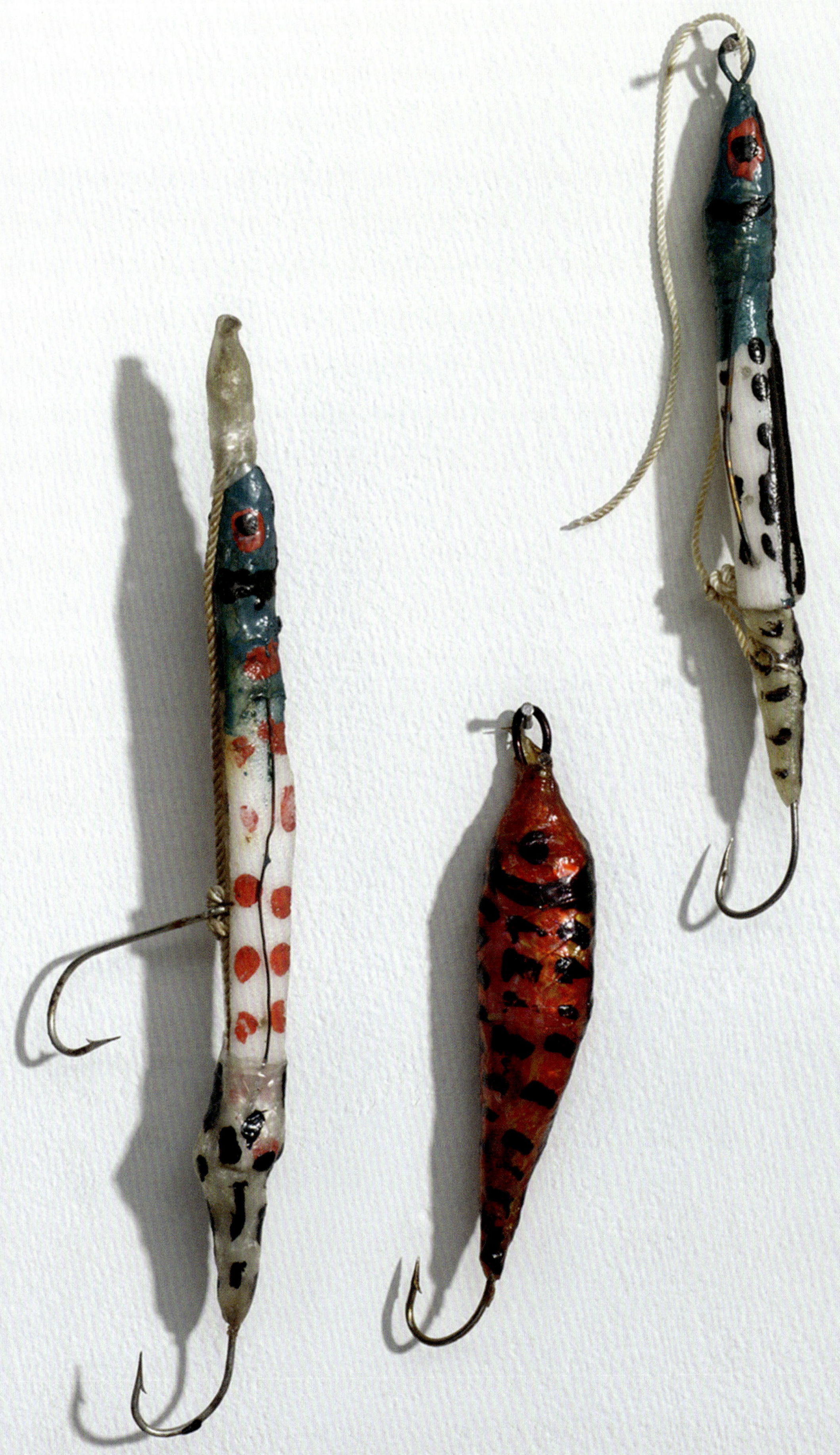

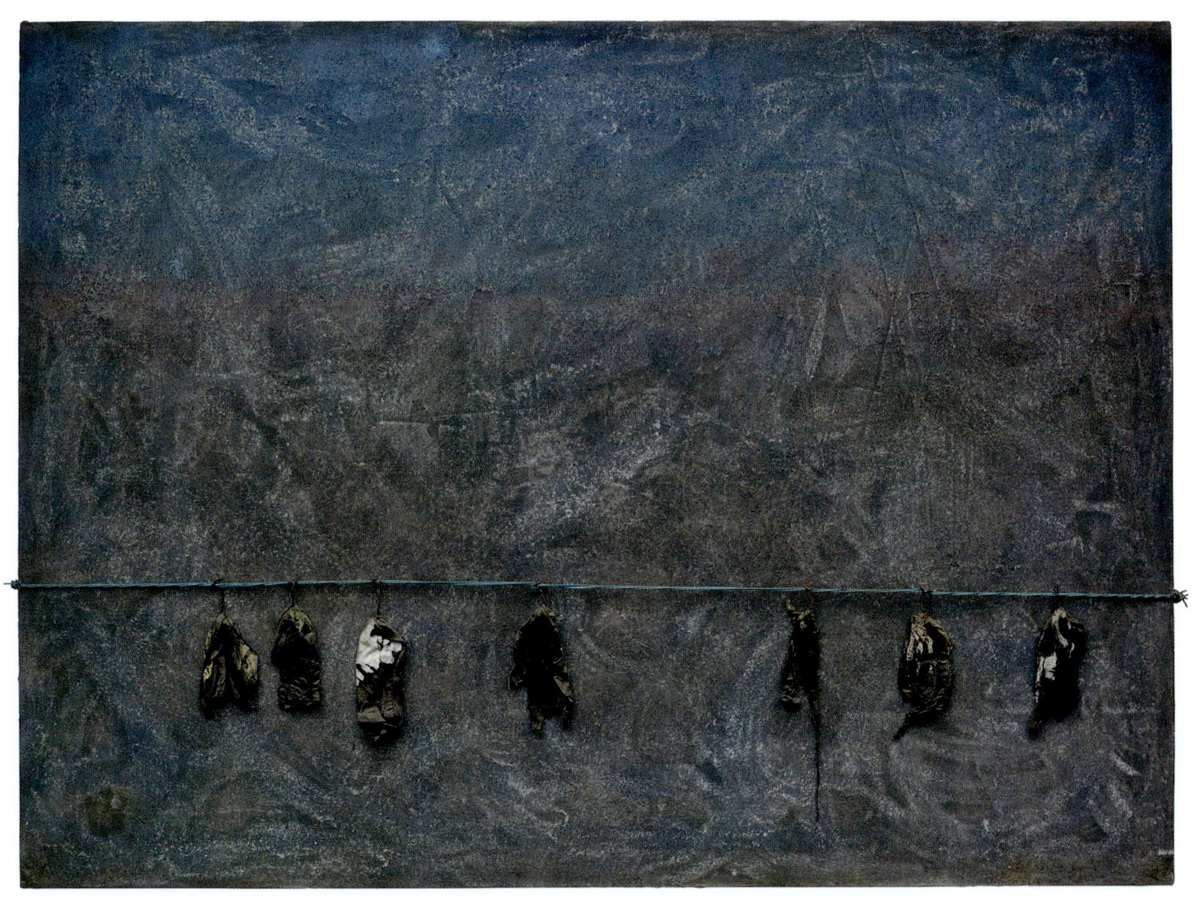

2
Thornton Dial
Fishing lures, mid-1980s
Fish hooks, heat-formed plastic, polyester resin and paint,
22.9 x 5.7 x 1.3 cm, 17.8 x 2.5 x 1.3 cm, 13.2 x 2.5 x 1.9 cm
Souls Grown Deep Foundation, Atlanta

3
Thornton Dial
Blue Skies: The Birds that Didn't Learn How to Fly, 2008
Cloth rags, rubber-coated copper wire, wire, screws and enamel
on canvas, 152.4 x 200.7 cm
Private collection, New York City

4
Thornton Dial
Mrs Bendolph, 2002
Clothing, bedding, carpet, enamel and spray paint
on canvas on wood, 213.4 x 127 x 10.2 cm
High Museum of Art, Atlanta. Museum purchase,
and gift of the Souls Grown Deep Foundation from
the William S. Arnett Collection

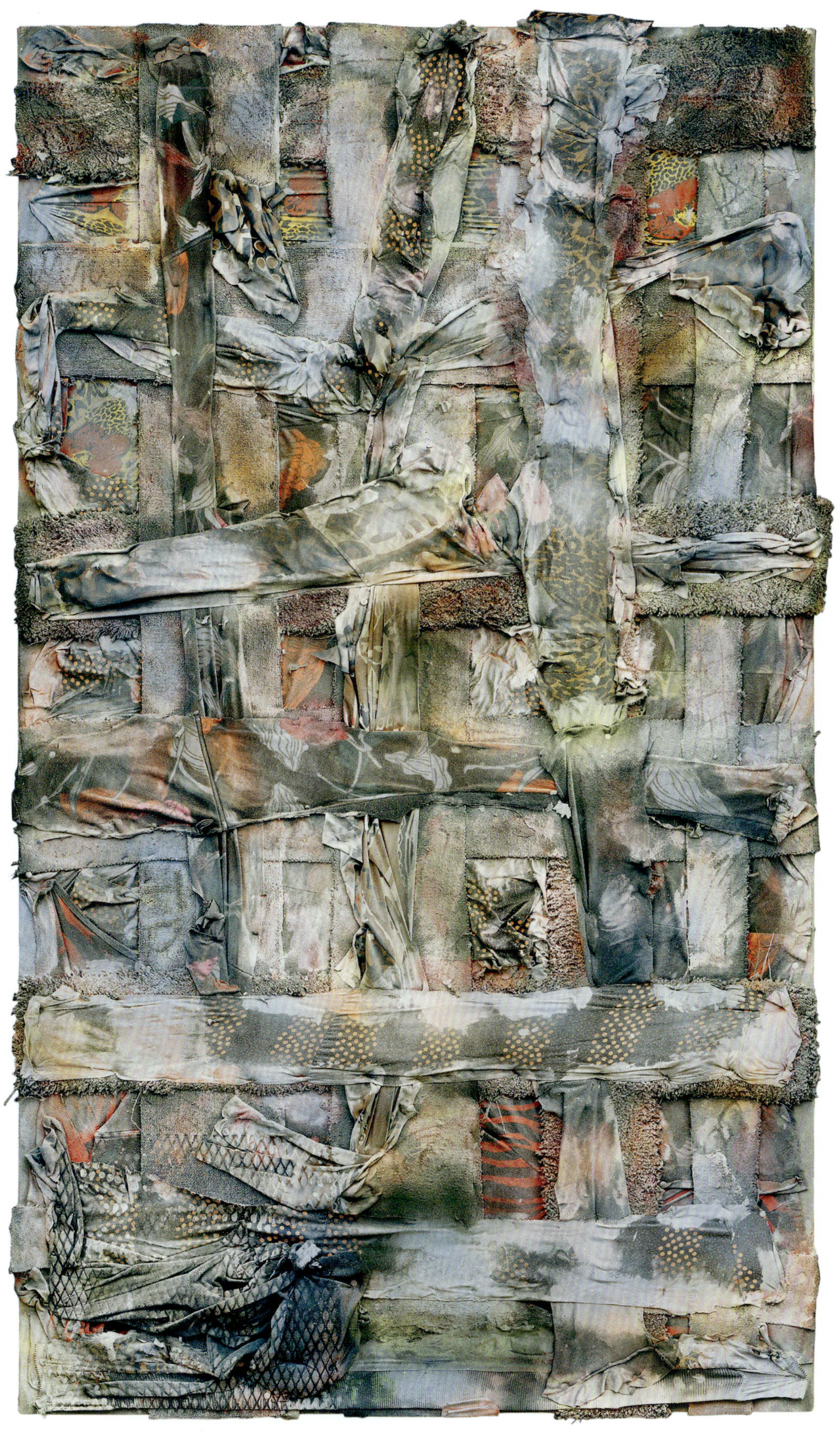

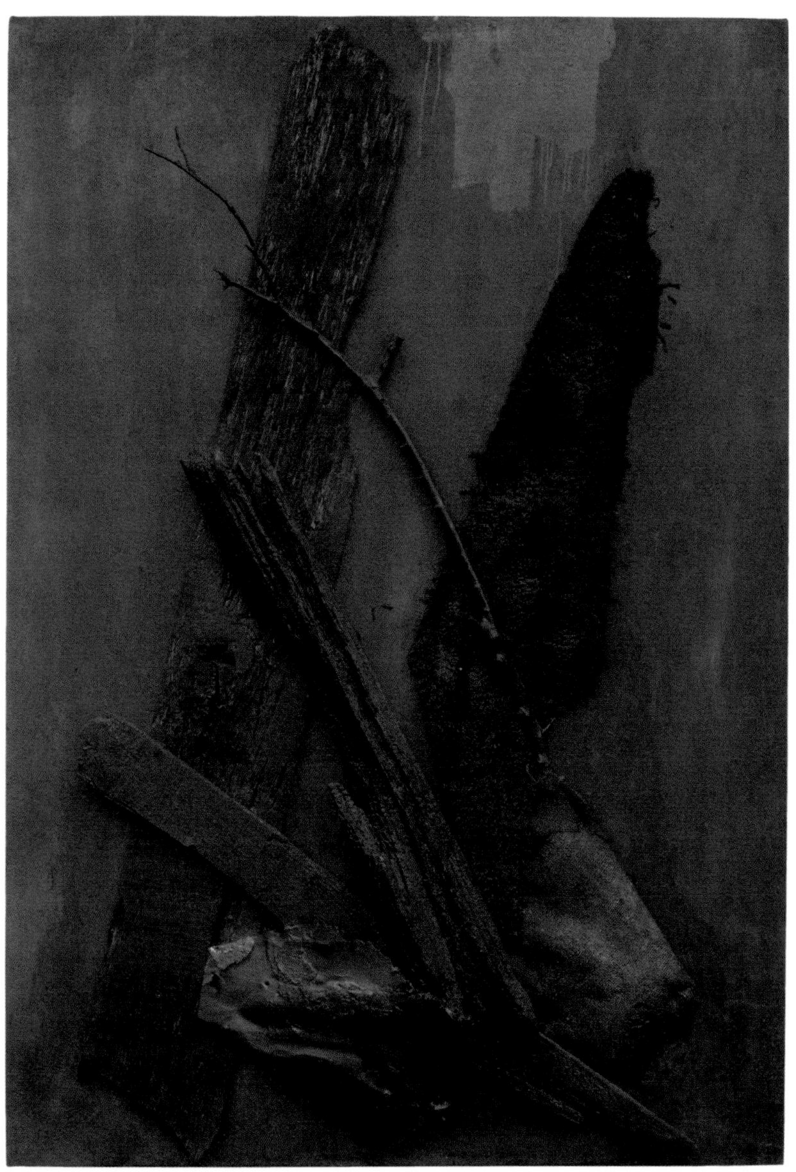

5
Thornton Dial
The Coming Dawn, 2011
Wood, tin, screws, nails, paint and carpet on wood,
each panel: 182.9 x 121.8 cm
Souls Grown Deep Foundation, Atlanta

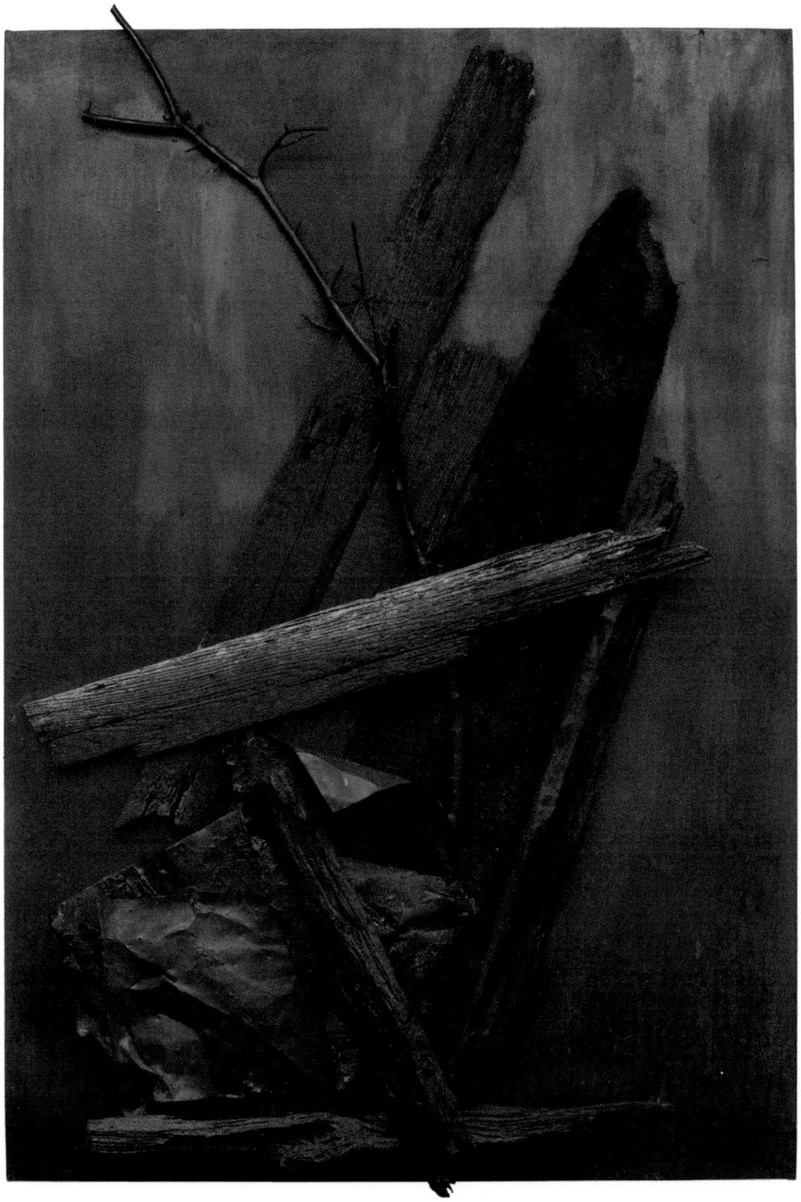

6
Thornton Dial
Tree of Life (In the Image of Old Things), **1994**
Found wood, roots, rubber tyre, wire, fabric, plastic air-freshener,
enamel and industrial sealing compound, 200.7 x 114.3 x 111.8 cm
Virginia Museum of Fine Arts, Richmond. Adolph D. and Wilkins
C. Williams Fund and partial gift of the Souls Grown Deep
Foundation from the William S. Arnett Collection, 2018.62

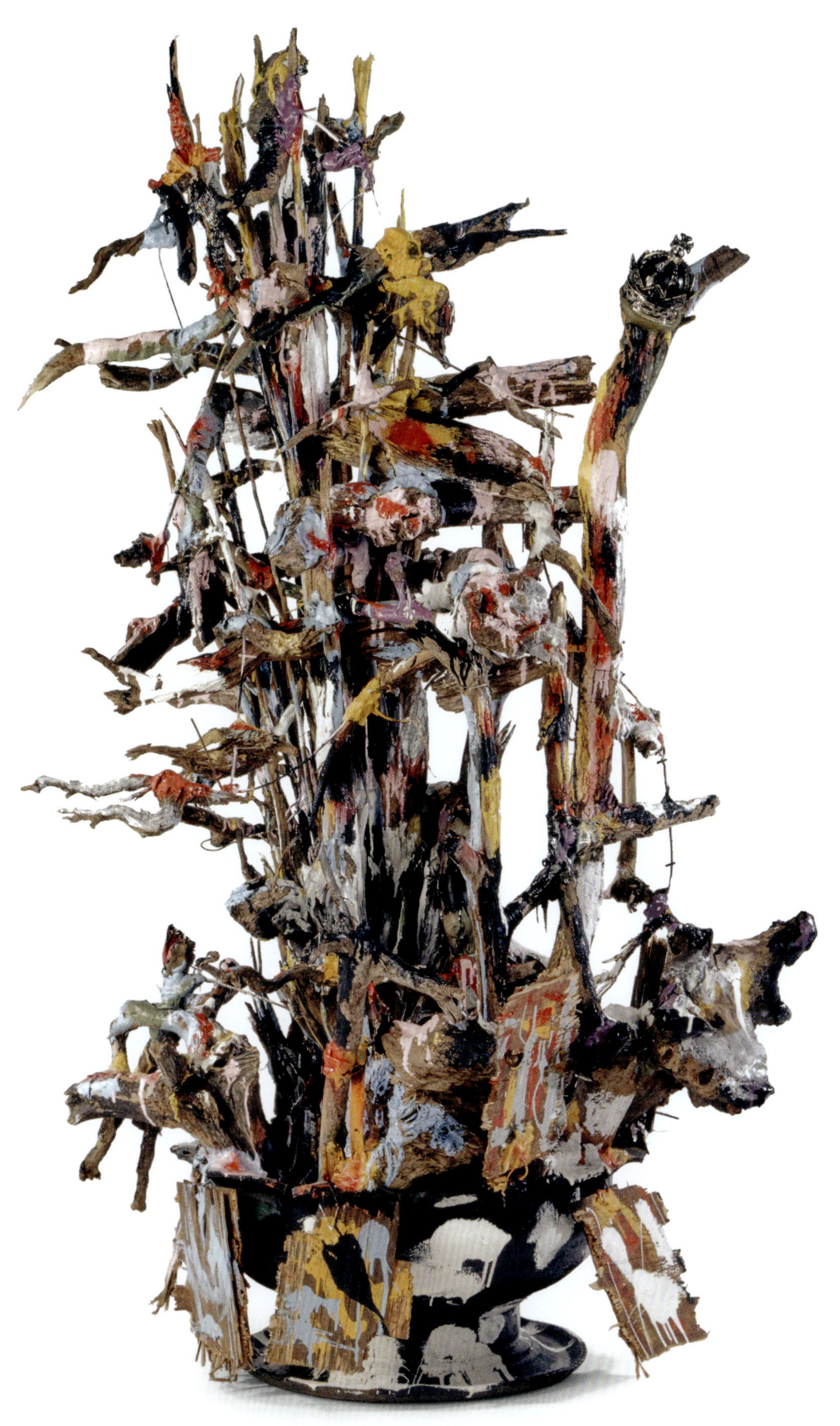

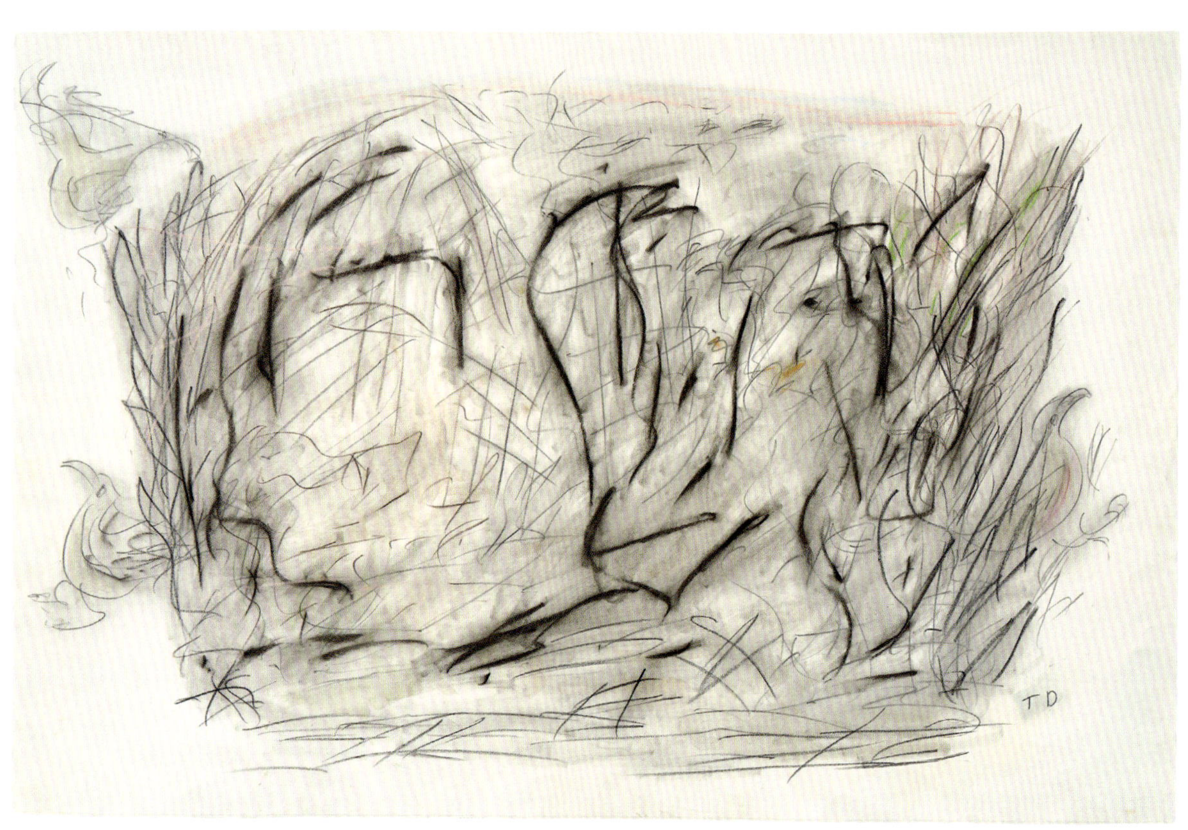

8

Thornton Dial
Cotton Field, 1996
Graphite, charcoal and watercolour on paper, 70 x 90 cm
From the collection of Susan and Stephen Pitkin, Rockford, Illinois

7
Thornton Dial
Katrina, 2005
Pencil, charcoal and watercolour on paper, 77.5 x 111.8 cm
Souls Grown Deep Foundation, Atlanta

9
Thornton Dial
Slavery, 2009
Graphite and watercolour on paper, 76 x 112 cm
From the collection of Susan and Stephen Pitkin, Rockford, Illinois

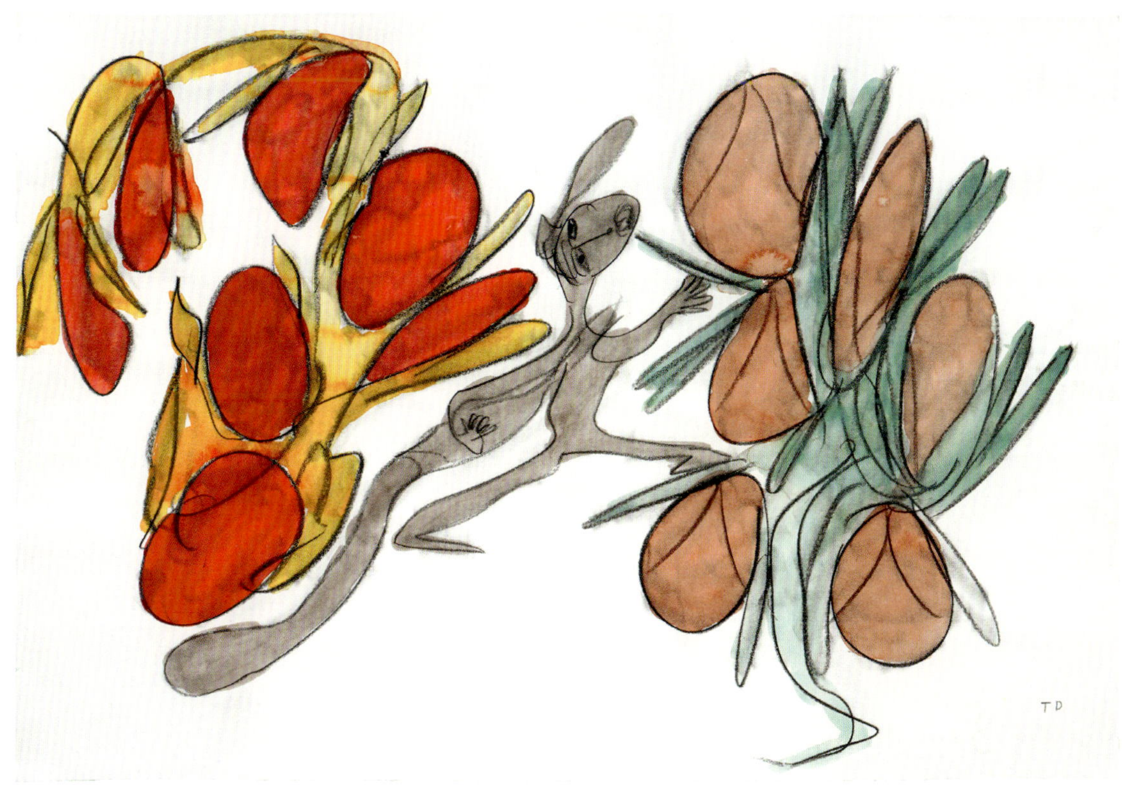

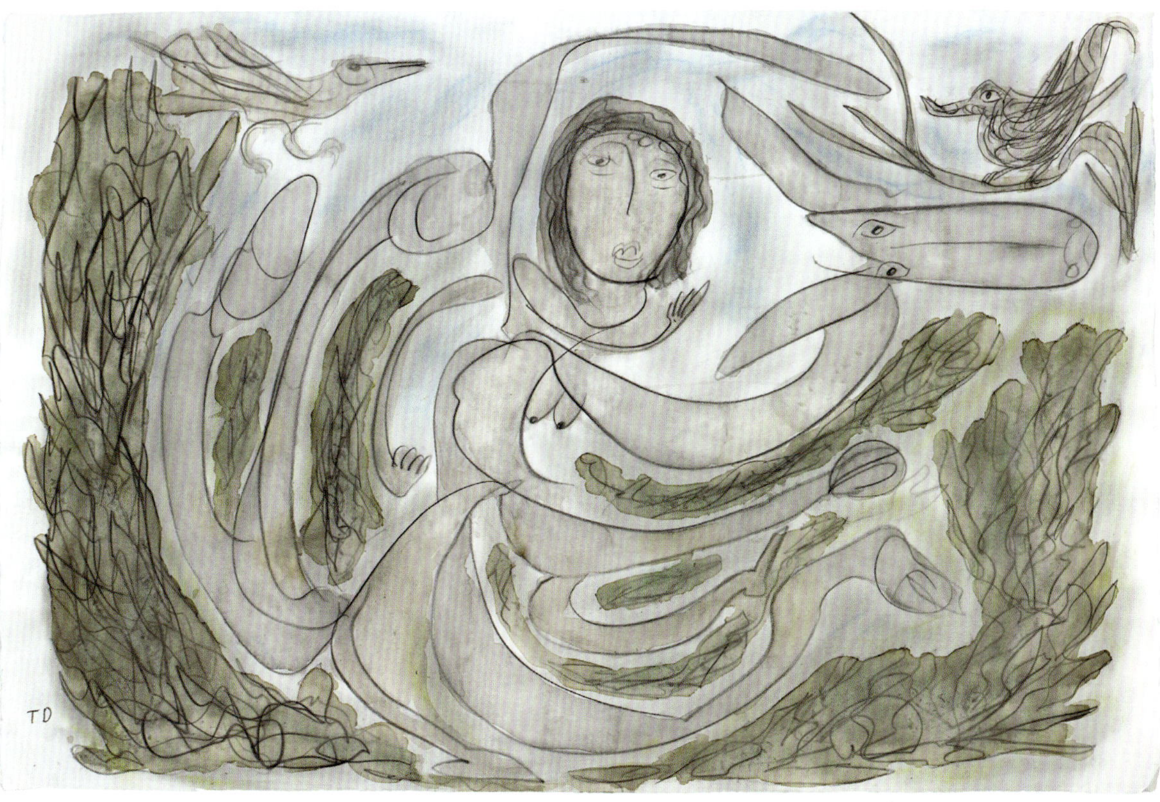

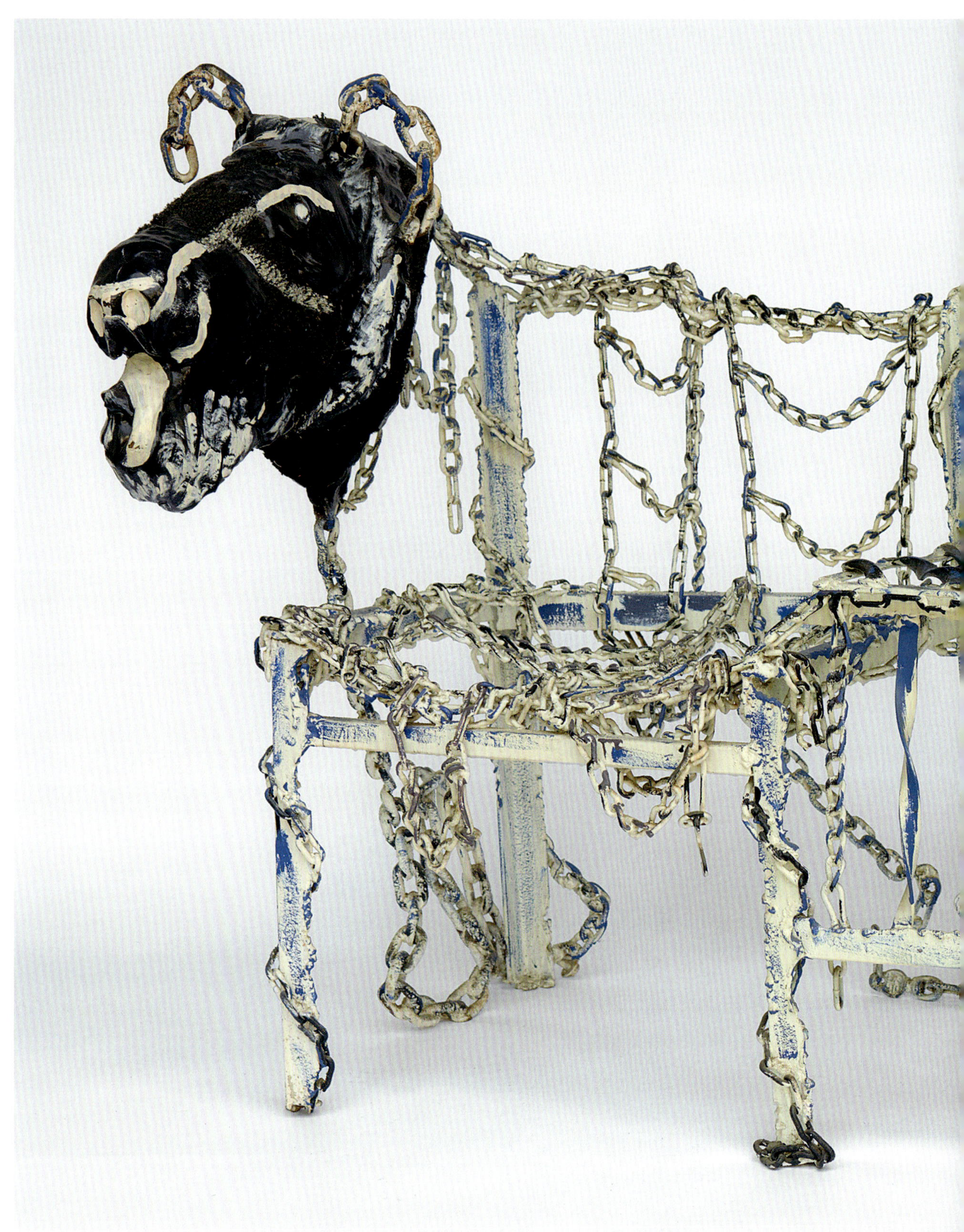

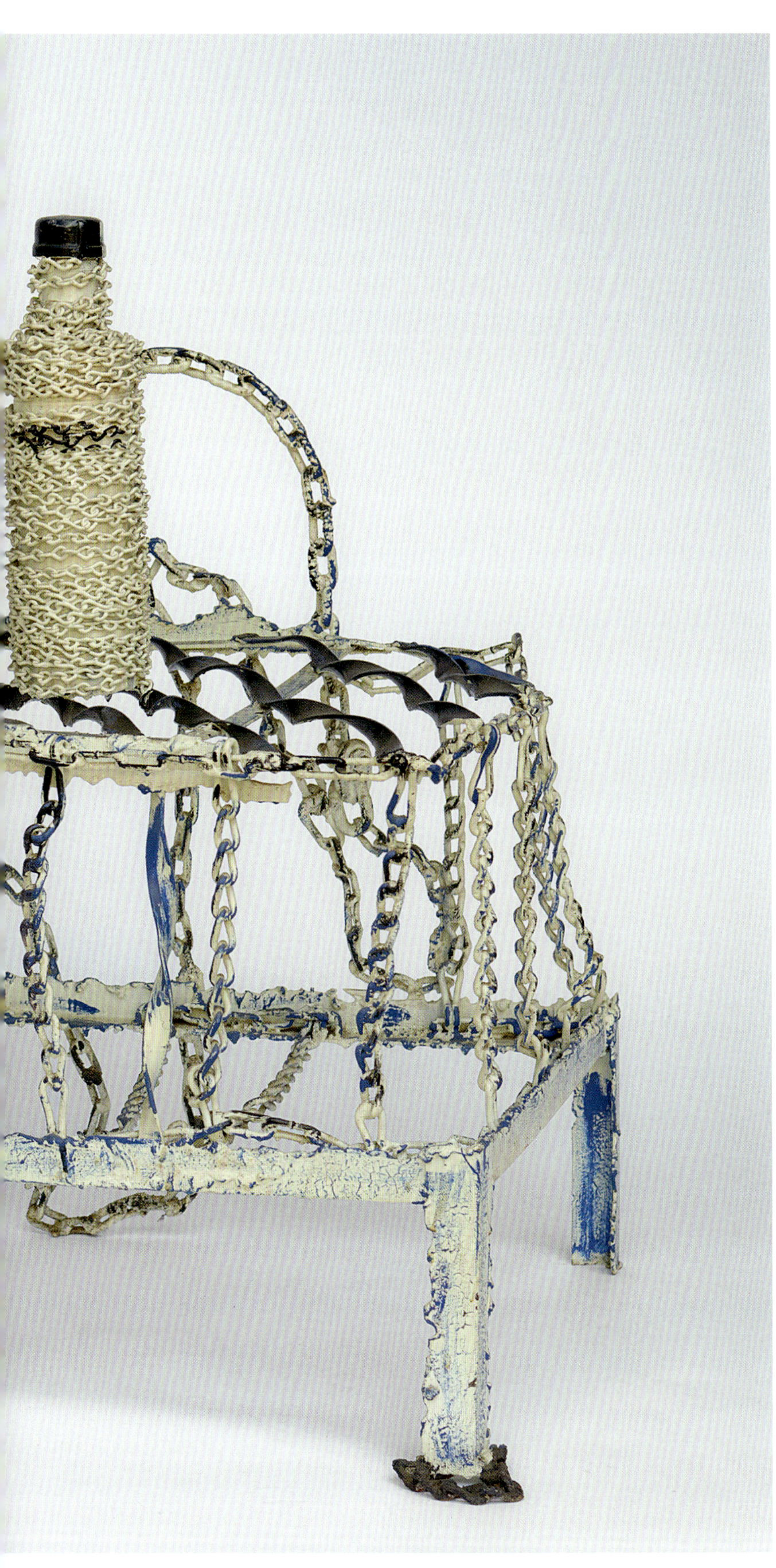

10
Thornton Dial Jr
King of the Jungle, 1990
Welded metal, carpet, industrial
sealing compound and enamel,
100.3 x 128.3 x 78.7 cm
Souls Grown Deep Foundation, Atlanta

Richard Dial

11
Richard Dial
Which Prayer Ended Slavery?, 1988
Welded steel, wire and paint, 147.3 x 127 x 53.3 cm
Souls Grown Deep Foundation, Atlanta

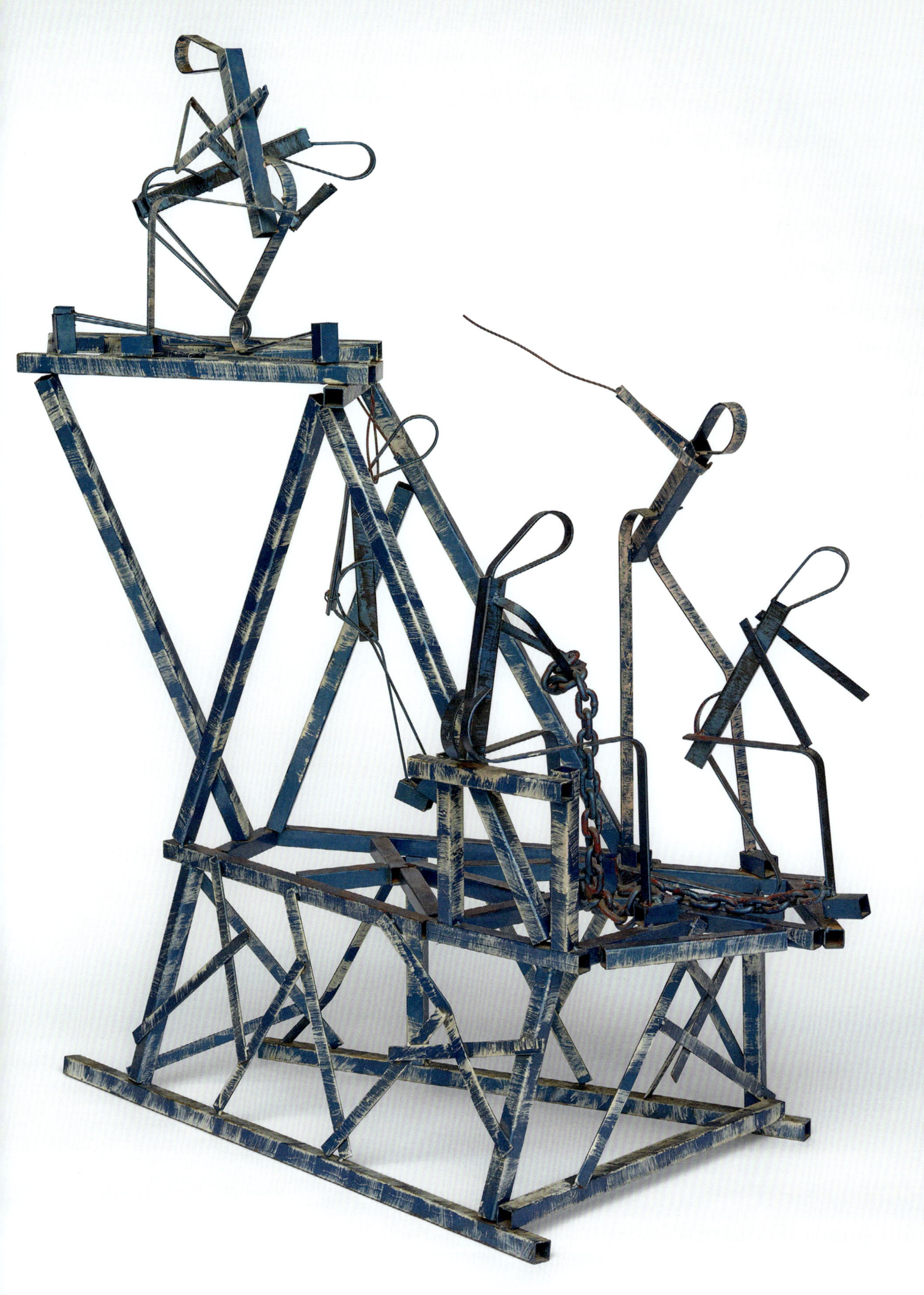

12
Mary Lee Bendolph
Burgle Boys, **2007**
Cotton and polyester, 226.1 x 200.7 cm
Courtesy of the artist Mary Lee Bendolph

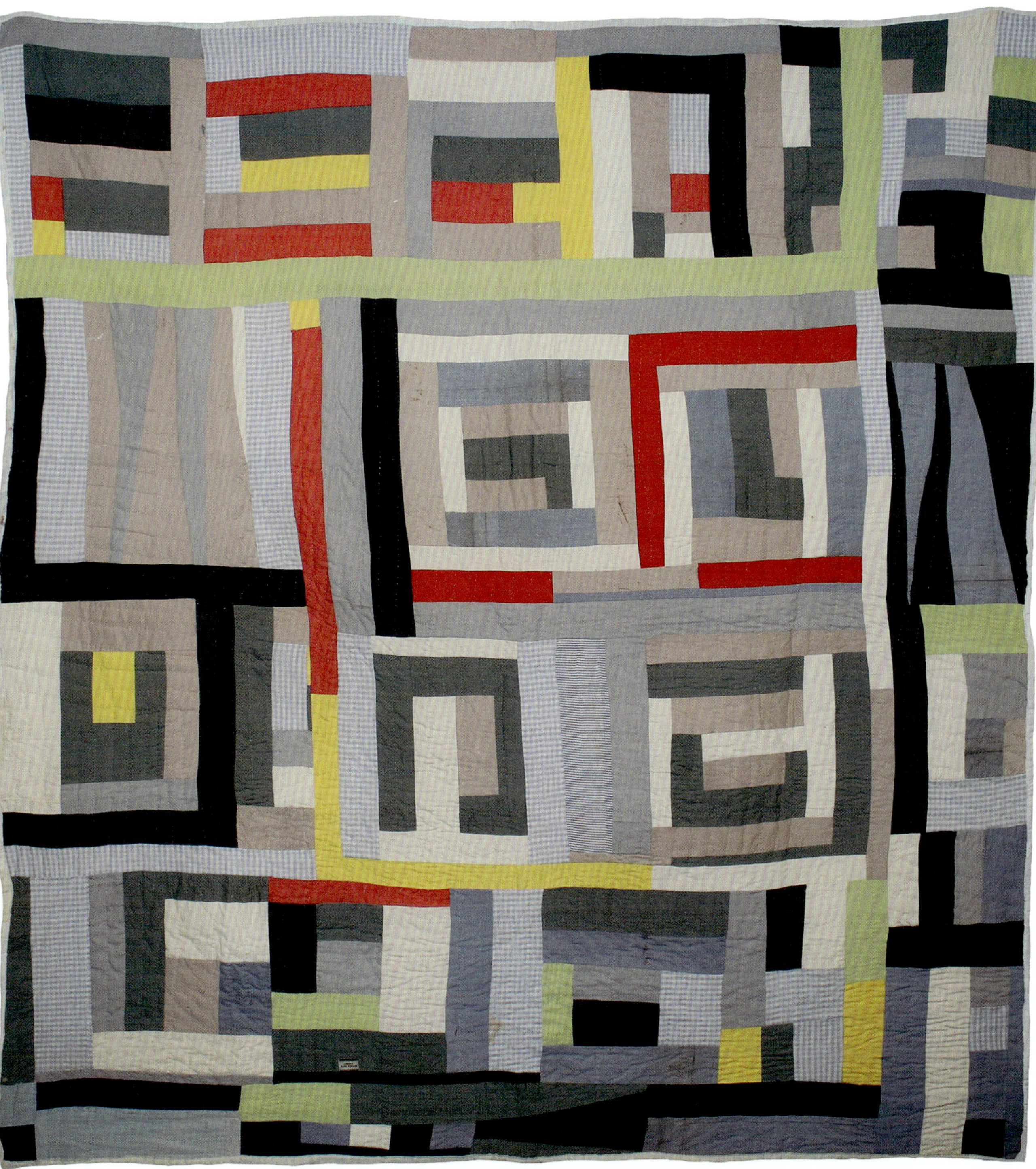

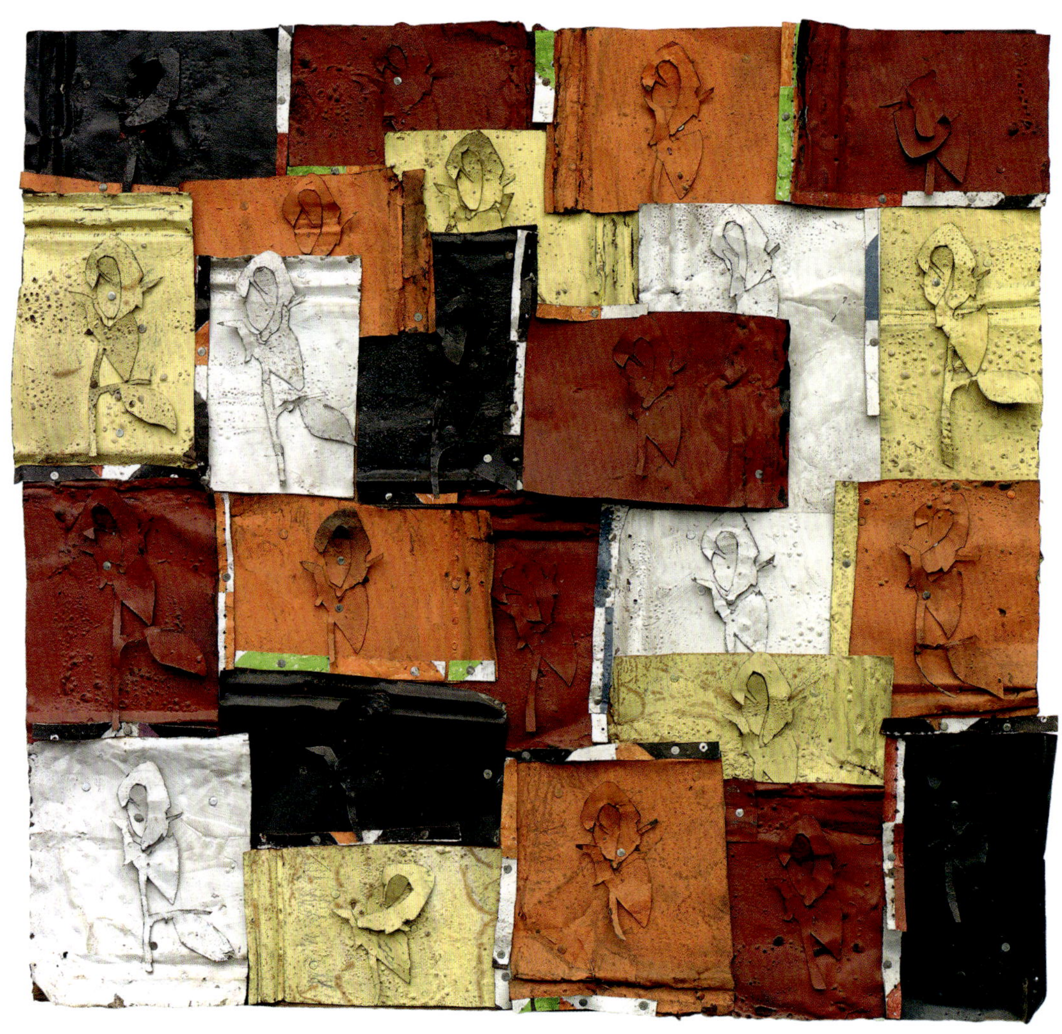

13
Ronald Lockett
Sarah Lockett's Roses, 1997
Cut tin, nails and enamel on wood, 129.5 x 123.2 x 3.8 cm
Souls Grown Deep Foundation, Atlanta

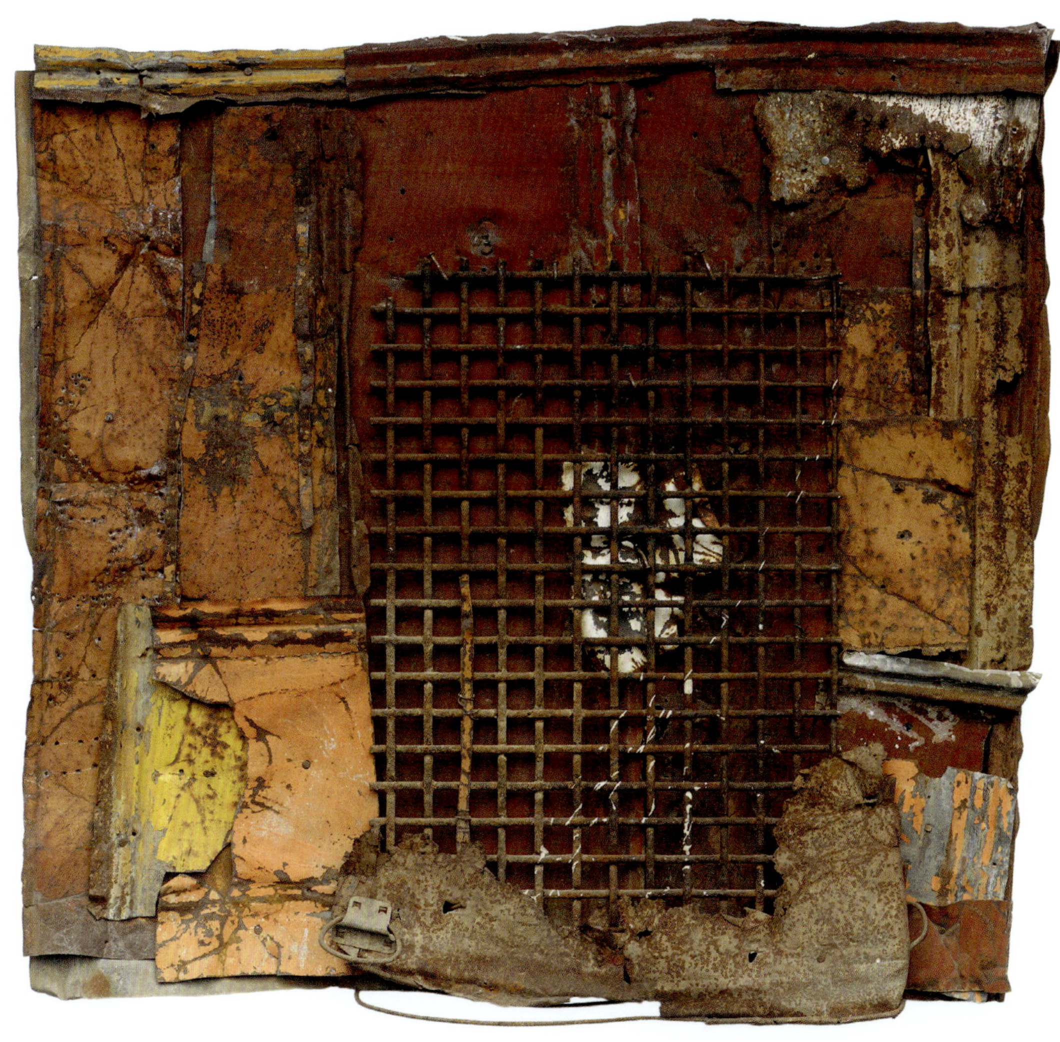

14
Ronald Lockett
Oklahoma, 1995
Found sheet metal, tin, wire, paint and nails on wood,
114.3 x 117.5 x 7.6 cm
Souls Grown Deep Foundation, Atlanta

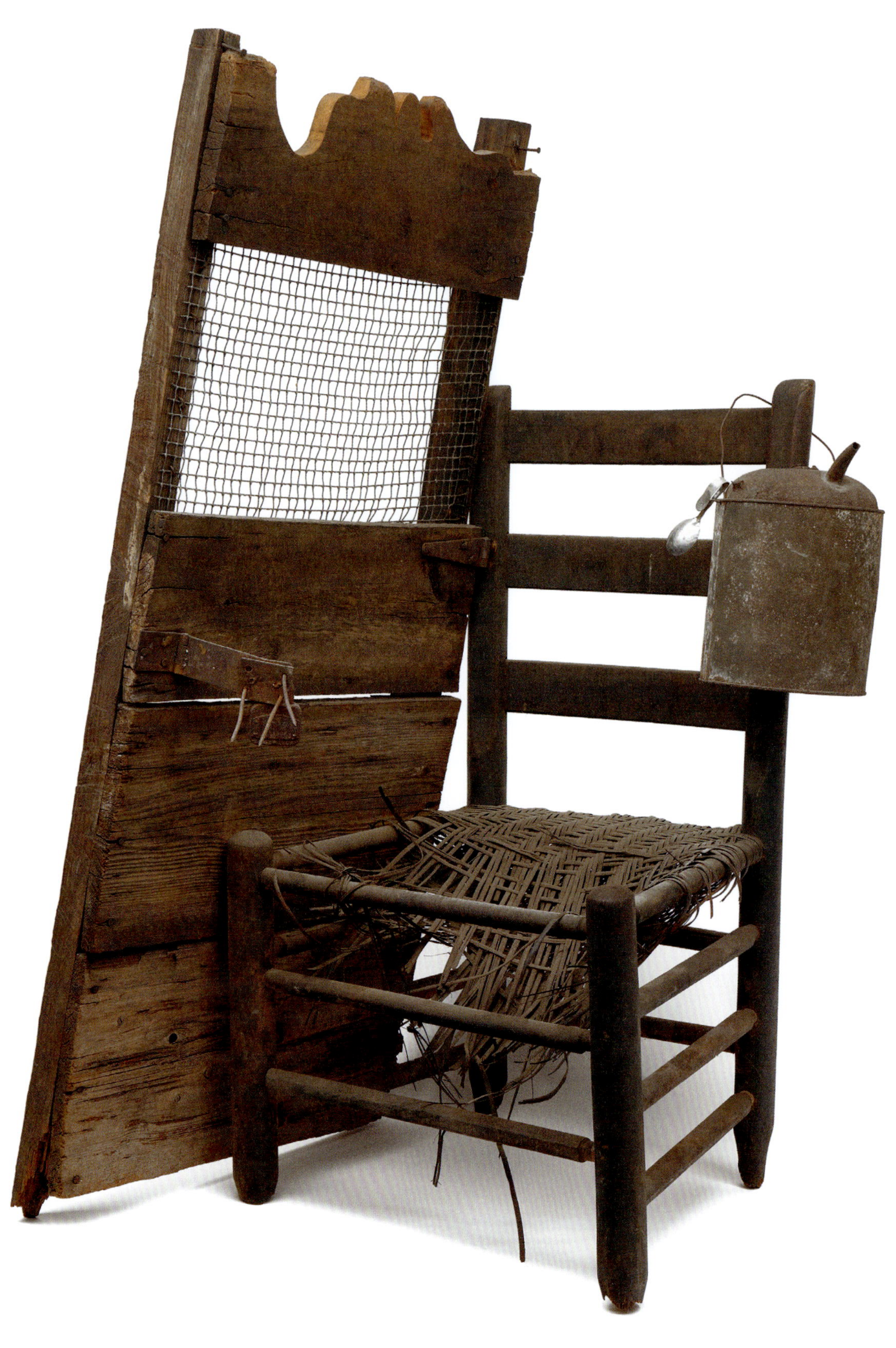

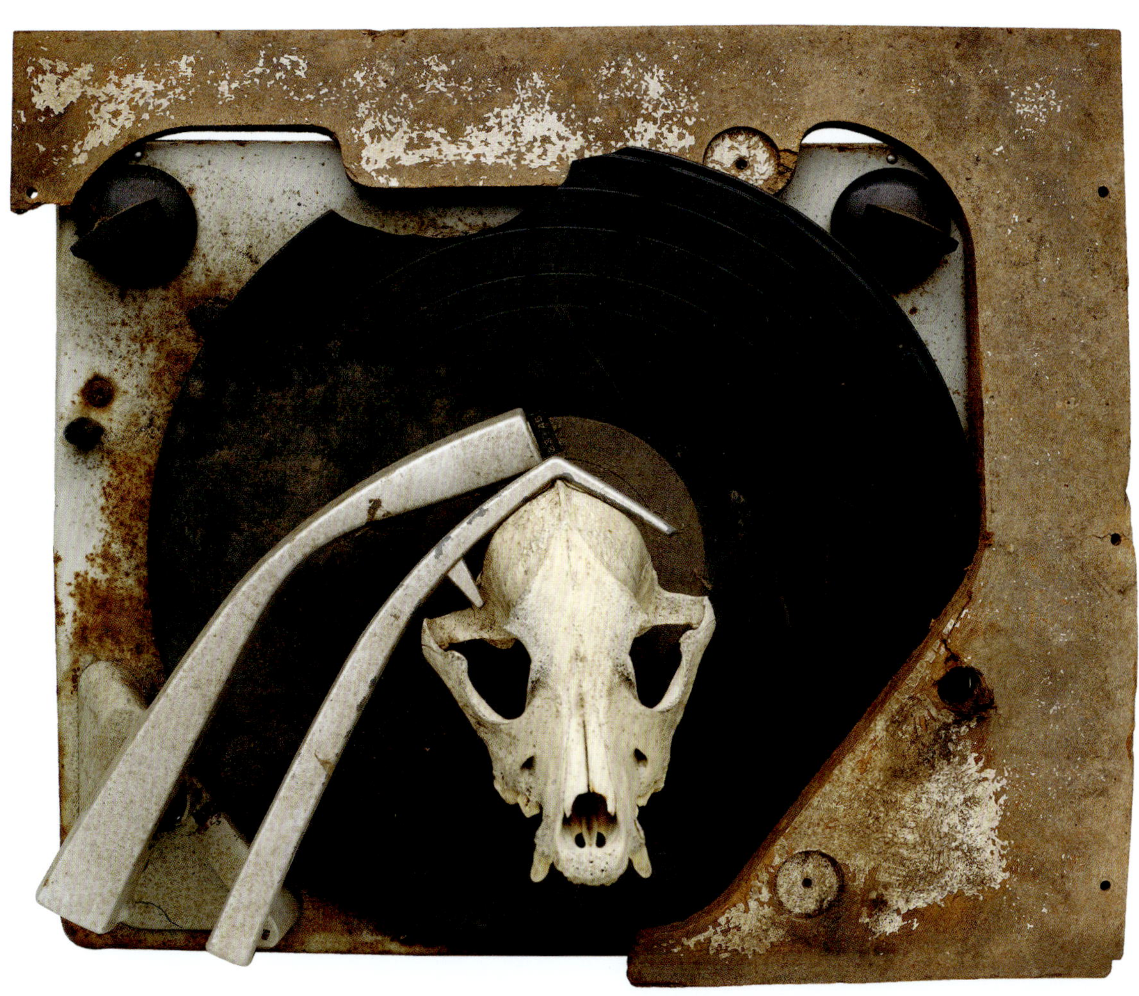

15
Lonnie Holley
Spirit of the Man by the Chicken House Door, 1984
Wooden chair, door and metal can, 116.8 x 90.2 x 43.2 cm
Souls Grown Deep Foundation, Atlanta

16
Lonnie Holley
Keeping a Record of It (Harmful Music), 1986
Salvaged phonograph top, phonograph record and animal skull,
34.9 x 40 cm
Souls Grown Deep Foundation, Atlanta

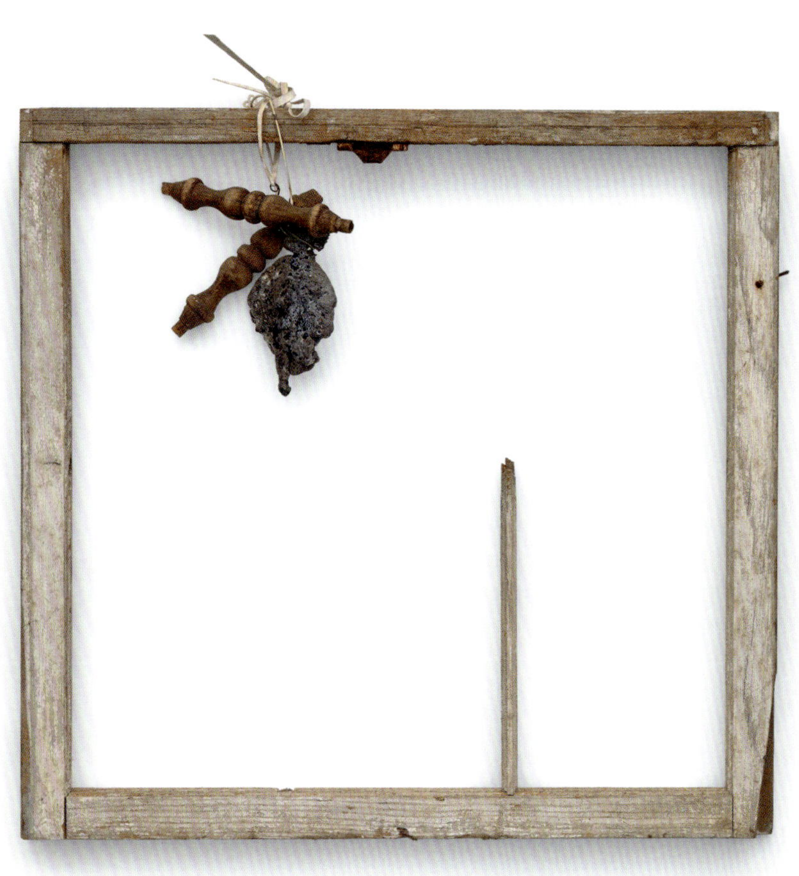

17
Lonnie Holley
The Pain that Broke Me, 1995
Window frame and found materials, 76.8 x 71.1 cm
Souls Grown Deep Foundation, Atlanta

18
Lonnie Holley
Carrying the Lighter Child, 1986
Enamel on wood, 186.7 x 121.9 cm
Souls Grown Deep Foundation, Atlanta

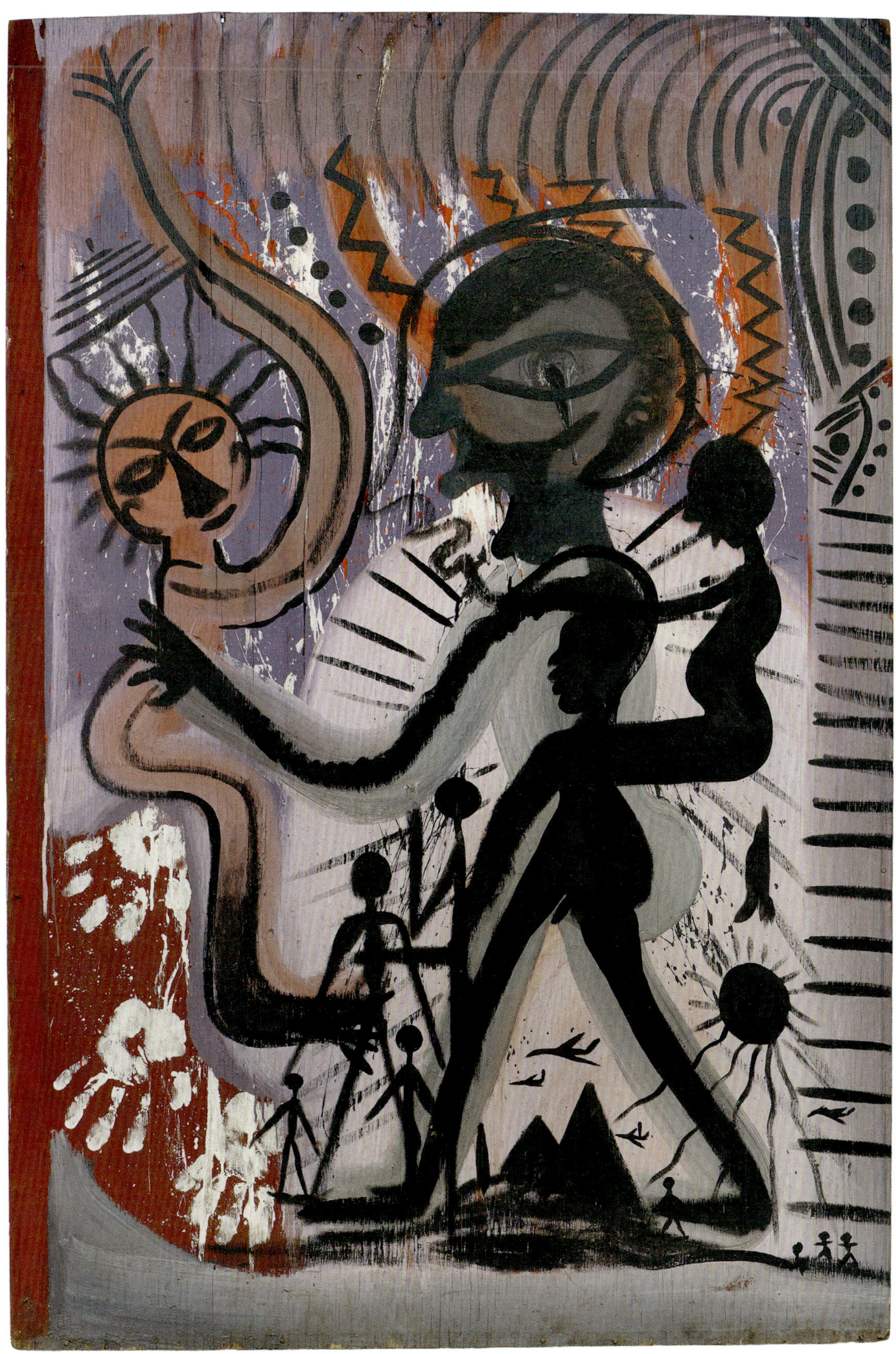

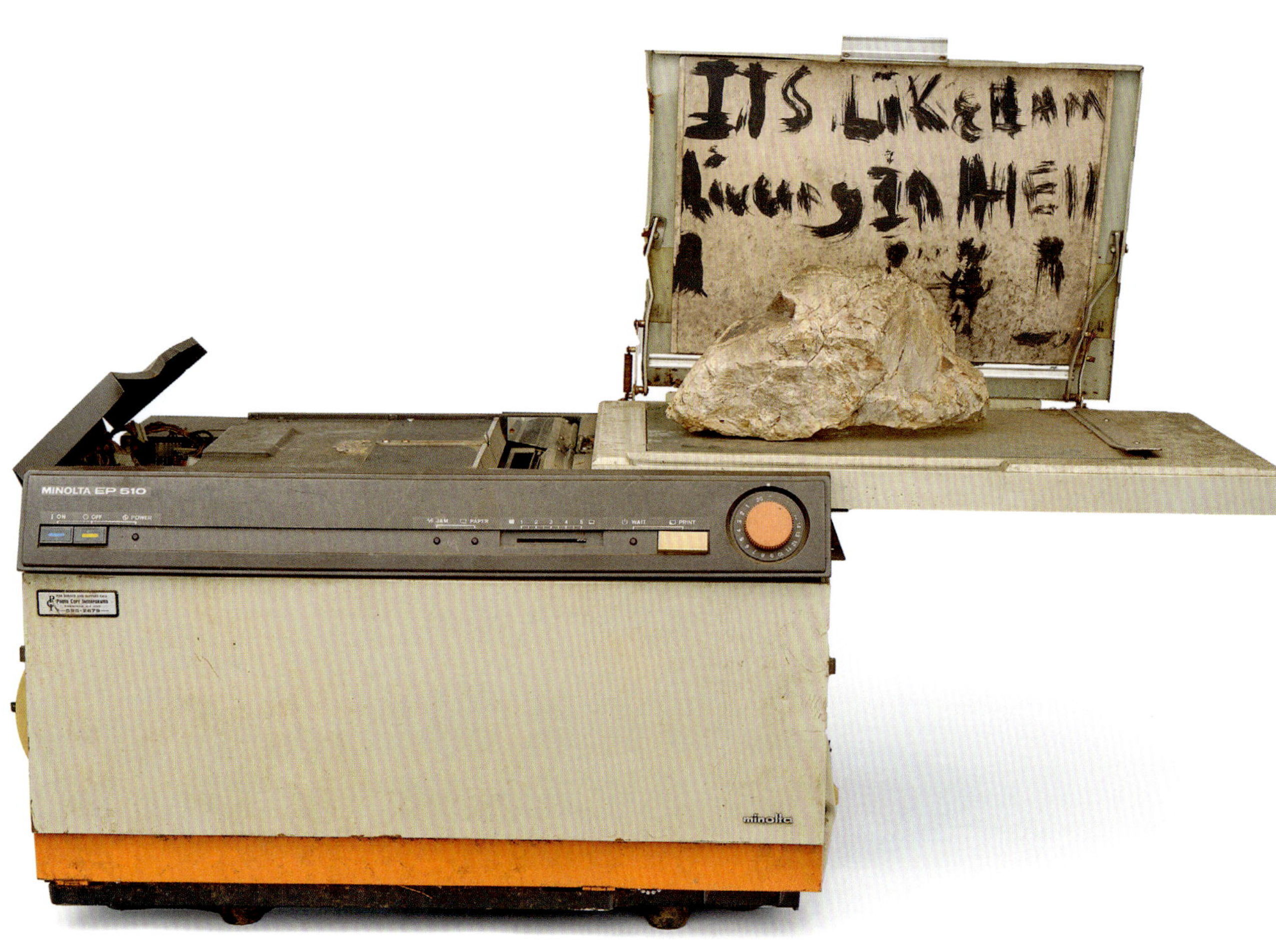
ITS LiKe I AM
living in HEll
MINOLTA EP 510
minolta

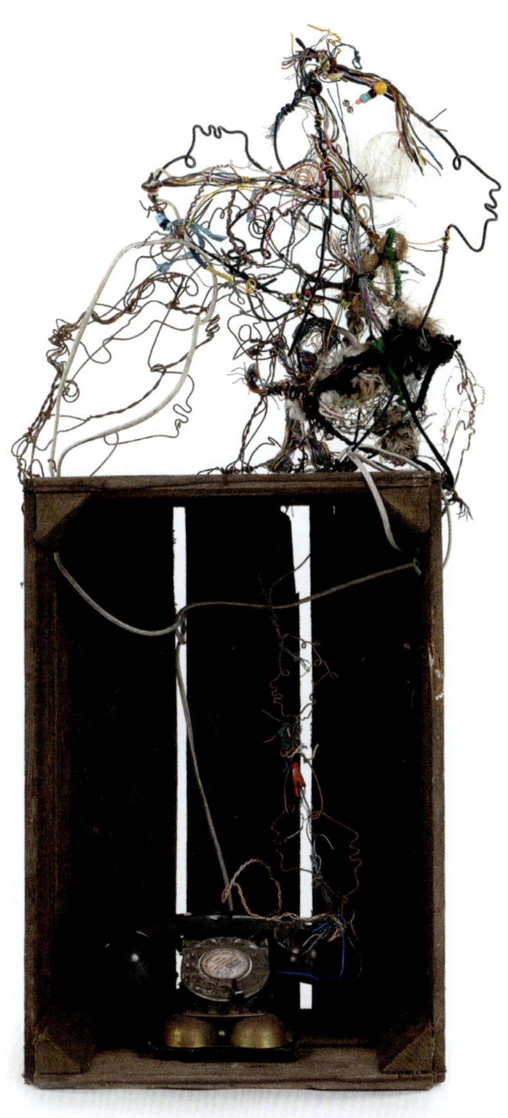

19
Lonnie Holley
Copying the Rock, 1995
Copier, rock and paint, 85.1 x 116.8 x 61 cm
Souls Grown Deep Foundation, Atlanta

20
Lonnie Holley
The Growth of Communication, 2022
Wooden milk crate, telephone, cotton thread,
telephone cables and wire, 98 x 44 x 30 cm
Zabludowicz Collection

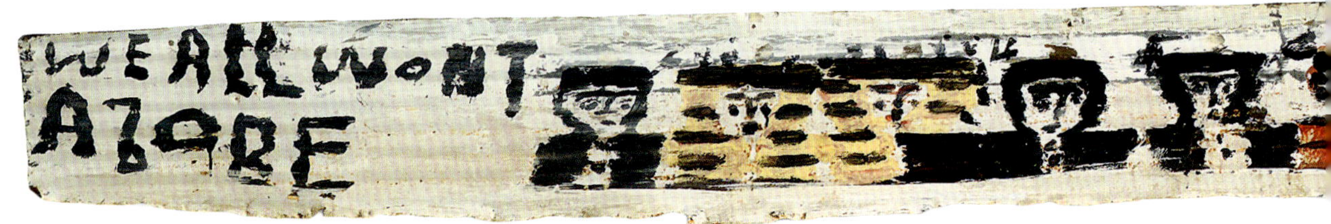

21
Mary T. Smith
We All Want a Jobe [We All Want a Job], **early 1980s**
Paint on corrugated tin, 27.9 x 367 cm
Souls Grown Deep Foundation, Atlanta

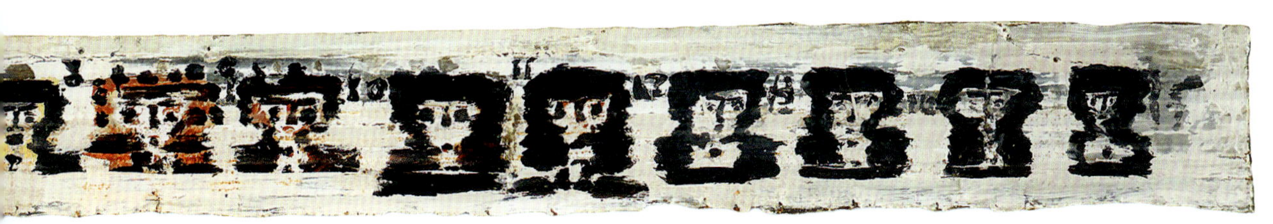

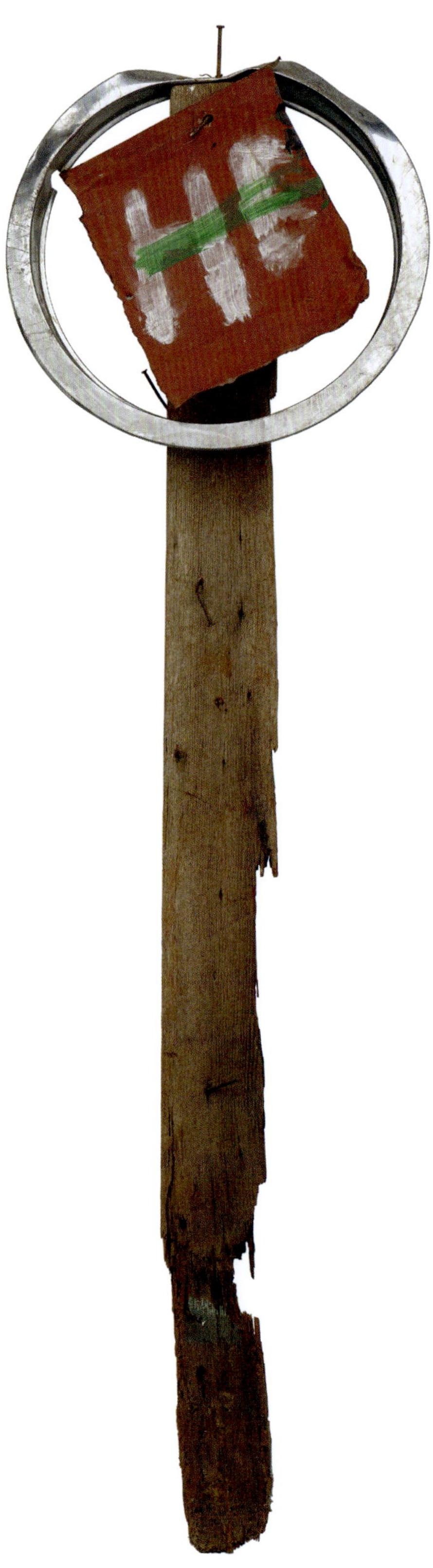

22
Mary T. Smith
He, c. 1980
Tyre rim, tin, paint, nails and wood, 154.9 x 41.9 cm
Souls Grown Deep Foundation, Atlanta

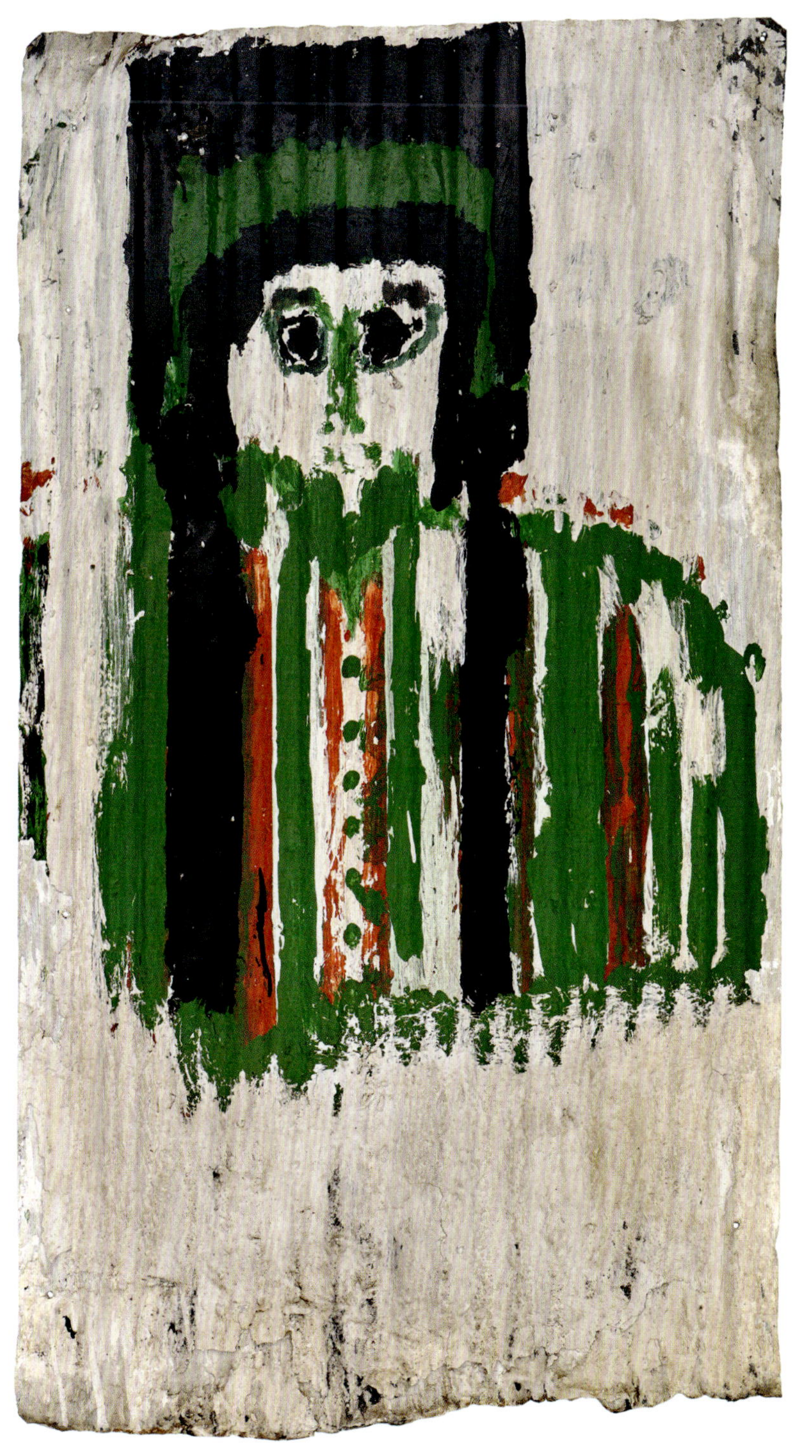

23
Mary T. Smith
Untitled, 1984
Paint on corrugated tin, 125.7 x 66 cm
Souls Grown Deep Foundation, Atlanta

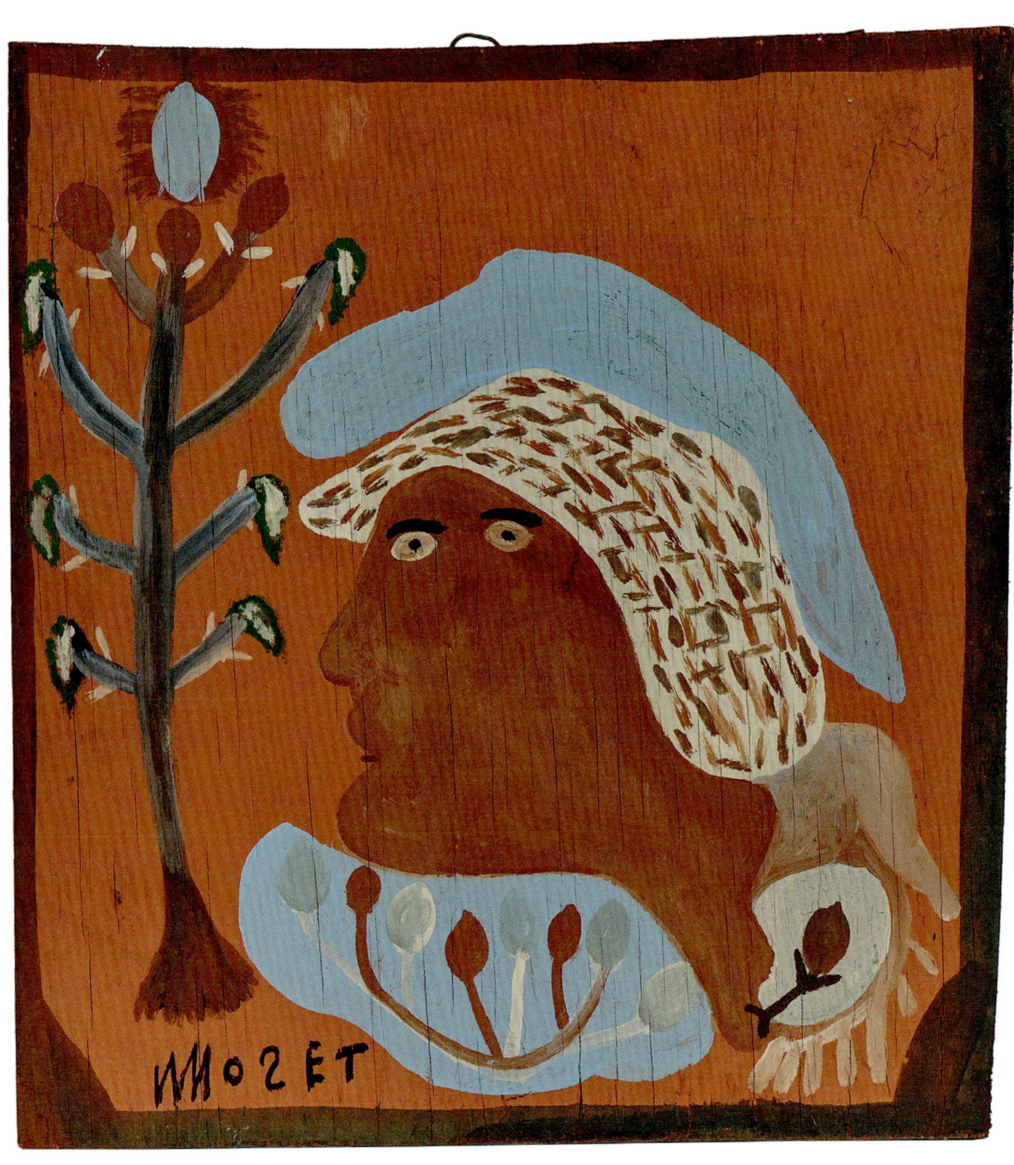

24
Mose Tolliver
Mary, 1986
House paint on wood, 50.8 x 45.7 cm
Souls Grown Deep Foundation, Atlanta

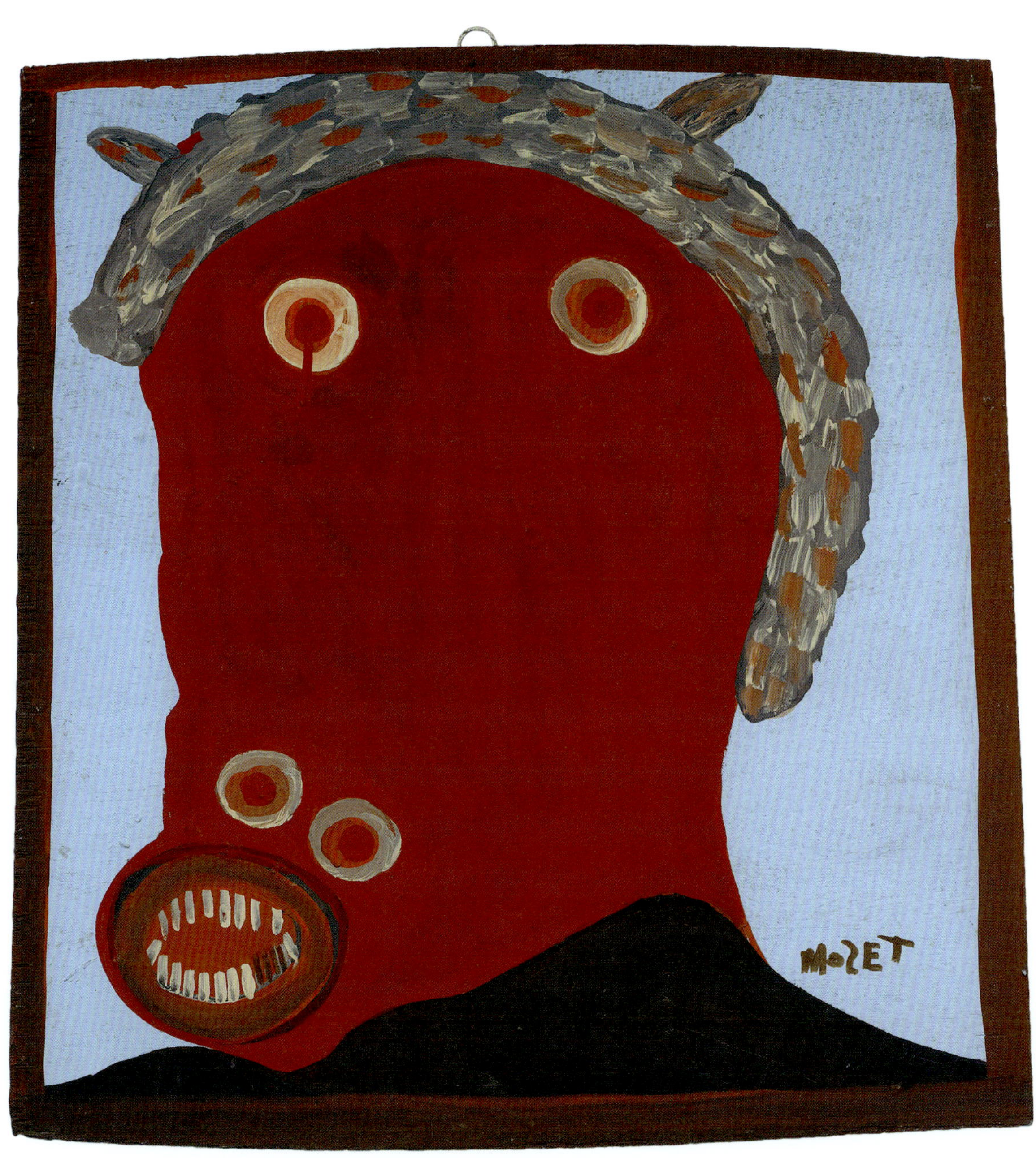

25
Mose Tolliver
Self-portrait, 1987
Paint on plywood, 71 x 60 cm
From the collection of Susan and Stephen Pitkin, Rockford, Illinois

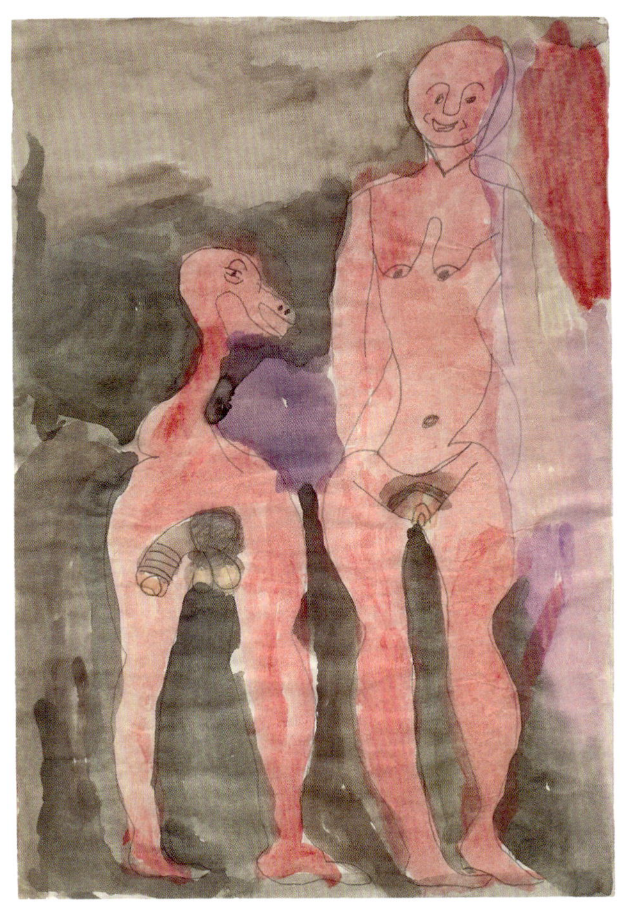

26
Georgia Speller
Untitled, 1985
Paint and pencil on paper, 45 x 30.5 cm
Souls Grown Deep Foundation, Atlanta

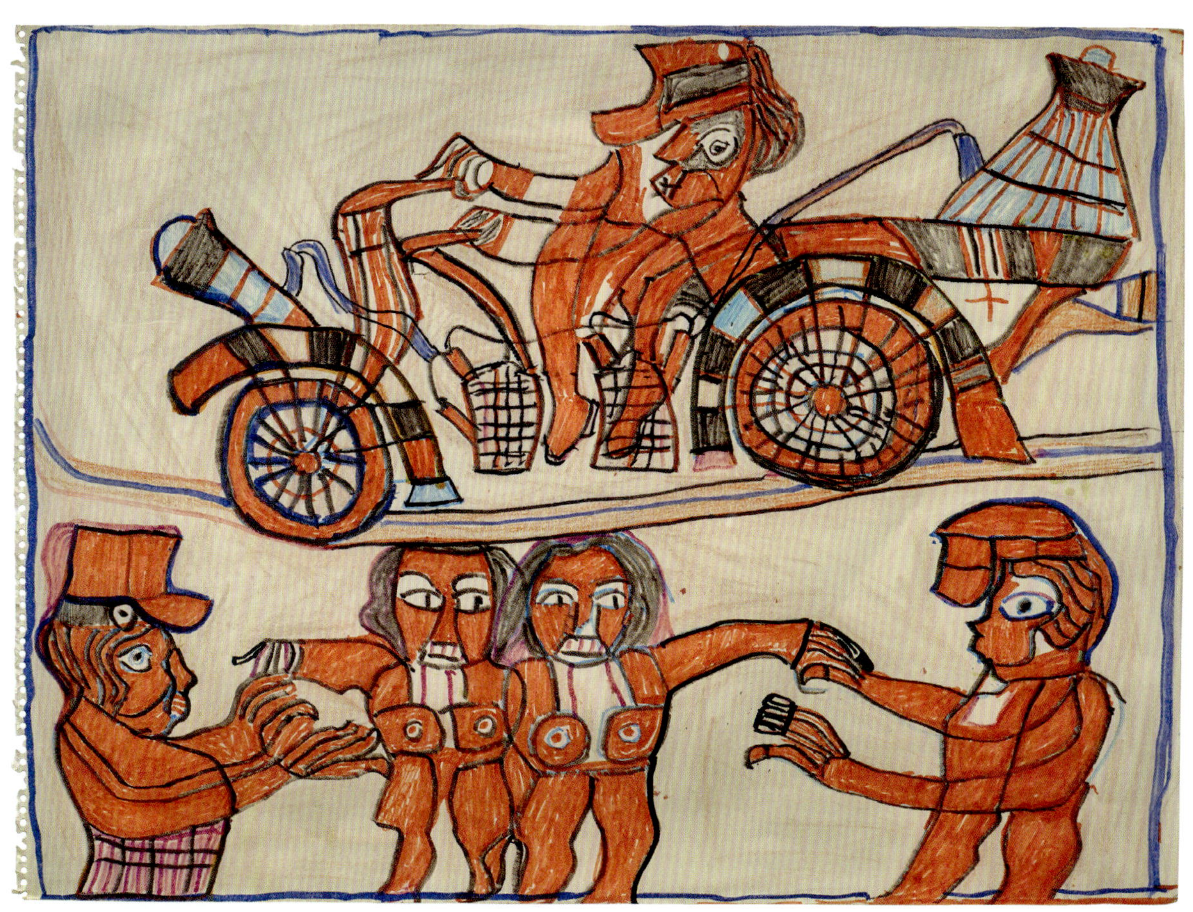

27
Henry Speller
People Looking at a Man on a Motorcycle, 1987
Marker, crayon and pencil on paper, 45.7 x 61 cm
Souls Grown Drep Foundation, Atlanta

Richard Burnside

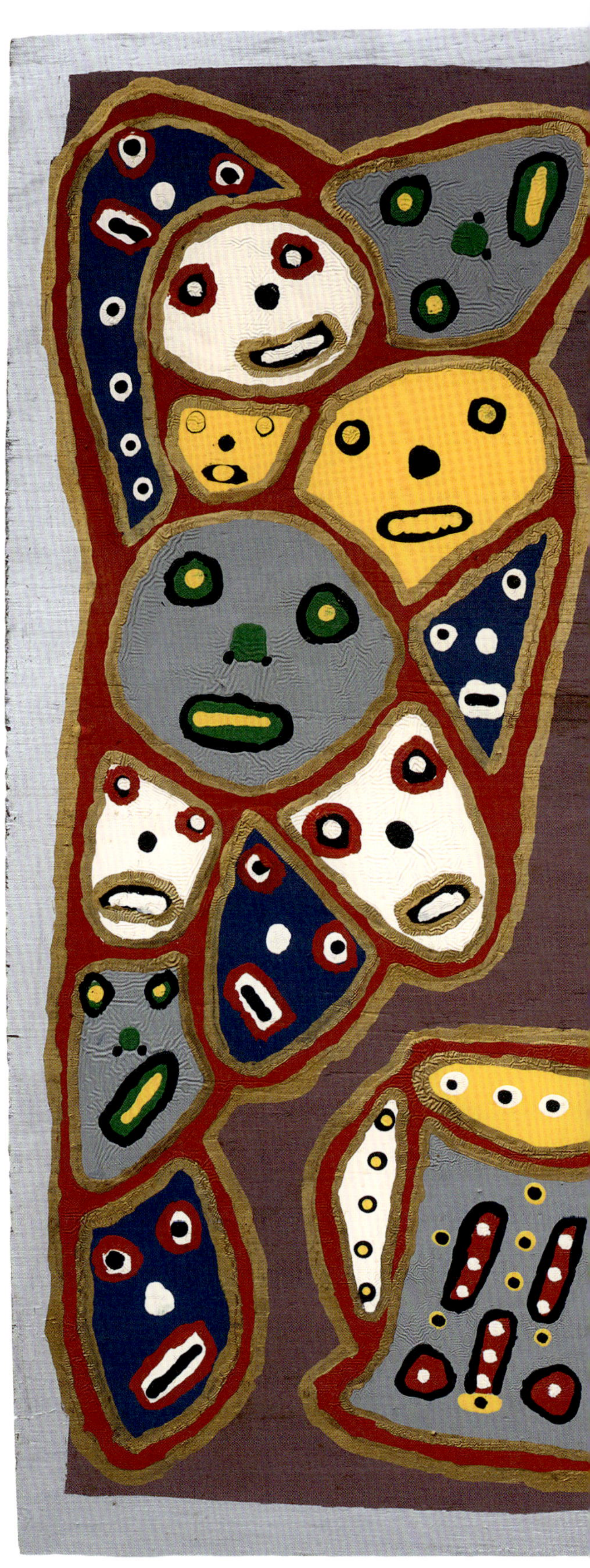

28
Richard Burnside
The Faces, 1988
Paint on wood, 59.7 x 71.8 cm
Souls Grown Deep Foundation, Atlanta

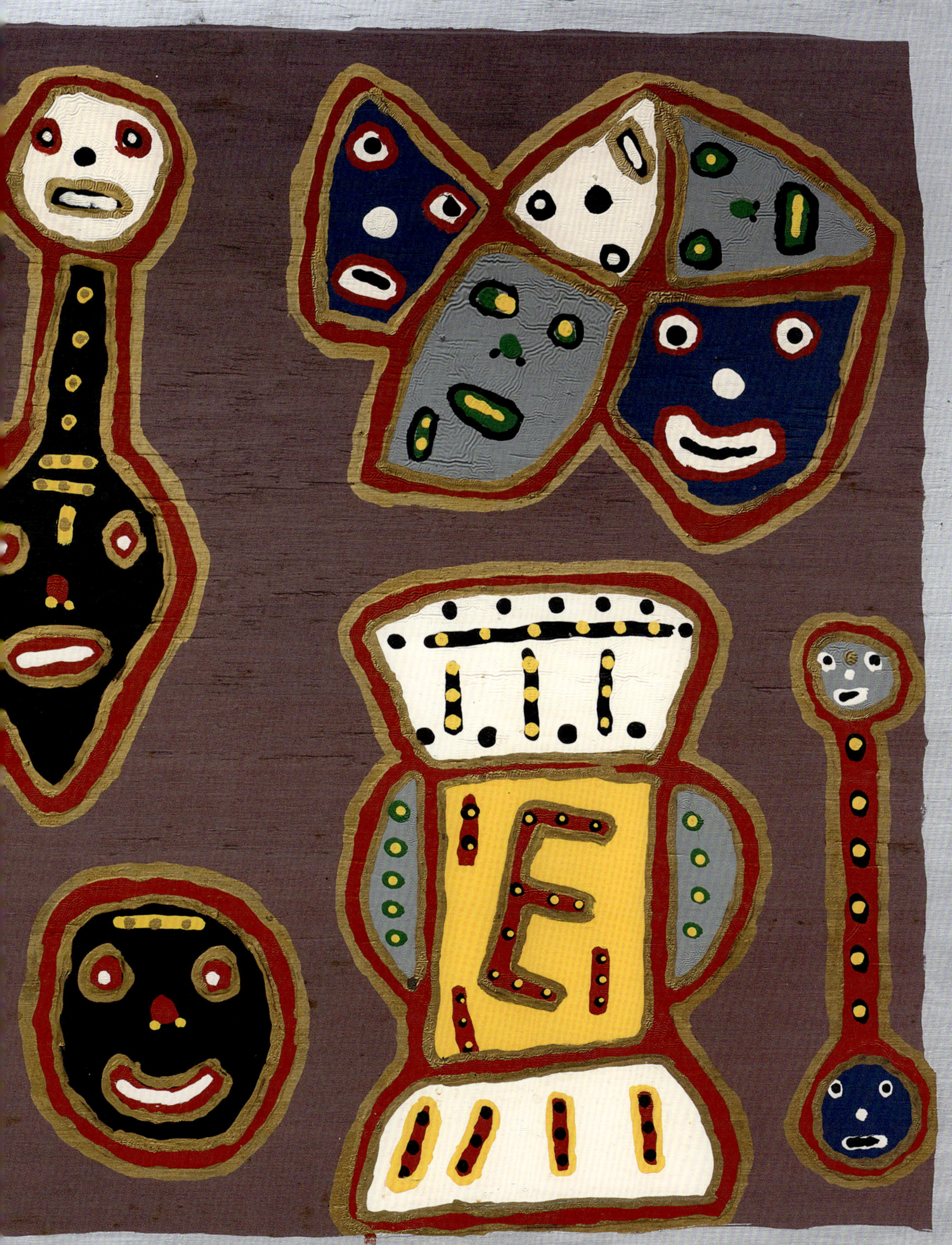

29
Sam Doyle
LeBe, late 1970s
Paint on tin, 95.2 x 67.9 cm
Souls Grown Deep Foundation, Atlanta

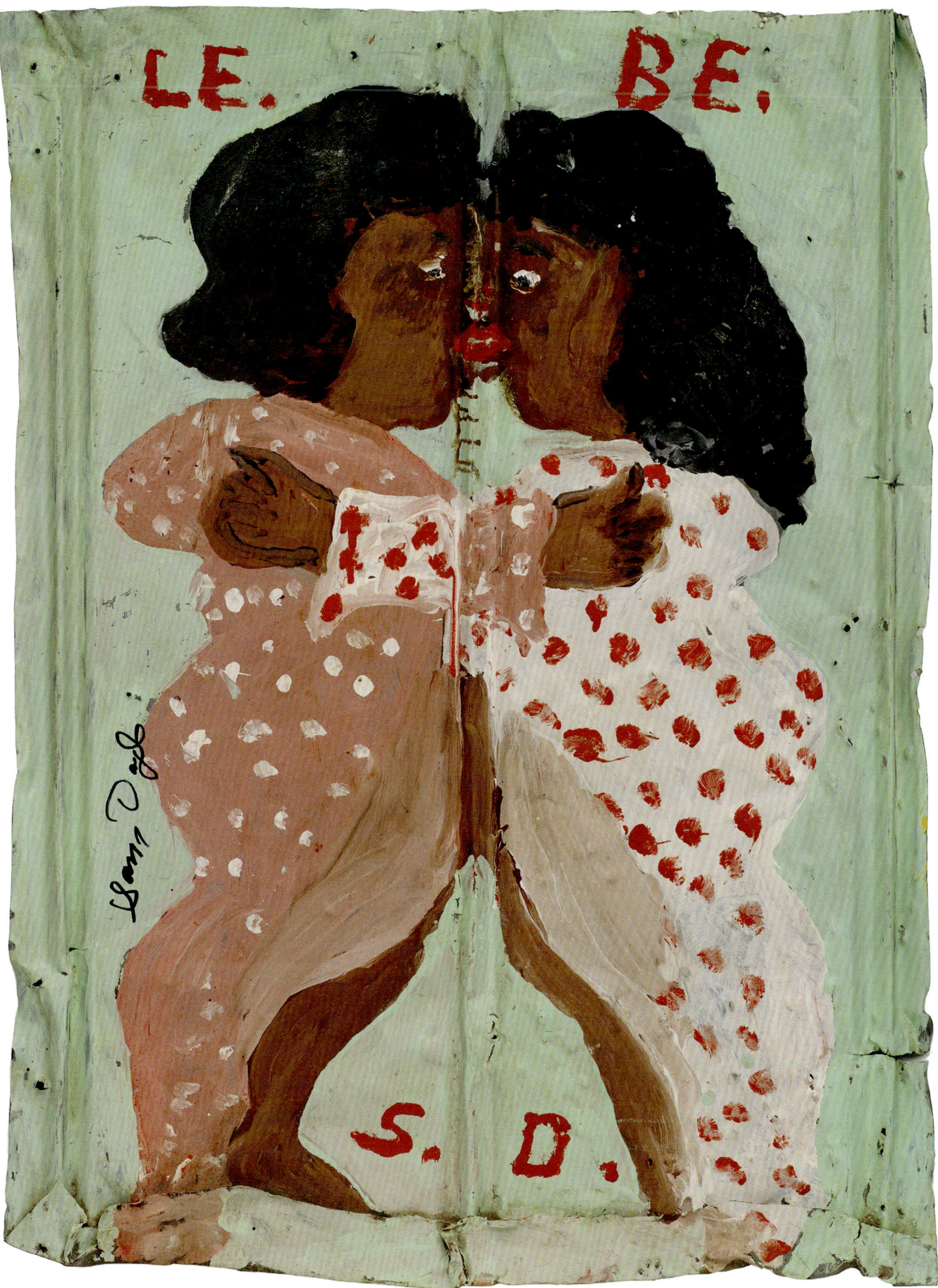
LE.
BE.
S. D.

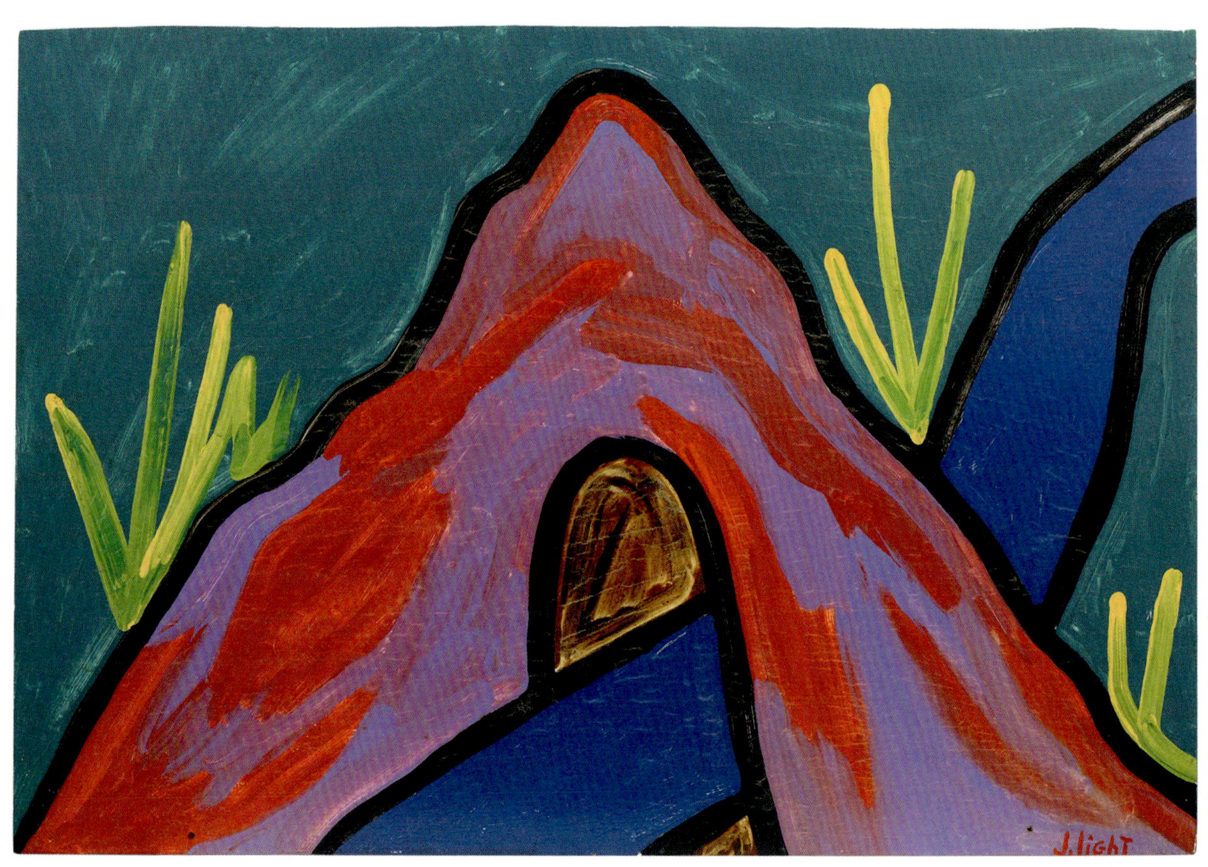

30
Joe Light
Blue River Mountain, 1988
Enamel on wood, 81.3 x 121.9 cm
Souls Grown Deep Foundation, Atlanta

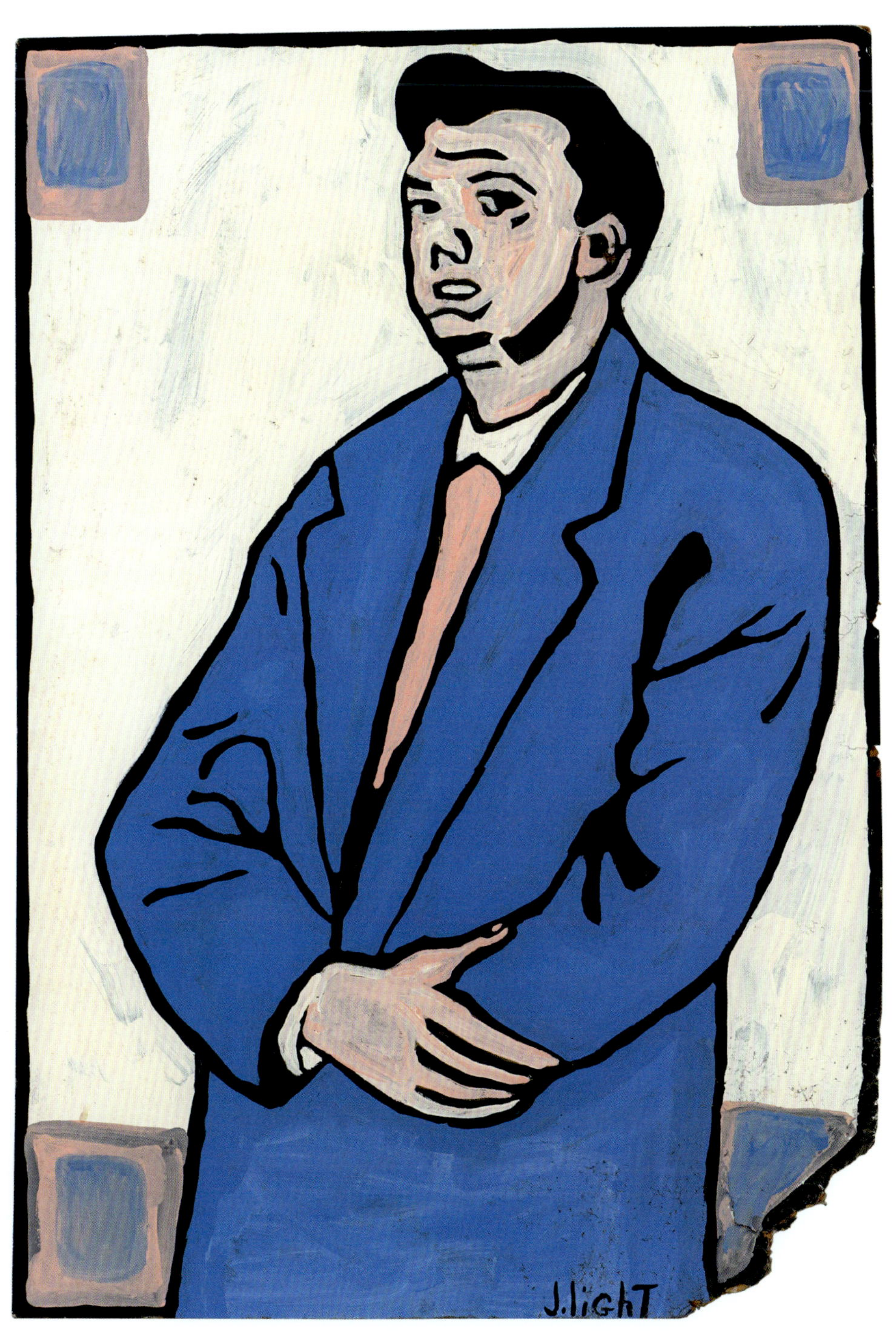

31
Joe Light
My Main Man Dan, 1988
Enamel on Masonite, 91.4 x 61 cm
Souls Grown Deep Foundation, Atlanta

32
Charles Williams
Lamp, early 1980s
Metal stool base, lamp, light bulb, pencil sharpener,
sprinkler head, metal clamp and paint, 132.1 x 45.7 x 66 cm
Souls Grown Deep Foundation, Atlanta

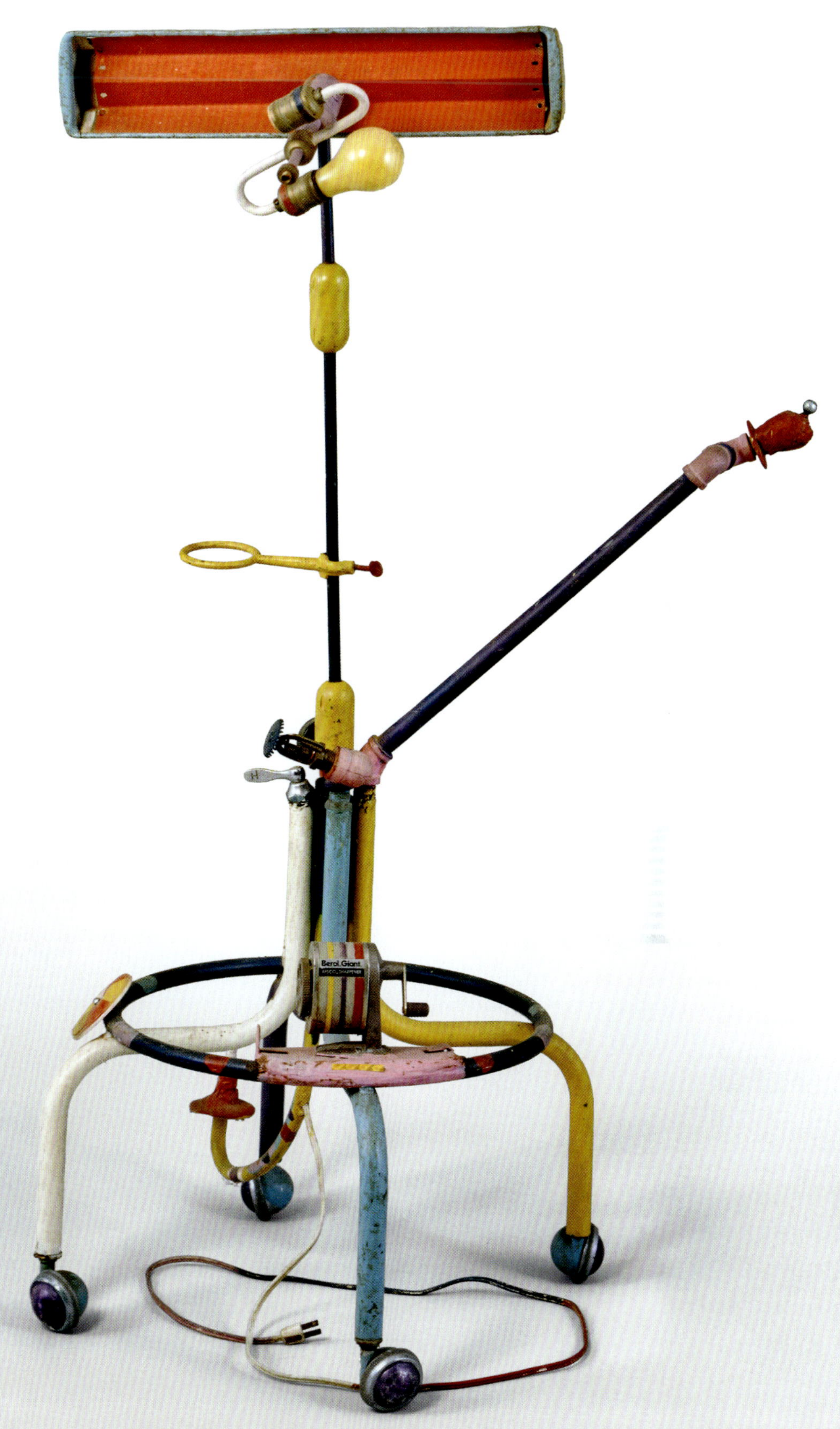

Berol Giant
APSCO SHARPENER

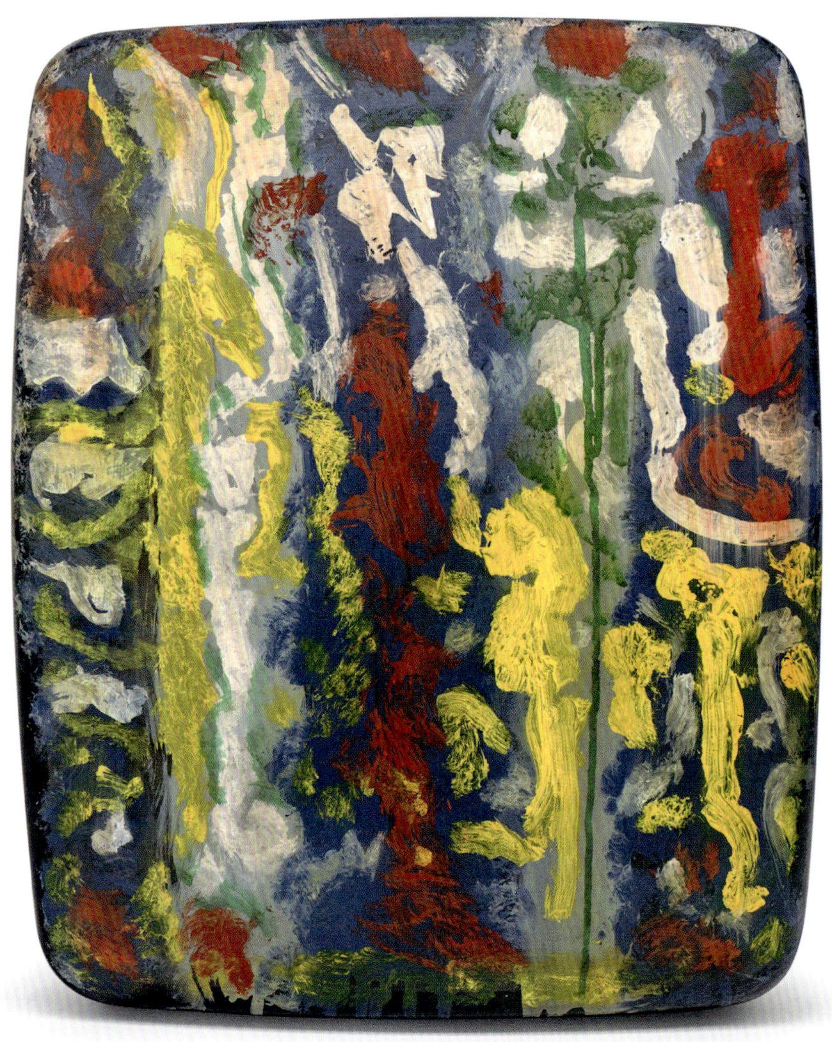

33
John B. Murray
Untitled, c. 1980
Marker, paint and paper tag on television picture tube,
41.9 x 33.7 x 31.7 cm
Souls Grown Deep Foundation, Atlanta

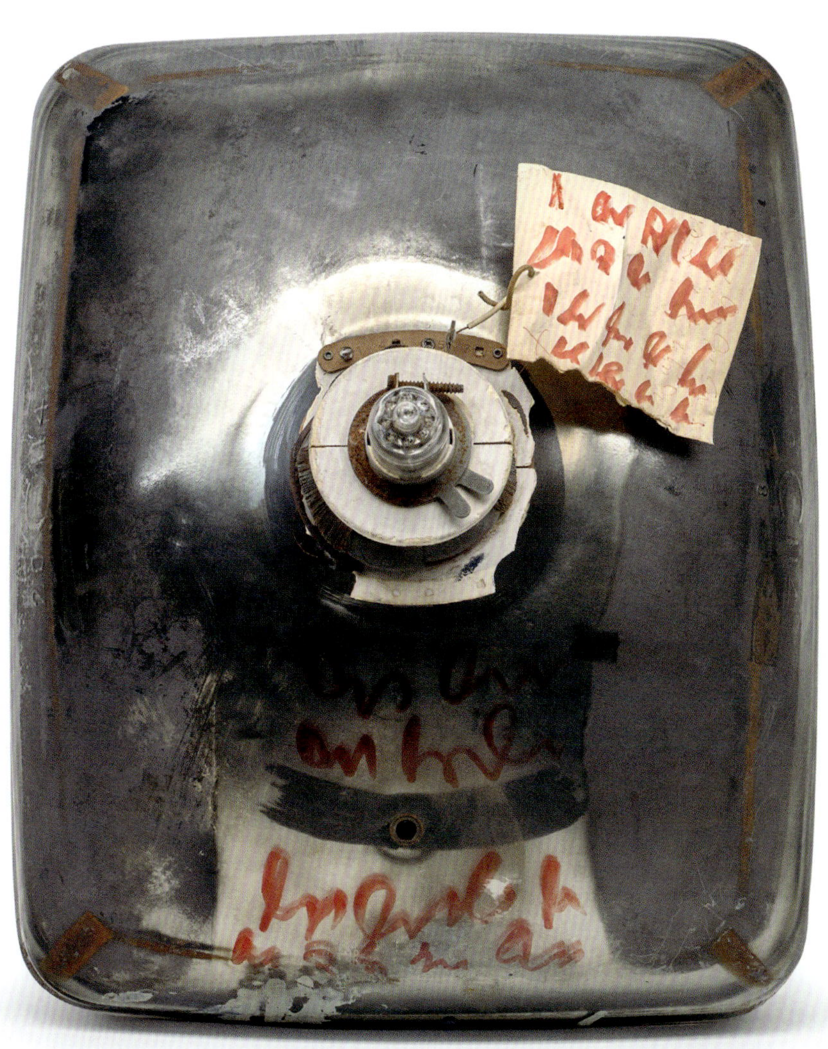

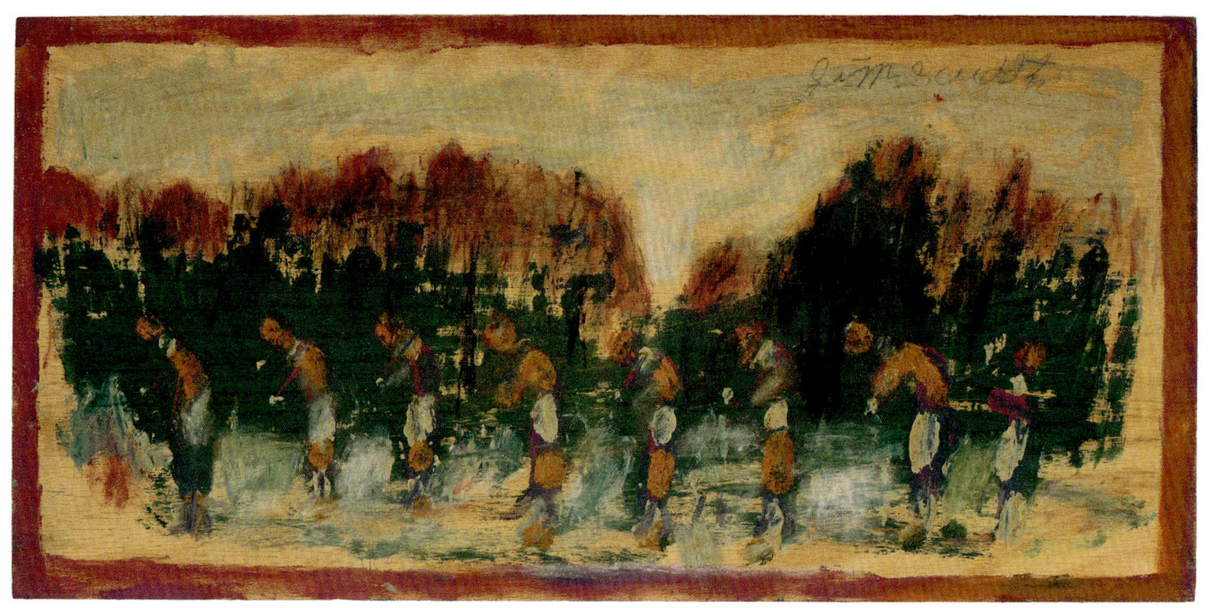

34
Jimmy Lee Sudduth
Africa, mid-1980s
Mud, blackberry juice, grass stain and white pigment on wood,
31.7 x 63.5 cm
Souls Grown Deep Foundation, Atlanta

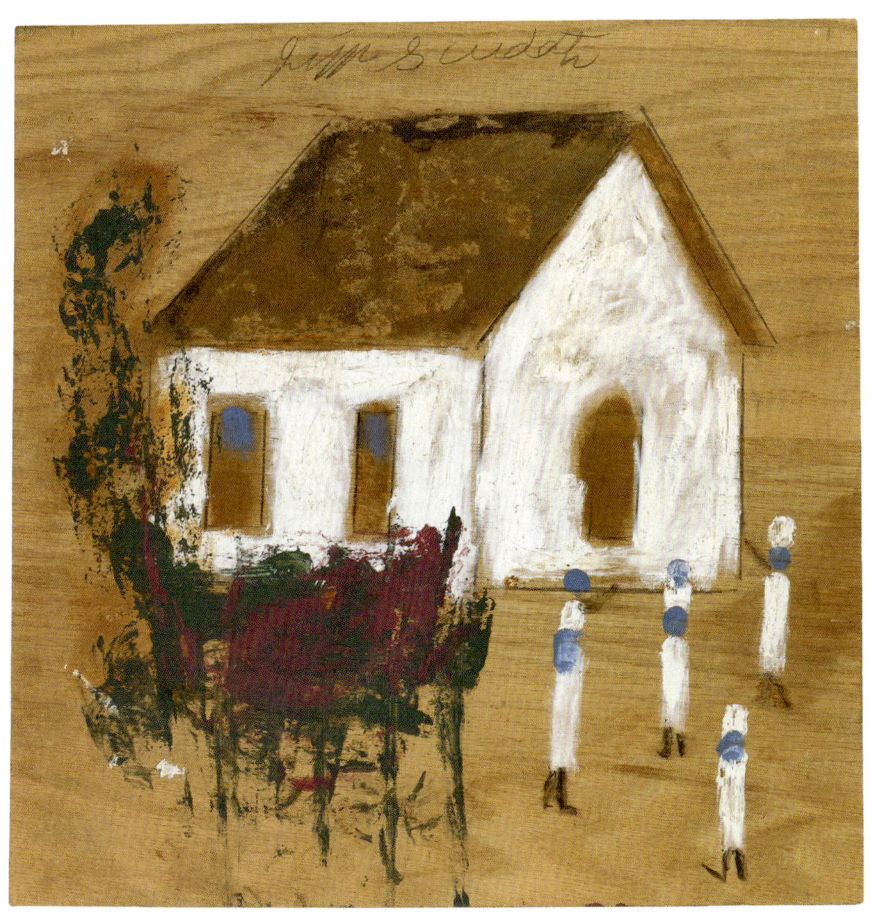

35
Jimmy Lee Sudduth
Caines Ridge Church, 1986
Mud, grass stain, berry juice, pencil and paint on wood,
45.7 x 43.8 cm
Souls Grown Deep Foundation, Atlanta

36
Jimmy Lee Sudduth
Atlanta, 1988
Mud, paint and white pigment on wood, 121.2 x 81.2 cm
Souls Grown Deep Foundation, Atlanta

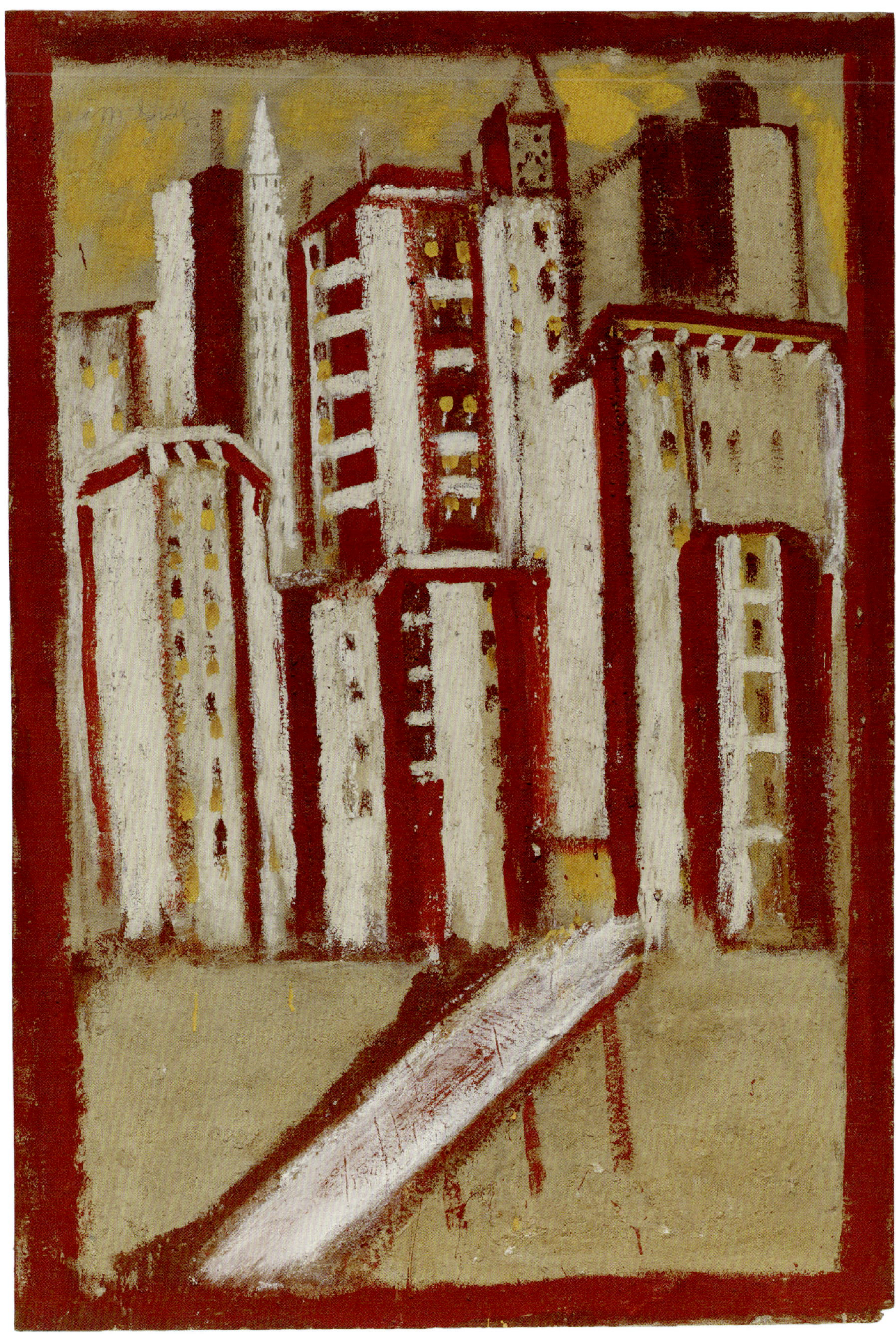

37
Hawkins Bolden
Untitled, 1998
Pot, drainpipe, cans, muffin tin, rubber hoses, nails,
wood and wire, 129.5 x 91.4 x 20.3 cm
Souls Grown Deep Foundation, Atlanta

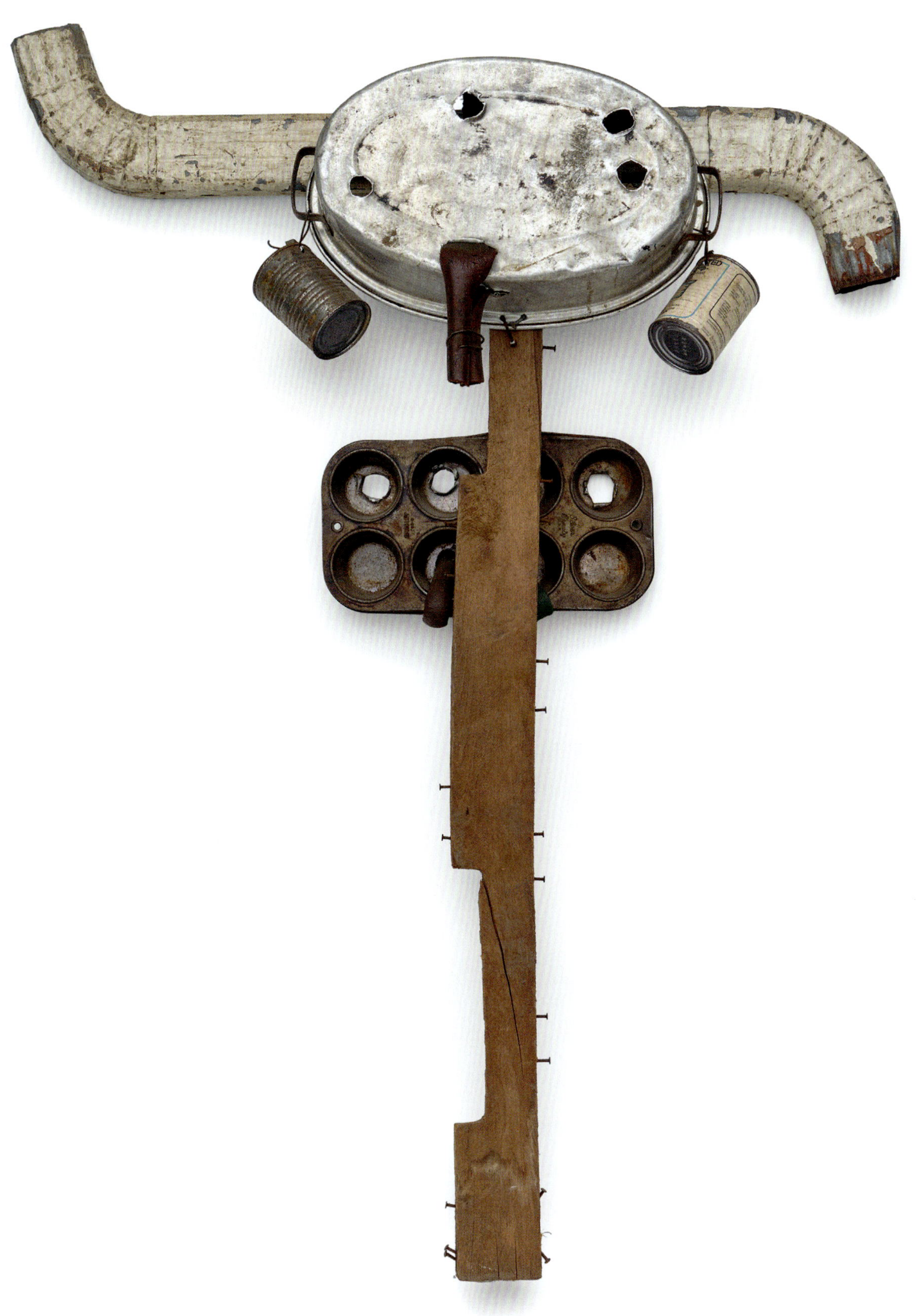

84

38
Archie Byron
Anatomy I, 1987
Sawdust-and-glue relief on wood, with wood frame,
123.8 x 123.8 cm
Souls Grown Deep Foundation, Atlanta

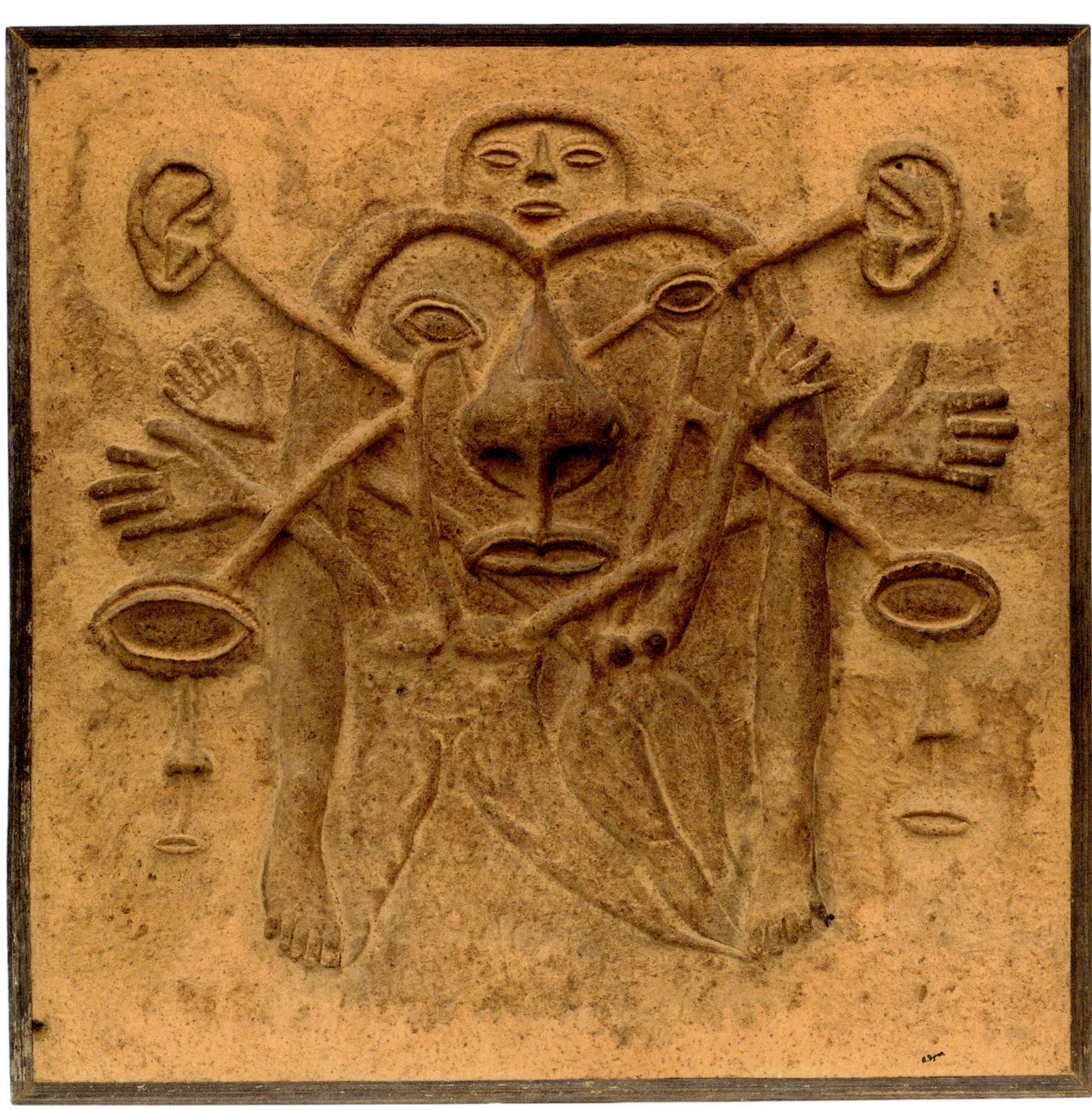

39
Bessie Harvey
Untitled, 1987
Tree root, salvaged wood plank, paste jewels, marbles,
modelling paste and paint, 76.2 x 58.4 x 17.8 cm
Souls Grown Deep Foundation, Atlanta

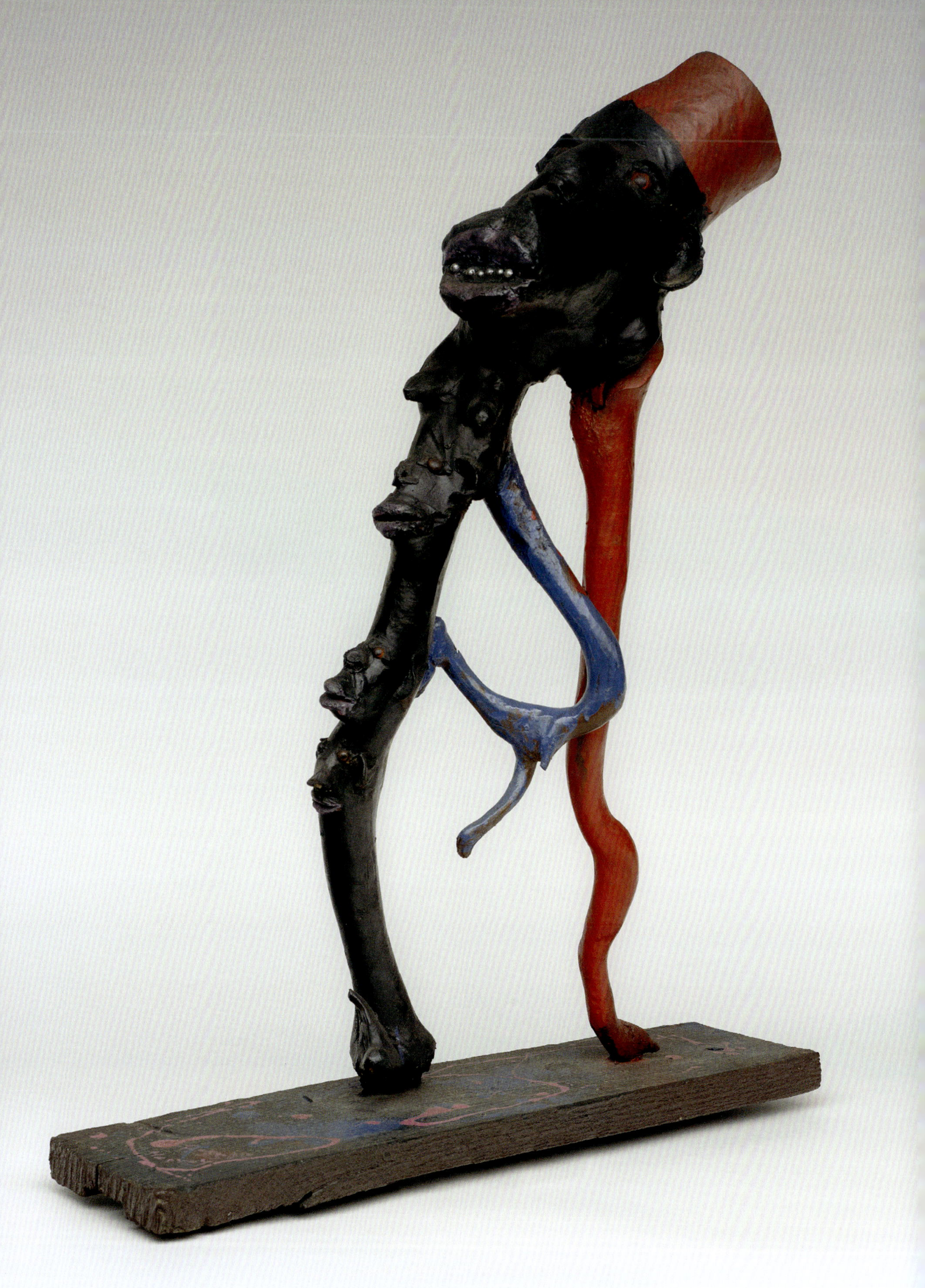

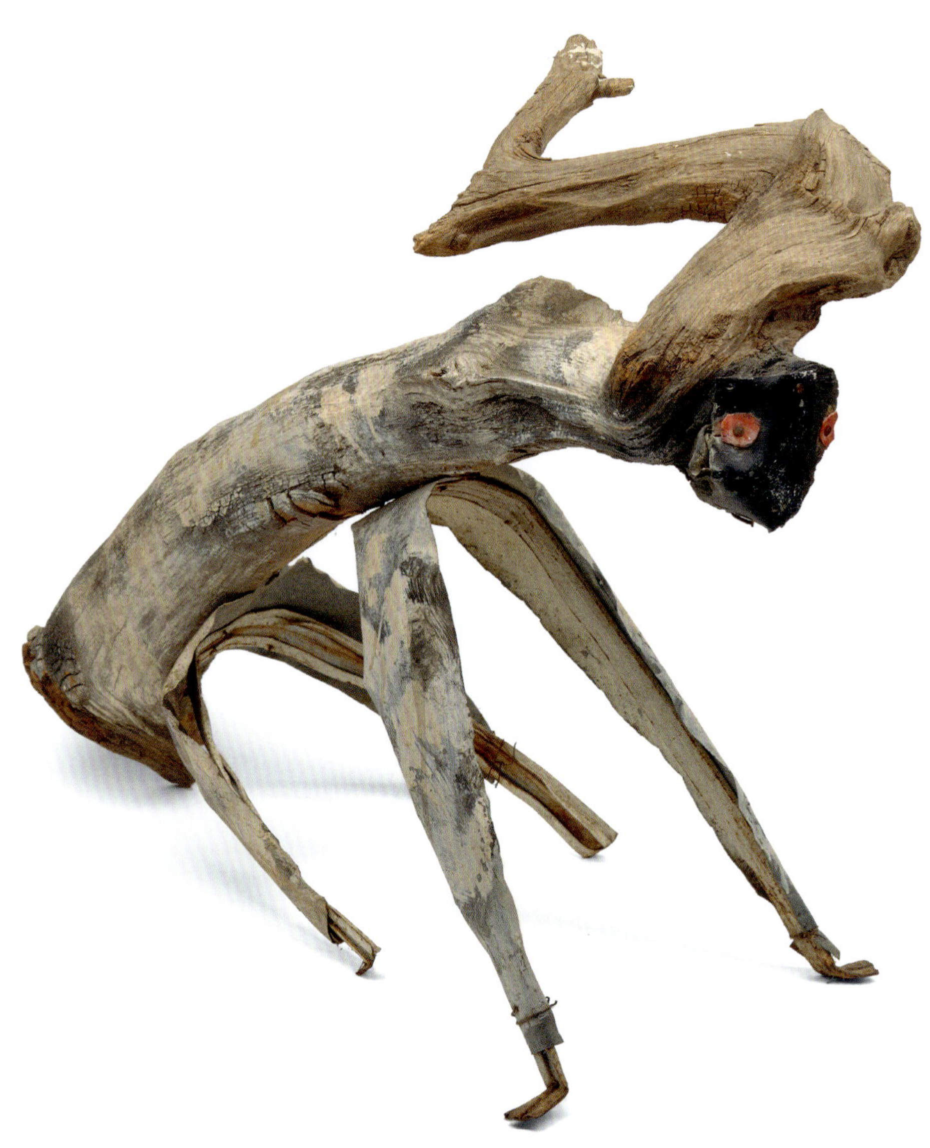

40
Ralph Griffin
Midnight, 1978
Found wood, tin, nails, plastic and paint, 94 x 96.5 x 48.3 cm
Souls Grown Deep Foundation, Atlanta

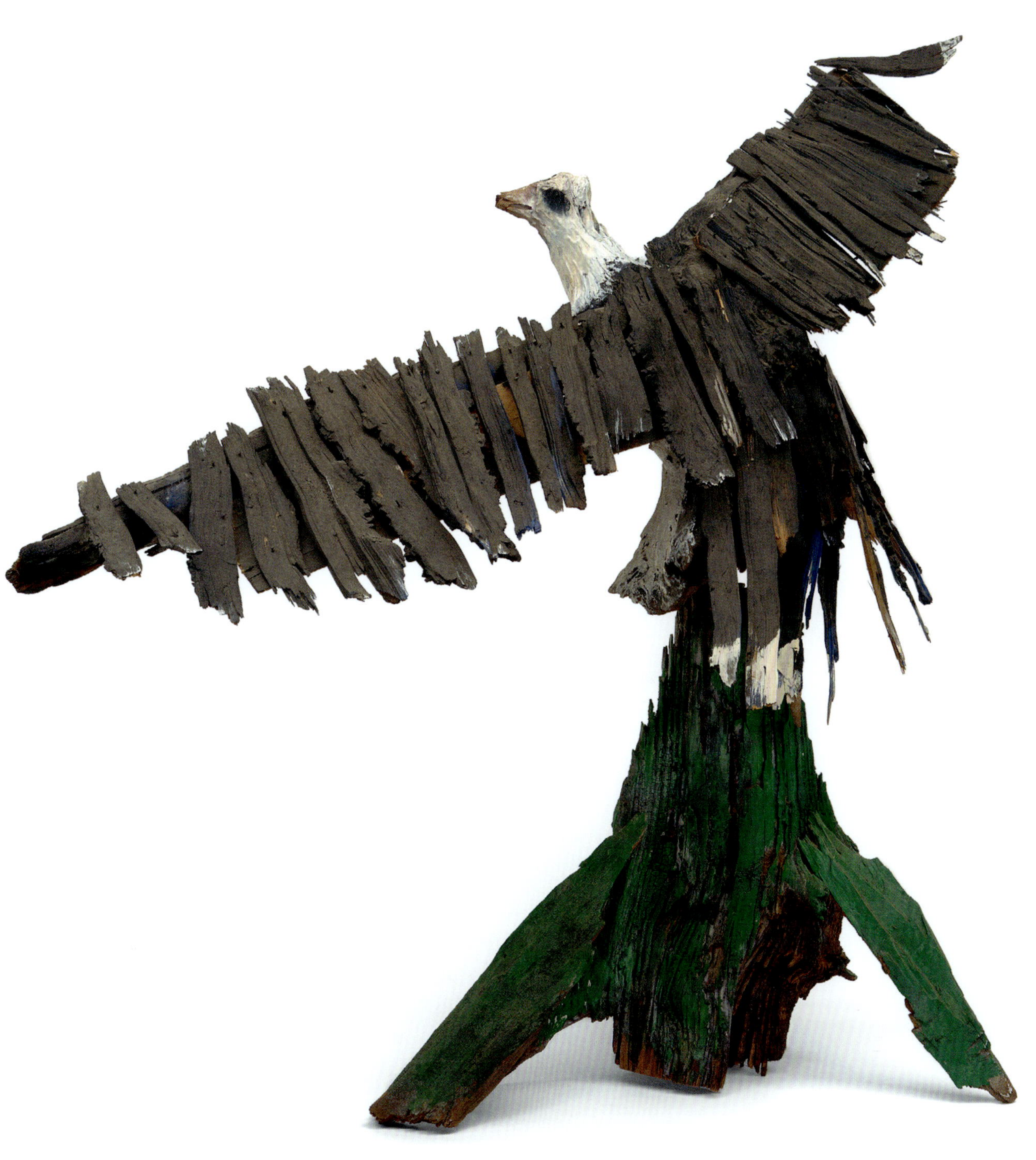

41
Ralph Griffin
Eagle, 1988
Found wood, nails and paint, 88.9 x 110.5 x 55.9 cm
Souls Grown Deep Foundation, Atlanta

42
Jesse Aaron
Untitled, c. 1972
Wood, hat and plastic eyes, 144.8 x 59.7 x 22.9 cm
Souls Grown Deep Foundation, Atlanta

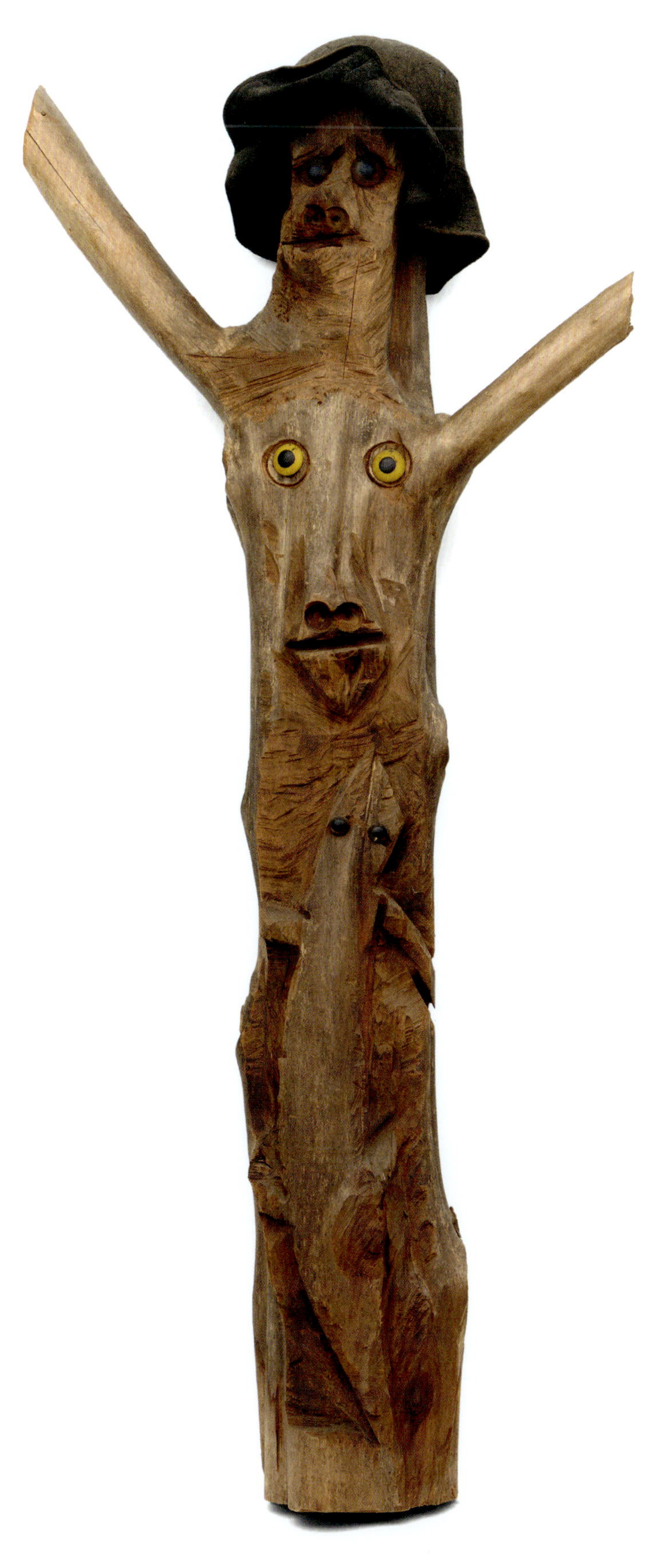

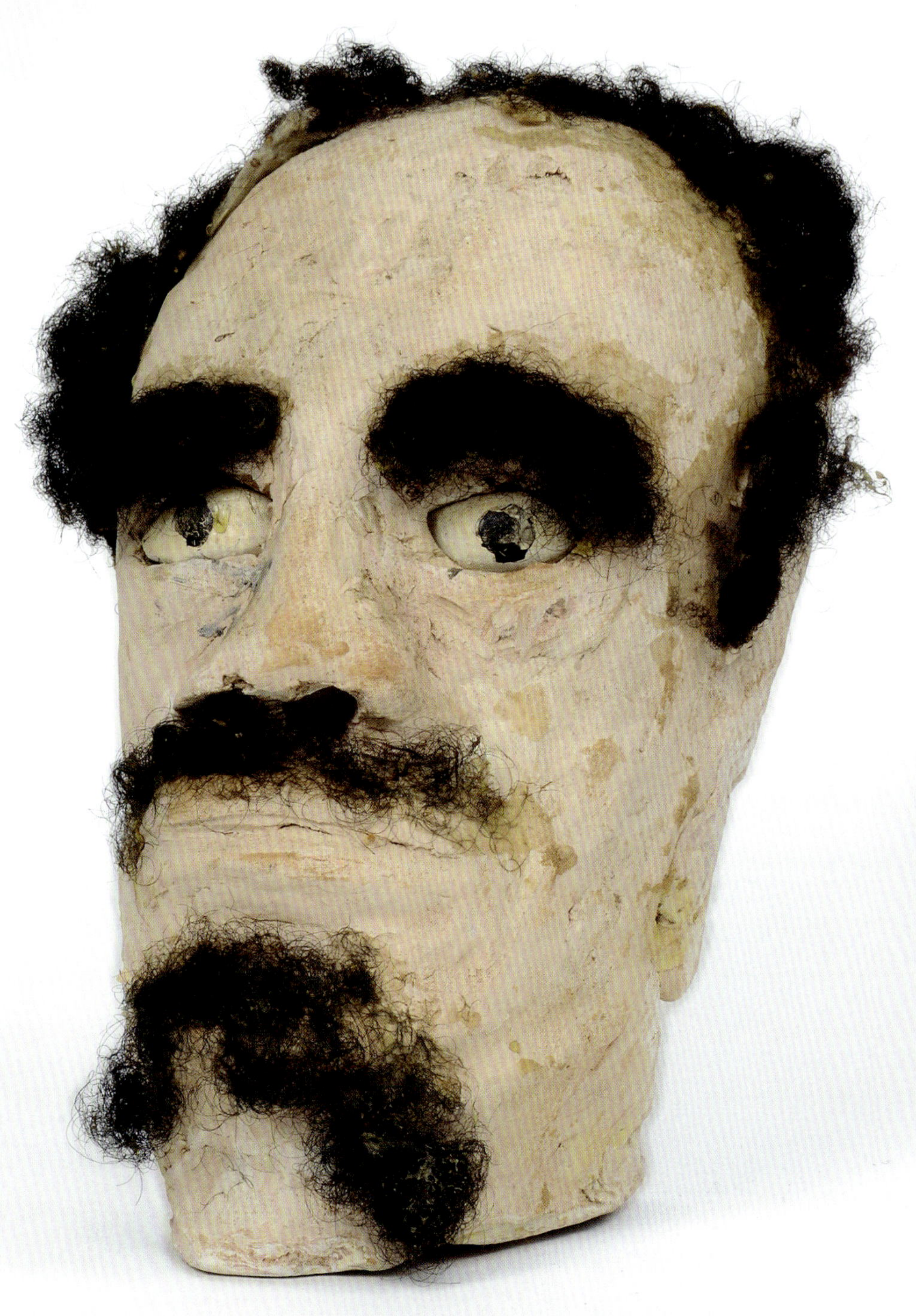

43
James 'Son Ford' Thomas
Untitled, 1985
Unfired clay, human hair and paint, 27.9 x 16.5 x 21.6 cm
Souls Grown Deep Foundation, Atlanta

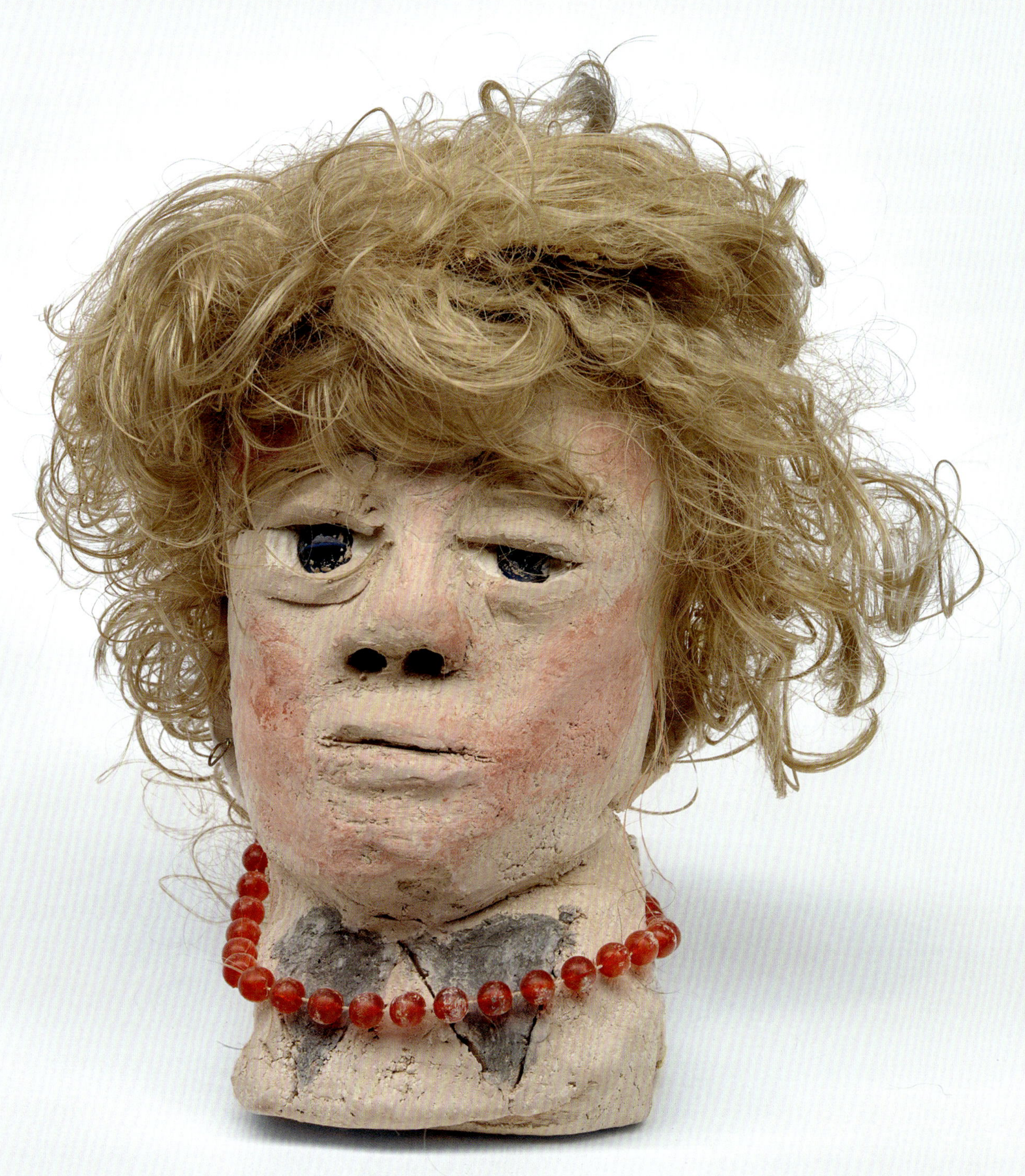

44
James 'Son Ford' Thomas
Untitled, 1989
Unfired clay, wig, glass marbles, wire, beads and paint,
25.4 x 15.2 x 20.3 cm
Souls Grown Deep Foundation, Atlanta

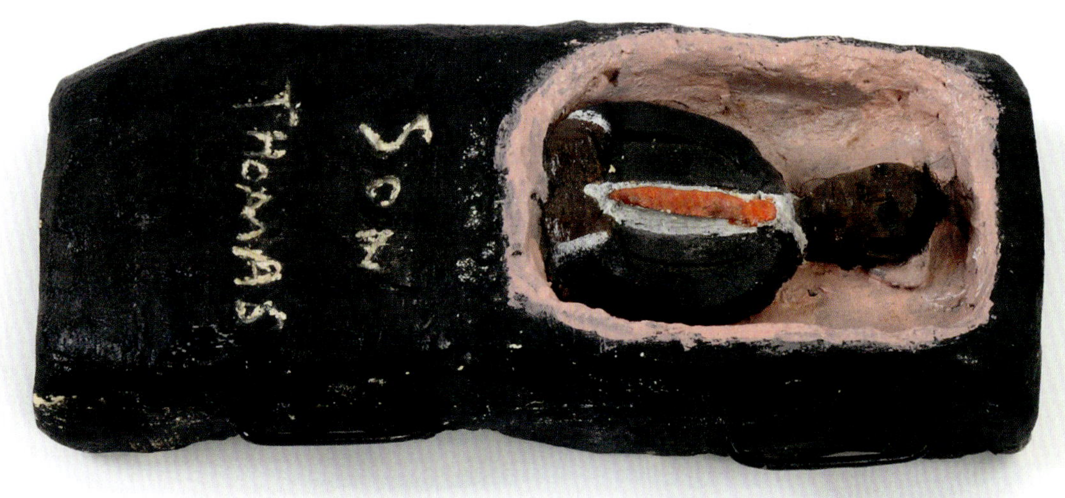

45
James 'Son Ford' Thomas
Untitled, **undated**
Unfired gumbo clay, paint and human hair, 3.2 x 18.4 x 8.3 cm
Thomas E. Scanlin Collection

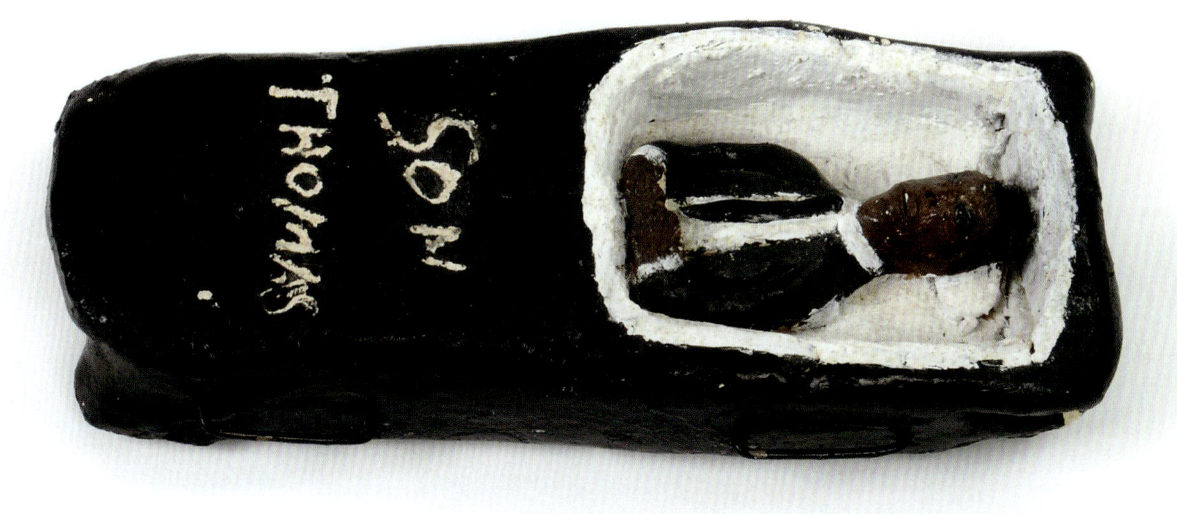

46
James 'Son Ford' Thomas
Untitled, undated
Unfired gumbo clay, paint and human hair, 3.8 x 19 x 7.6 cm
Thomas E. Scanlin Collection

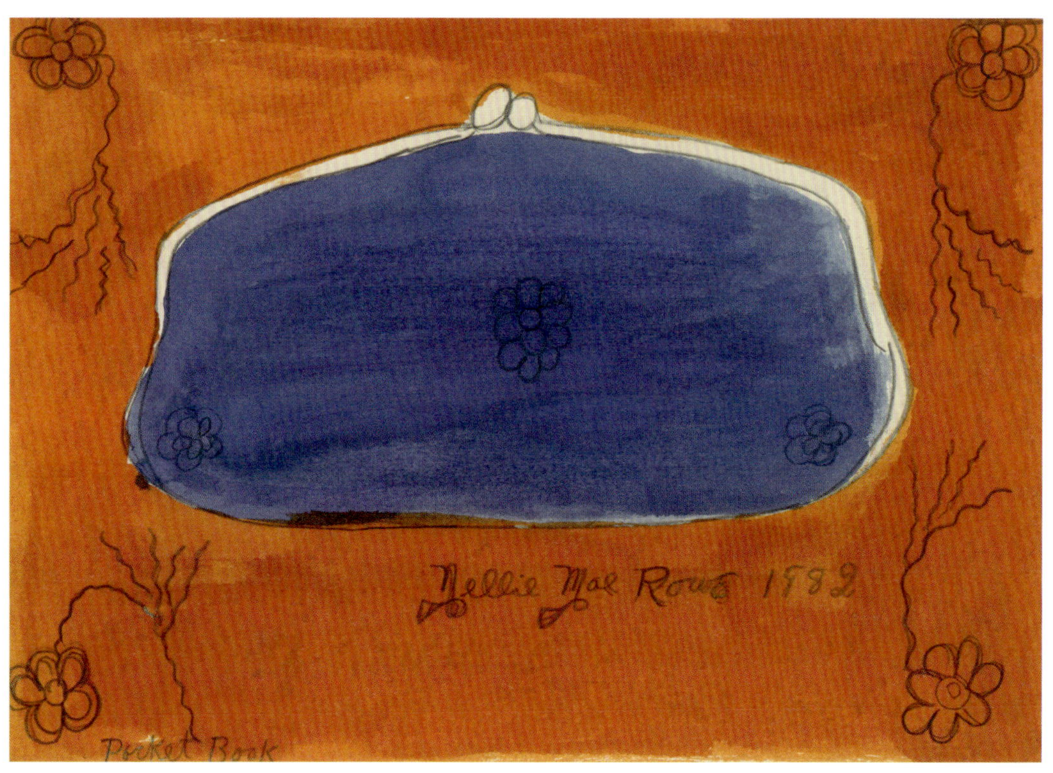

47
Nellie Mae Rowe
Pocketbook, 1982
Paint and pencil on paper, 26.7 x 35.6 cm
Souls Grown Deep Foundation, Atlanta

48
Nellie Mae Rowe
Woman Wearing a Fish Hat, 1980
Acrylic and graphite on wood, 52.7 x 30.5 cm
Souls Grown Deep Foundation, Atlanta

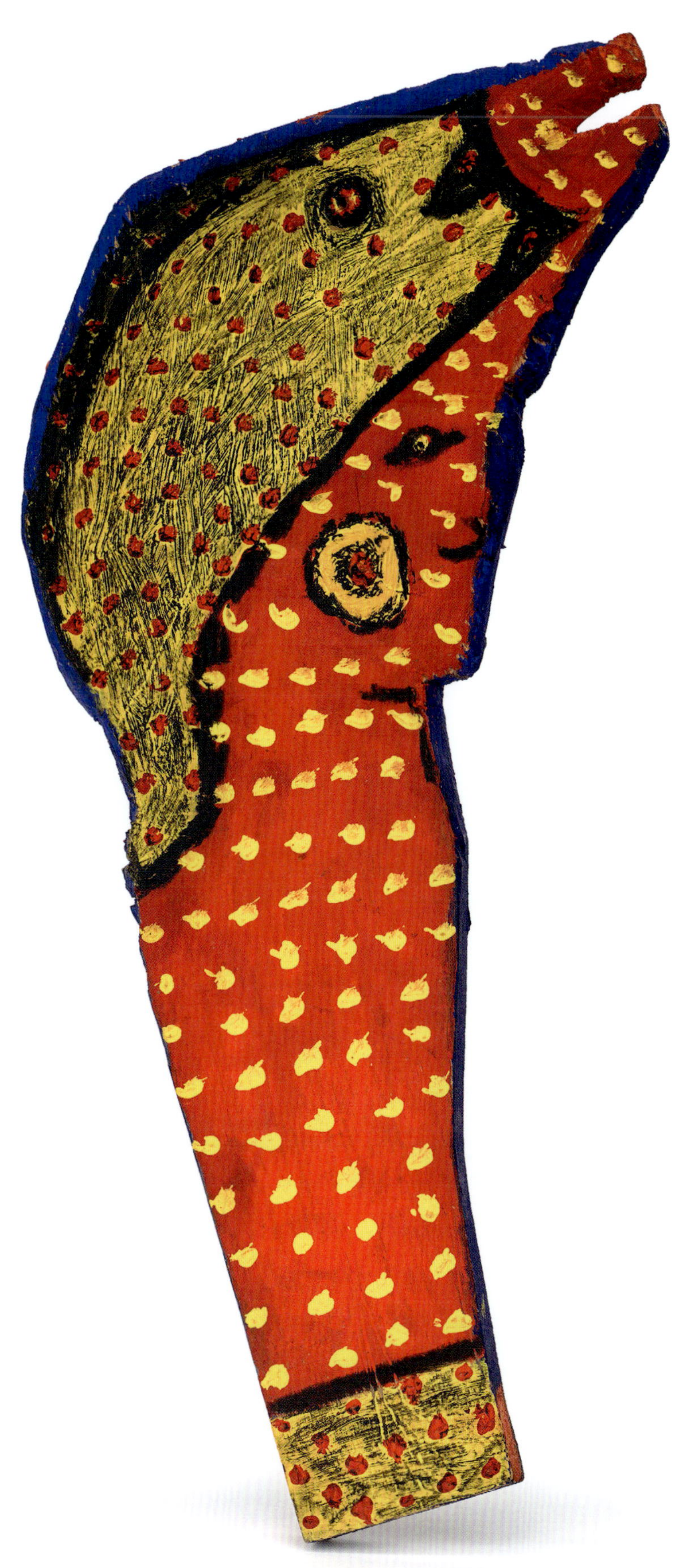

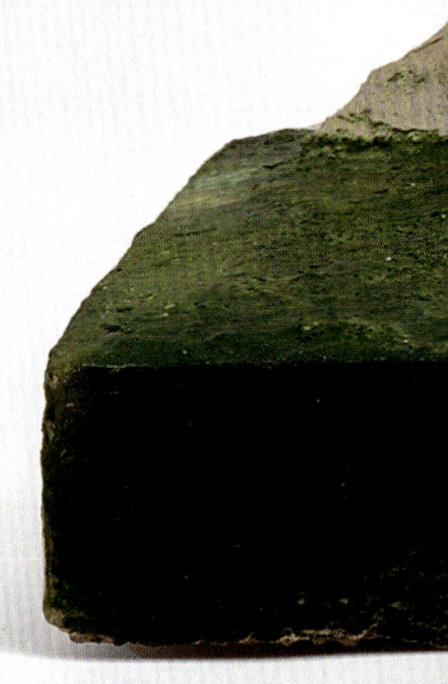

49
Eldren M. Bailey
Dancers, 1960s
Concrete, plaster and paint, 74.9 x 73.7 x 43.2 cm
Souls Grown Deep Foundation, Atlanta

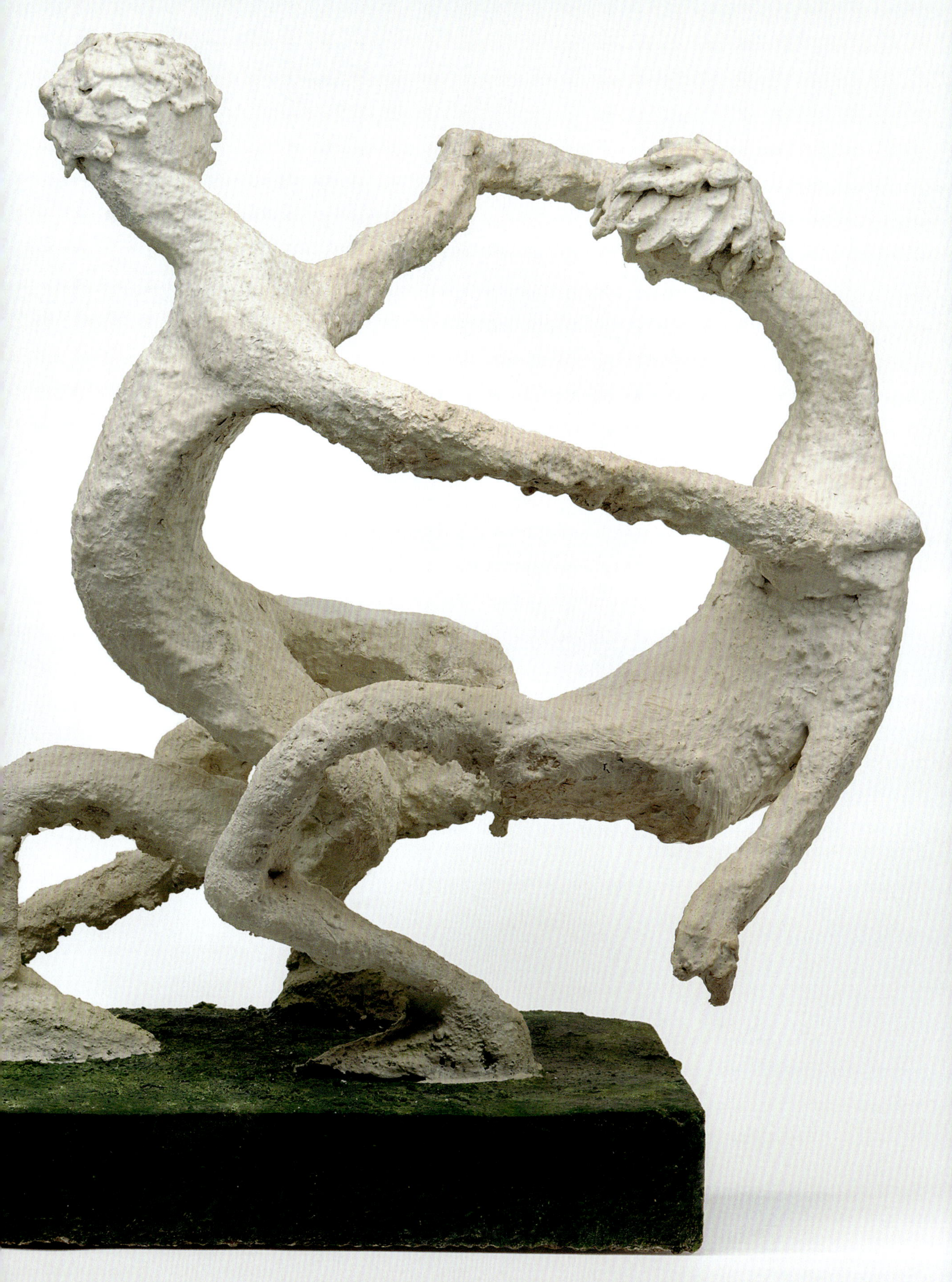

50
Charlie Lucas
Three-Way Bicycle, c. 1985
Bicycle wheels, metal machine parts and electrical wiring,
181.6 x 119.4 x 55.9 cm
Souls Grown Deep Foundation, Atlanta

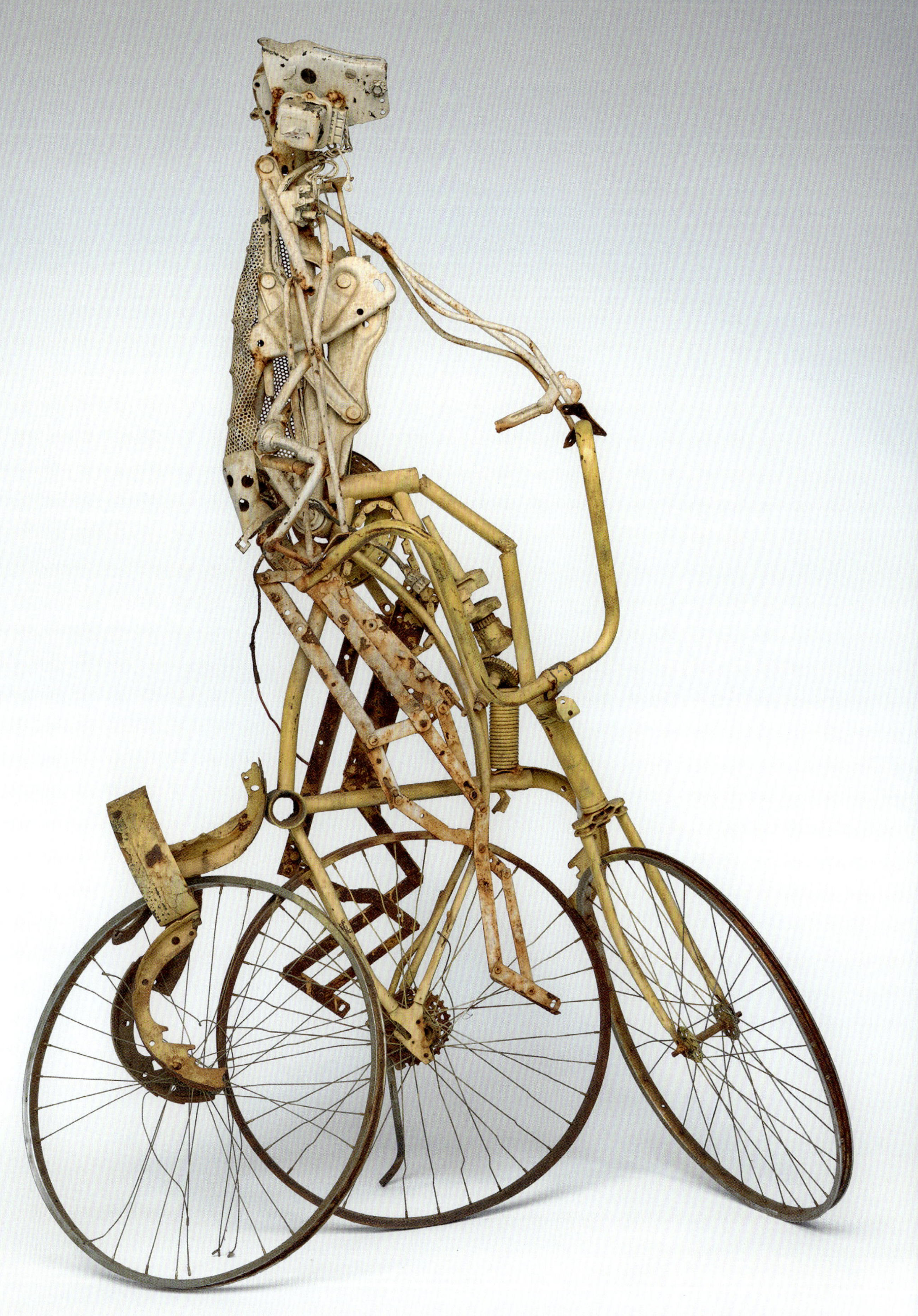

51
Joe Minter
And He Hung His Head and Died, 1999
Welded found metal, 243.8 x 194.3 x 87.6 cm
Souls Grown Deep Foundation, Atlanta

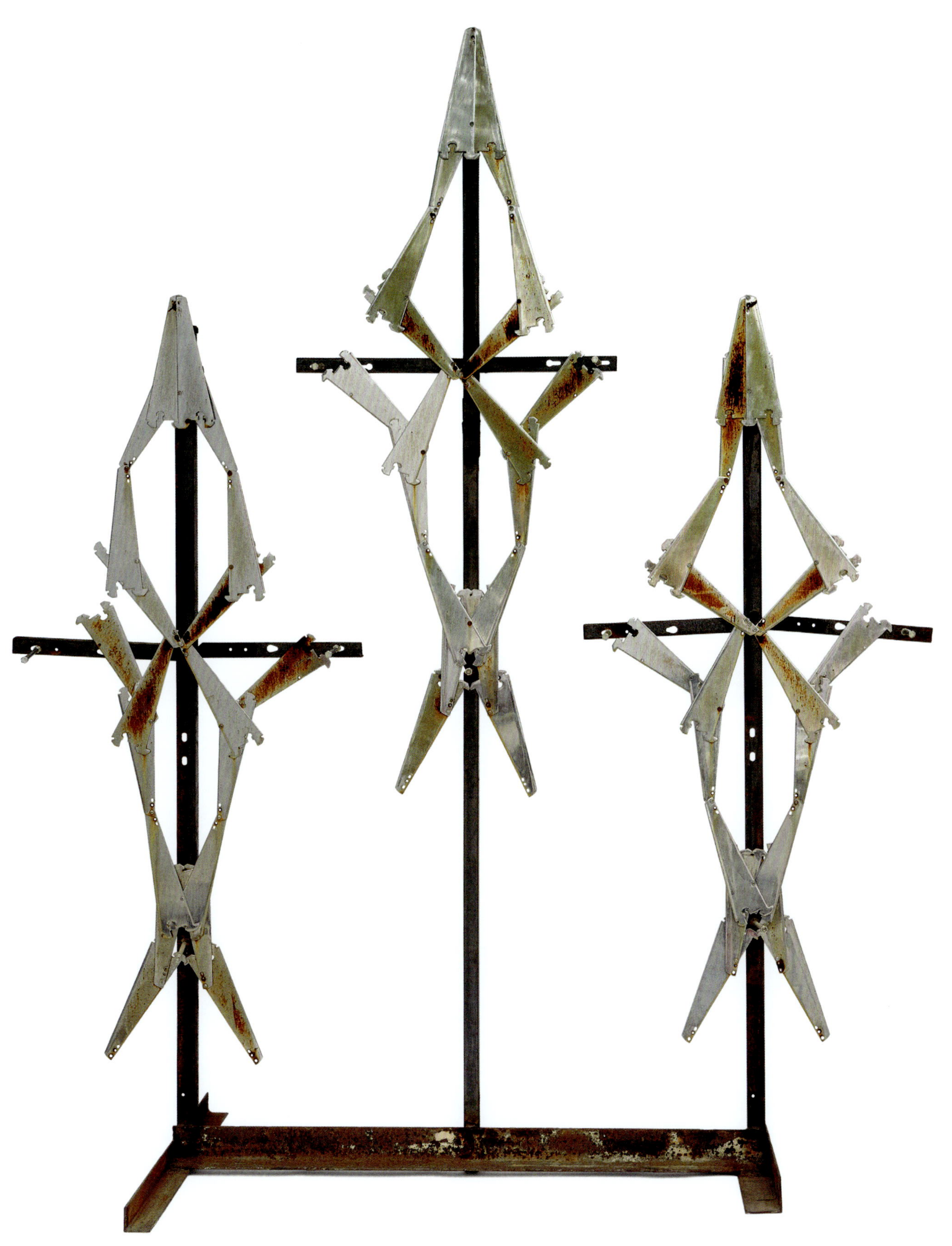

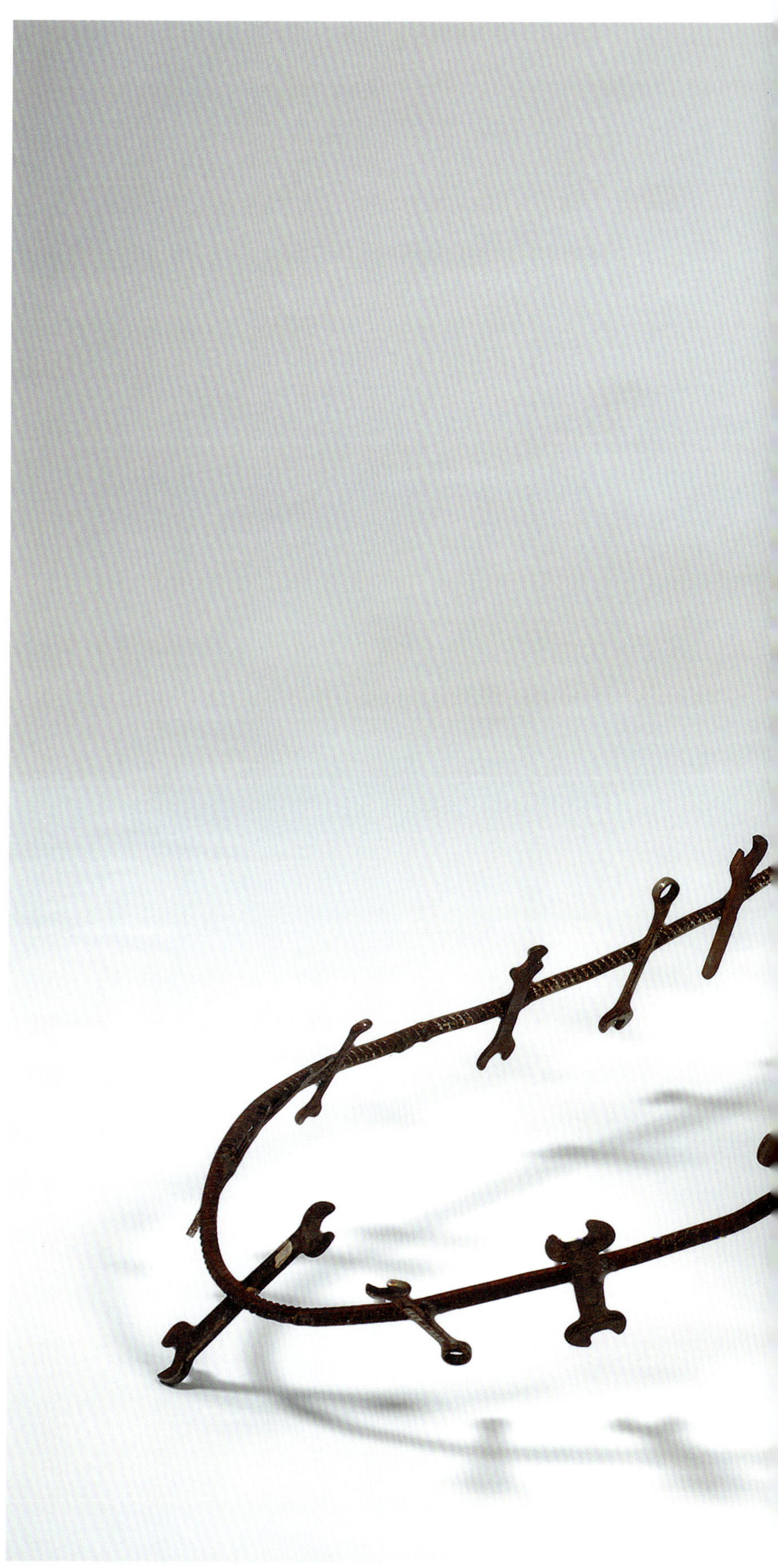

52
Joe Minter
Where is My Hammer?, 1996
Welded found metal,
93.9 x 182.8 x 132 cm
Souls Grown Deep Foundation, Atlanta

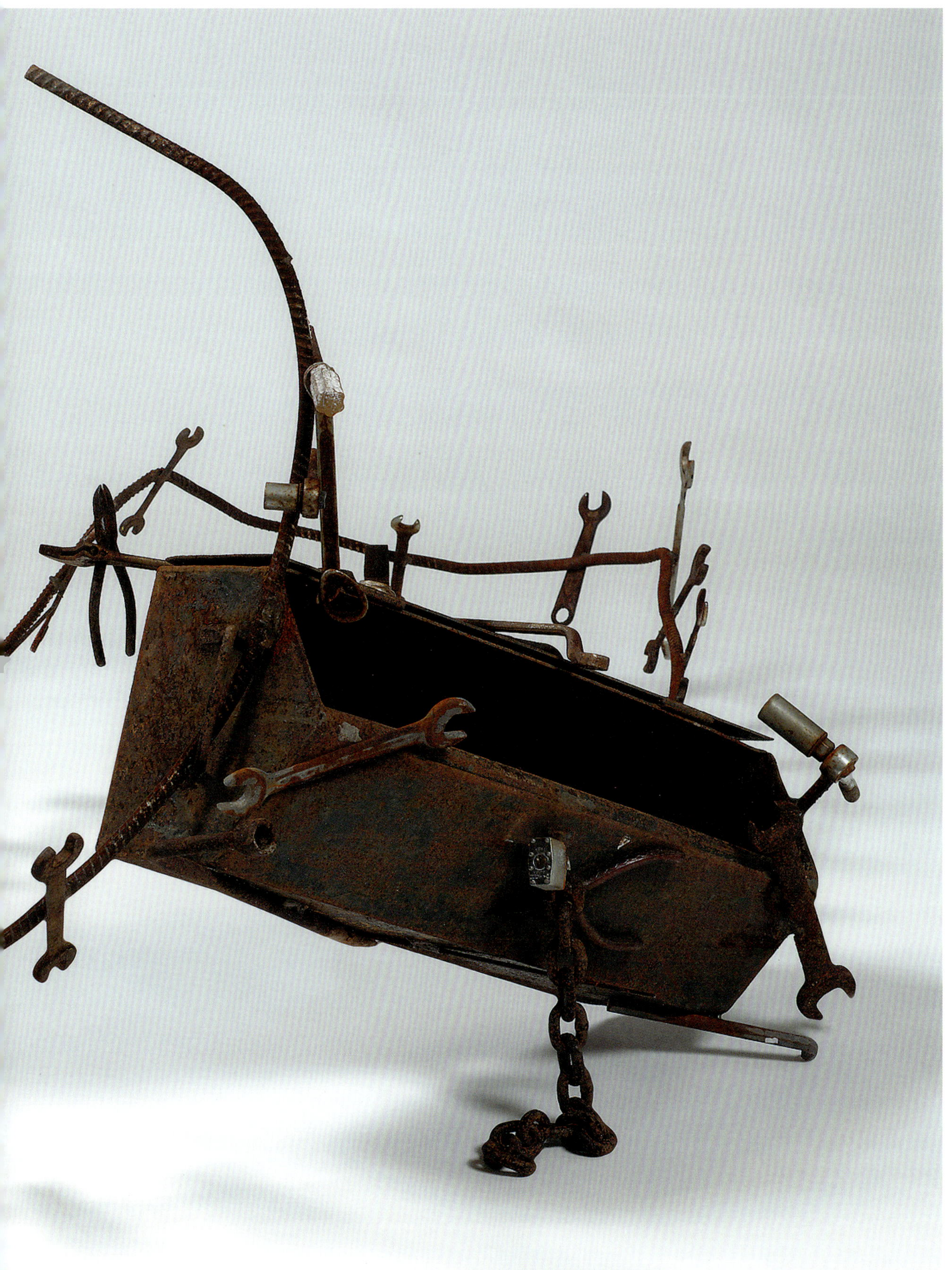

53
Purvis Young
Untitled (Jail Scene), 1980s
House paint with an assemblage of other materials on found
wood and board, with frame made by the artist, 204 x 122 x10 cm
Courtesy of the Graham Fleming & Maciej Urbanek Collection, in
memory of Larry T. Clemons

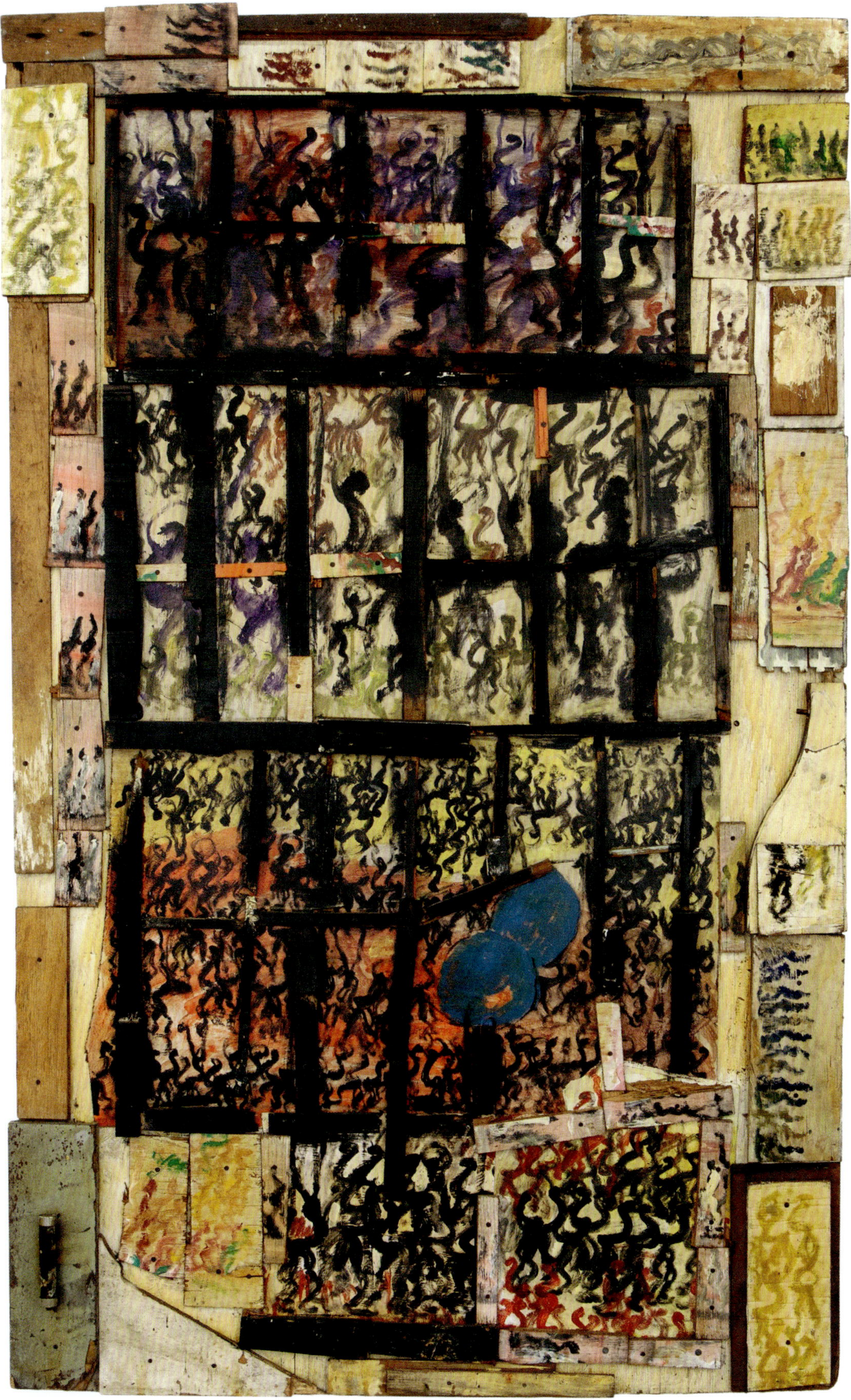

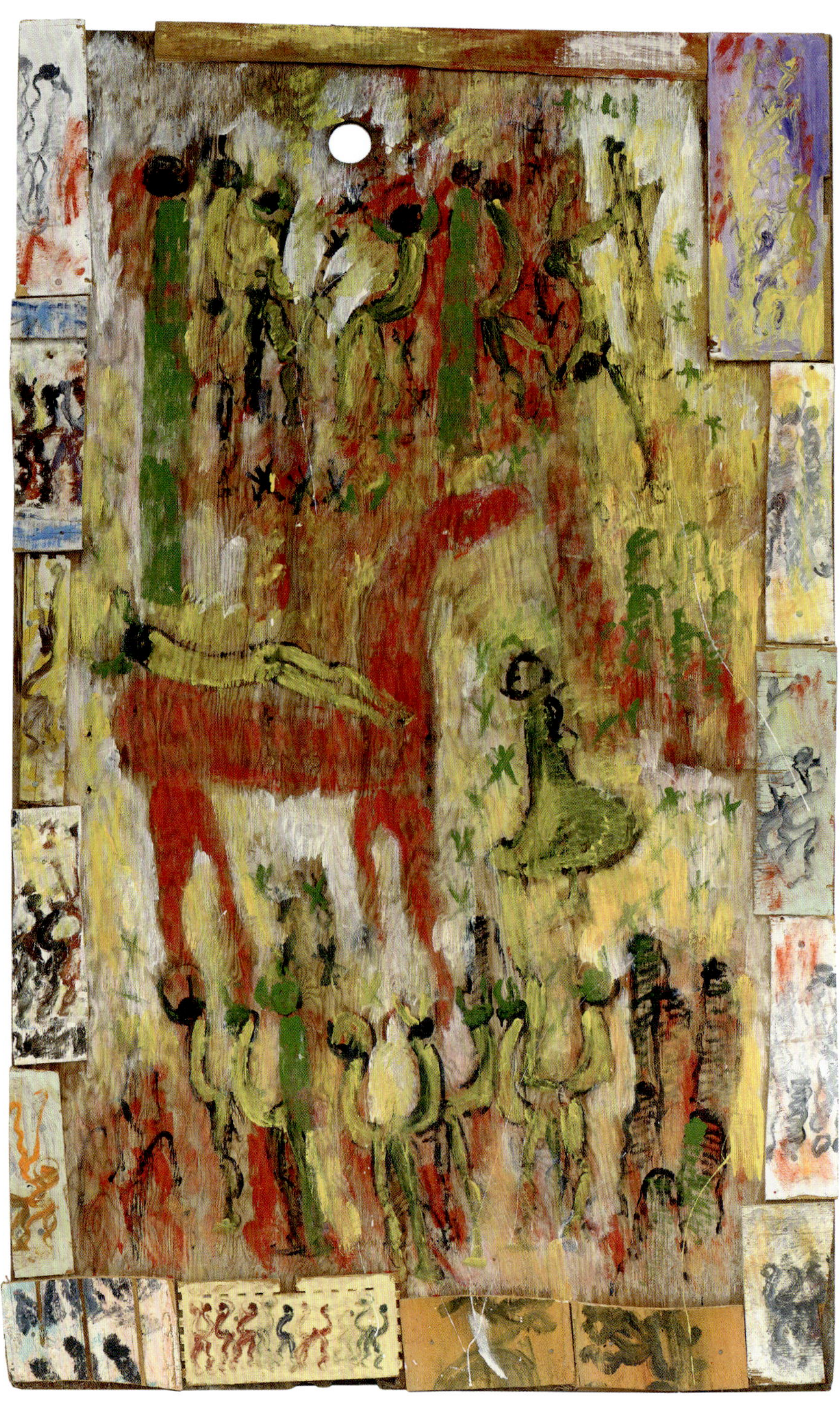

54
Purvis Young
Carrying the Angel to the People, 1994
Paint and wood on wood, 203.2 x 124.5 cm
Souls Grown Deep Foundation, Atlanta

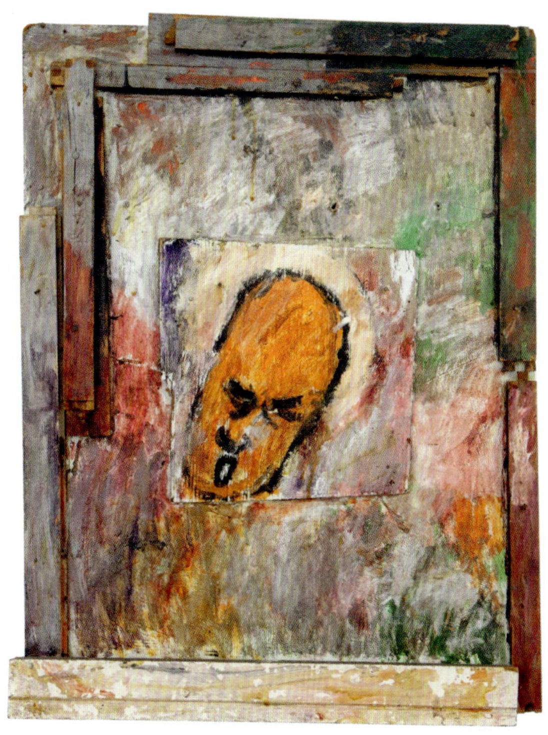

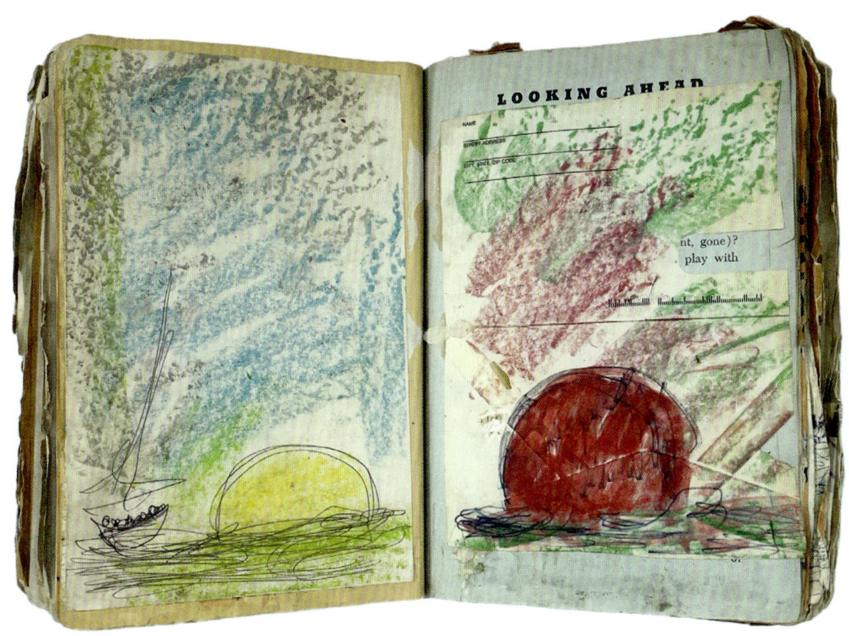

55
Purvis Young
Untitled (Baby), 1980s
Paint on found board with frame made by the artist, 76.5 x 56.5 cm
Courtesy of the Graham Fleming & Maciej Urbanek Collection,
in memory of Larry T. Clemons

56
Purvis Young
Artist's book of sunrises and sunsets, undated
Works on paper glued into an English text book
Courtesy of the Graham Fleming & Maciej Urbanek Collection,
in memory of Larry T. Clemons

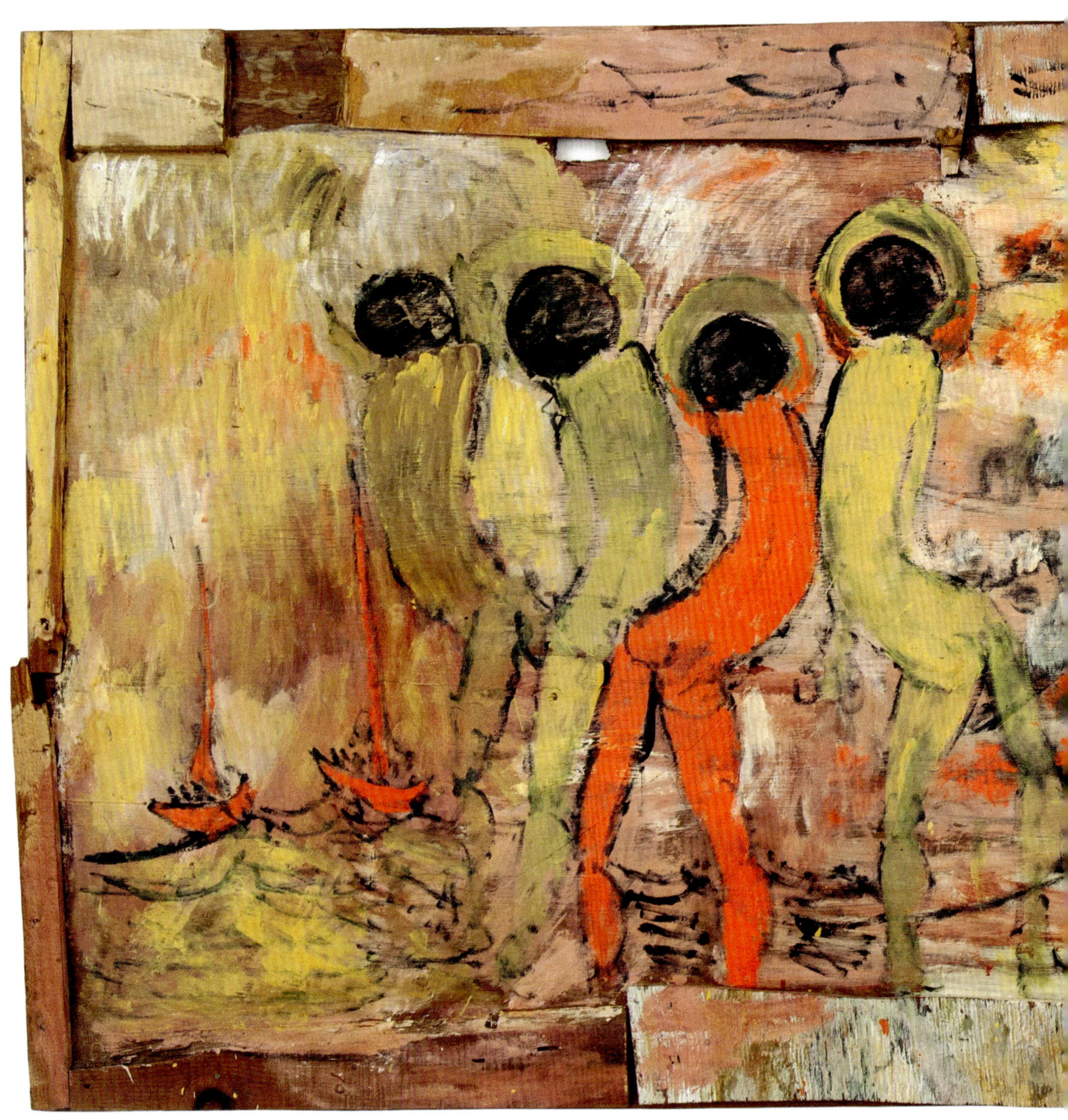

57
Purvis Young
Untitled (Narrative Scene), 1980s
Paint on found board with frame made by the artist, 121 x 245 x 8 cm
Courtesy of the Graham Fleming & Maciej Urbanek Collection,
in memory of Larry T. Clemons

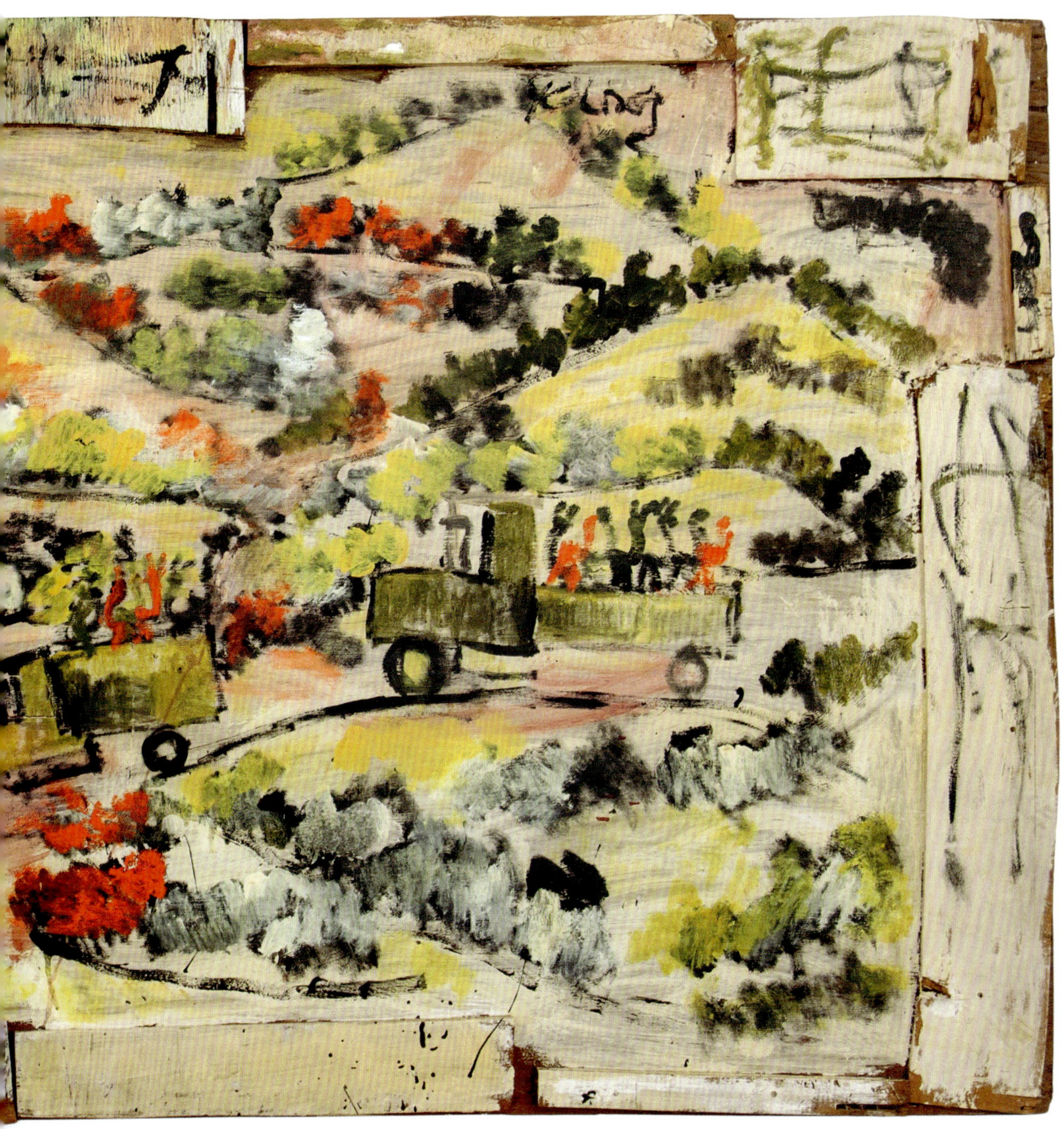

58
Rachel Carey George
'Housetop' – sixteen-block 'Half-Log Cabin' variation, **1930s**
Cotton, denim, wool and rayon, 200.7 x 190.5 cm
Souls Grown Deep Foundation, Atlanta

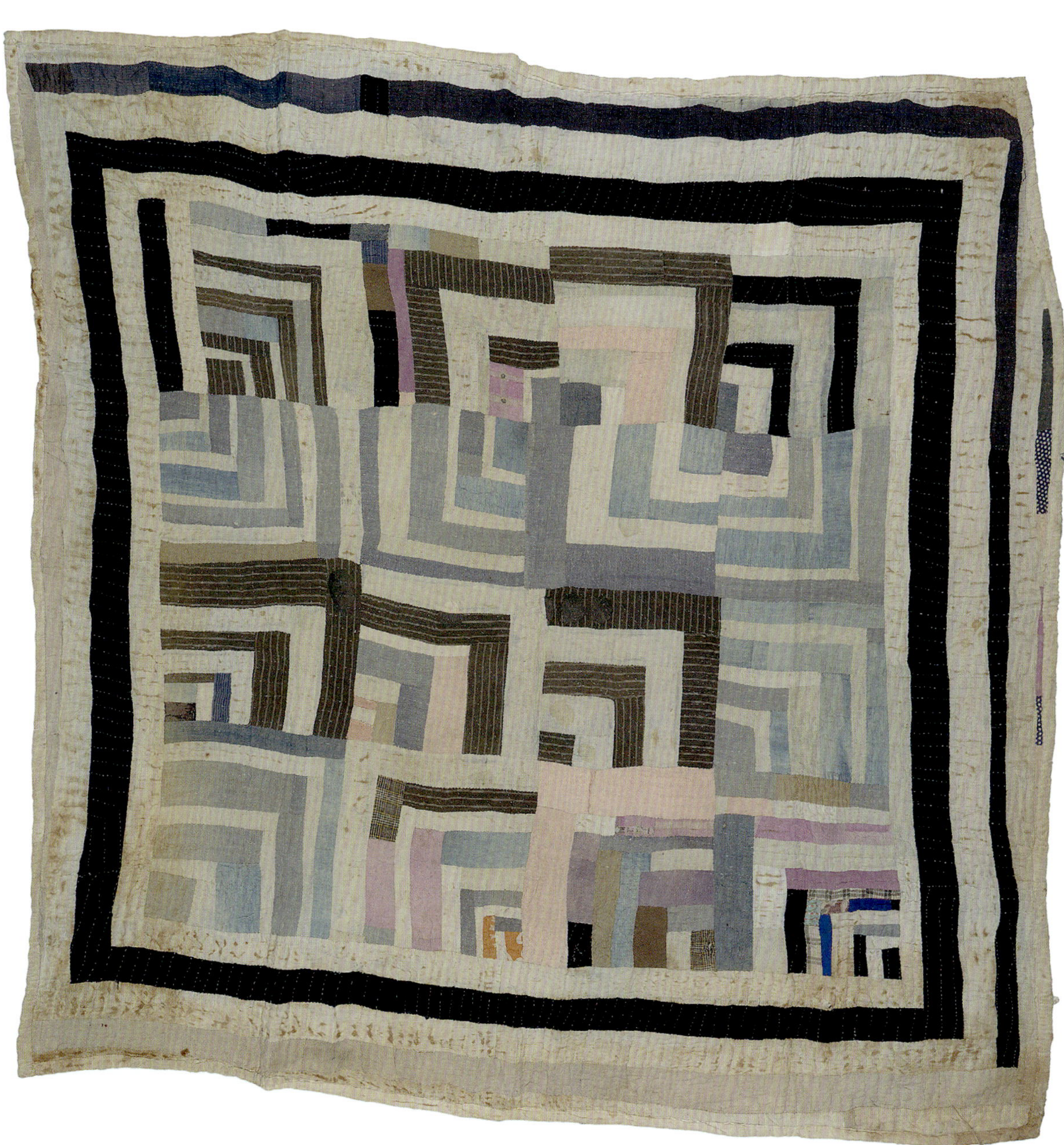

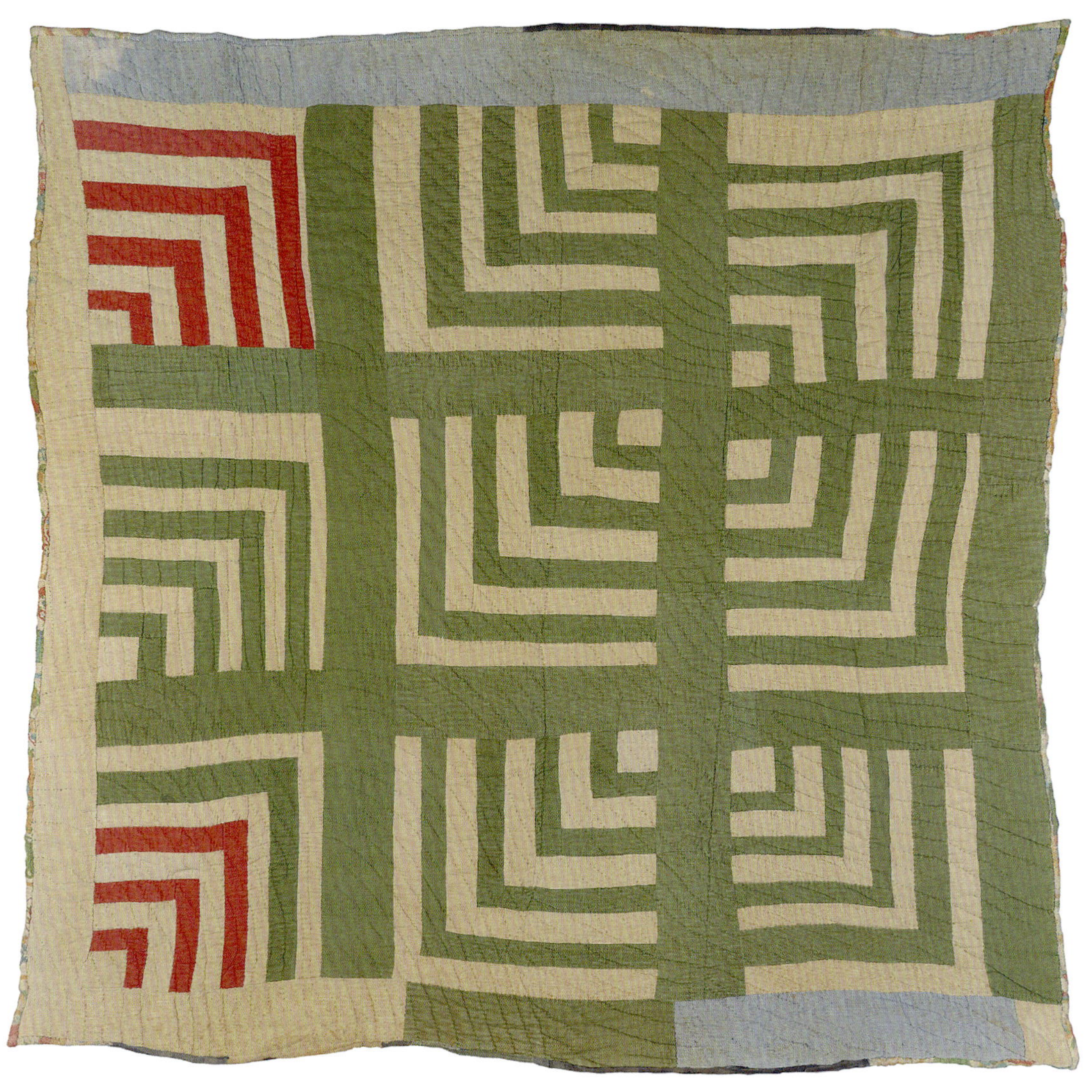

59
Martha Jane Pettway
'Housetop' – nine-block 'Half-Log Cabin' variation, c. 1945
Corduroy, 182.9 x 182.9 cm
Souls Grown Deep Foundation, Atlanta

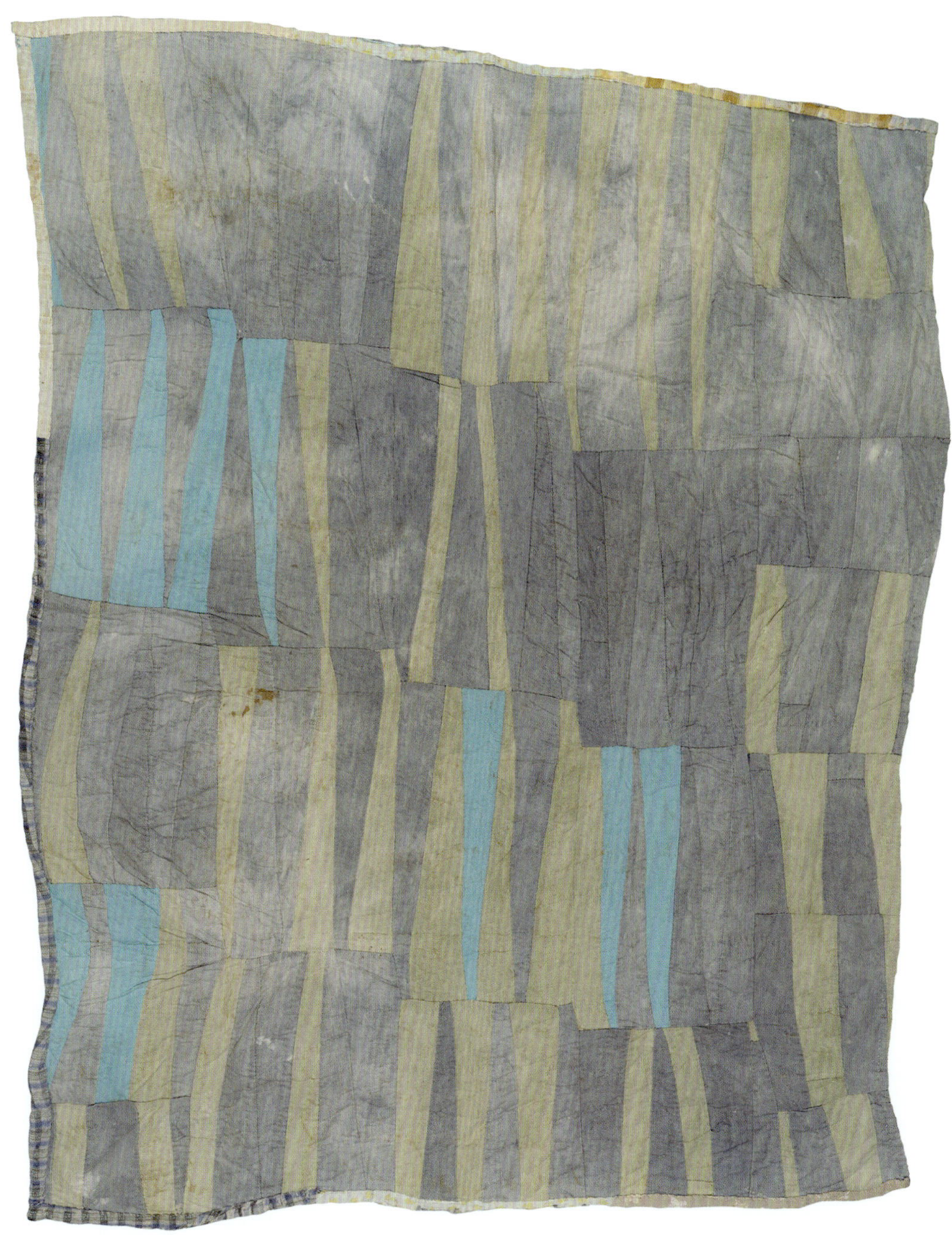

60
Loretta Pettway
String-pieced Quilt, 1960
Cotton twill and synthetic materials (men's clothing), 238.8 x 193 cm
Souls Grown Deep Foundation, Atlanta

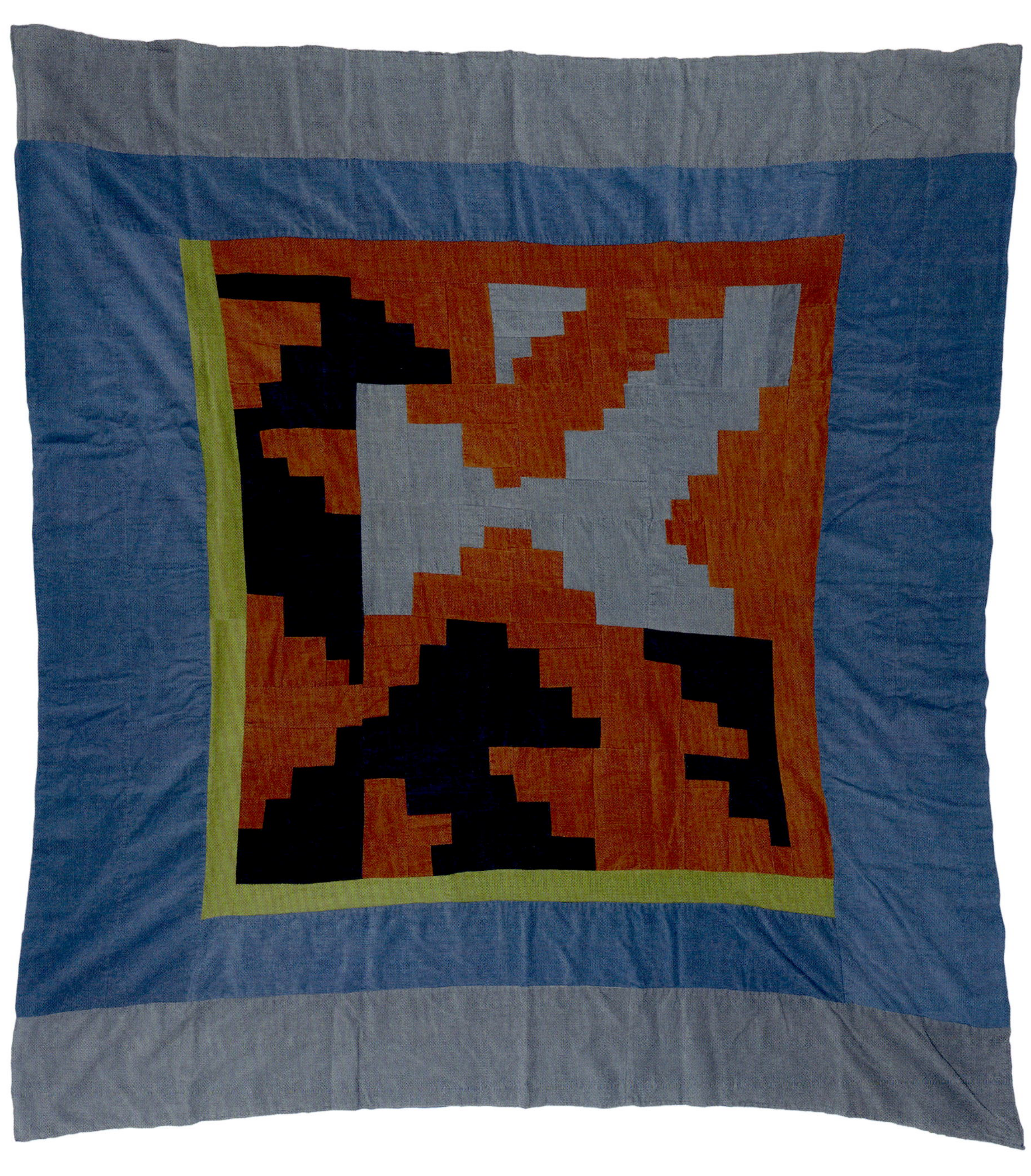

61
Flora Moore
'Log Cabin' variation, c. 1975
Corduroy, 210.8 x 233.7 cm
Souls Grown Deep Foundation, Atlanta

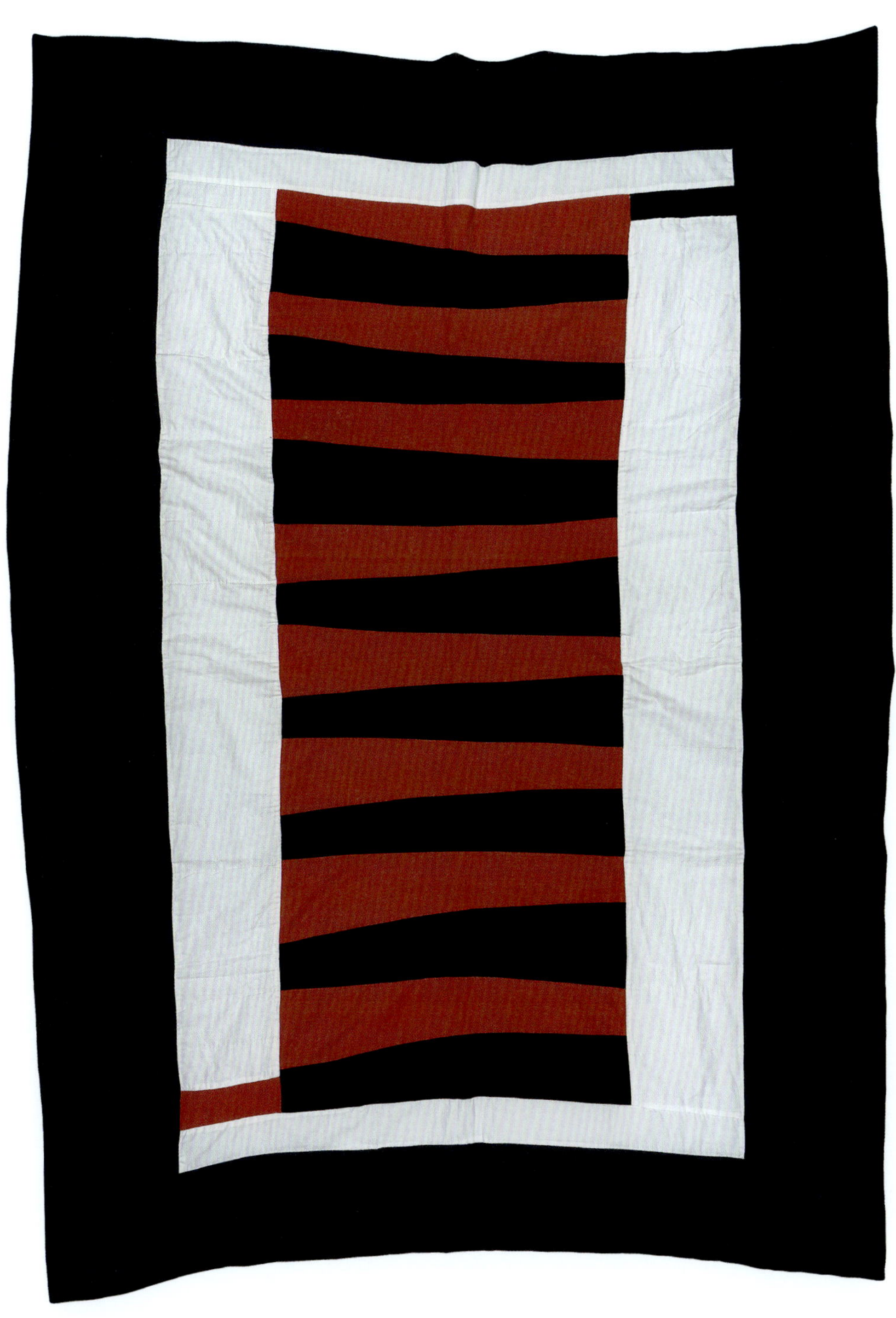

62
Loretta Pettway Bennett
Medallion, 2005
Cotton and twill, 215.9 x 154.9 cm
Souls Grown Deep Foundation, Atlanta

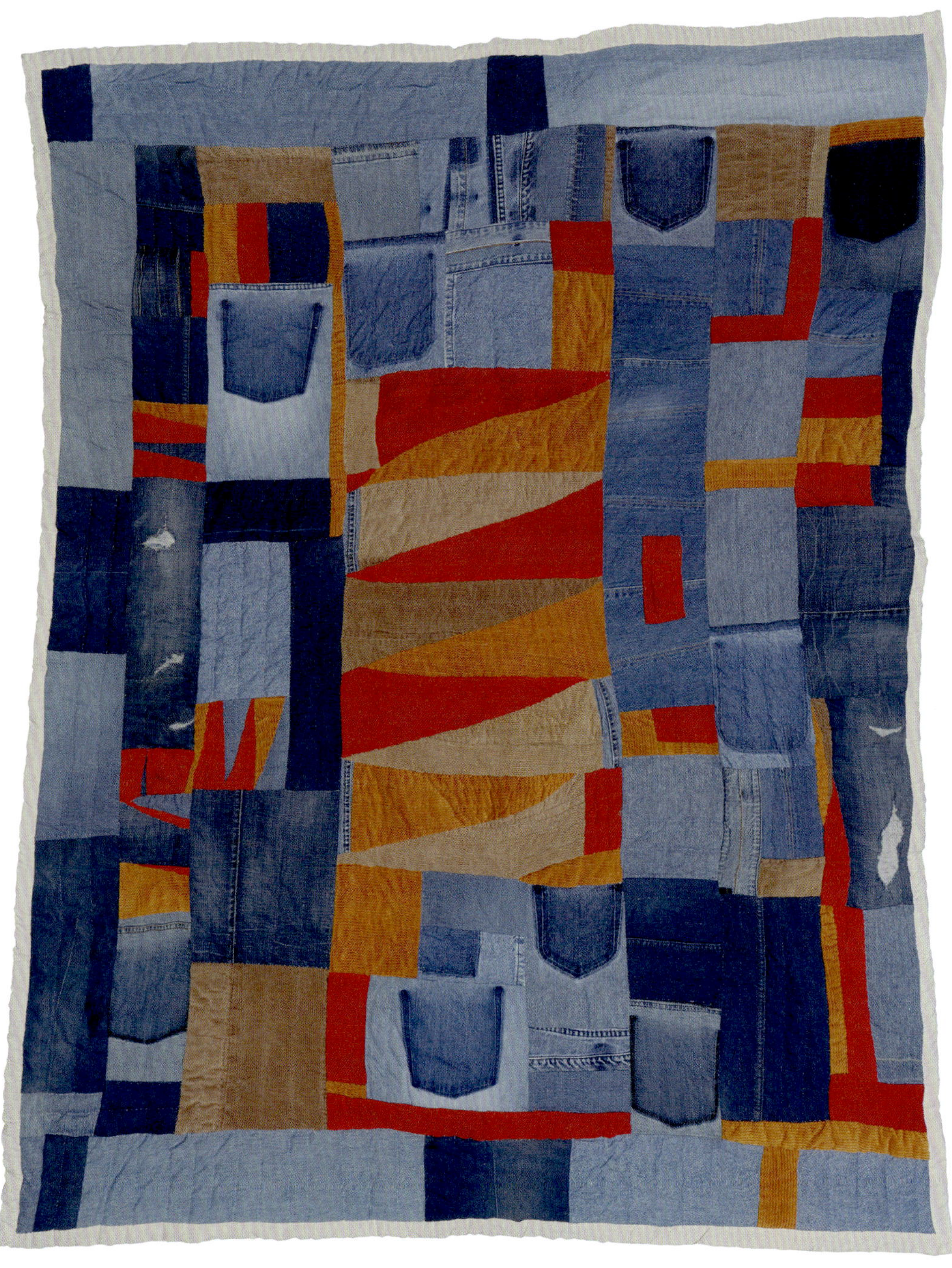

63
Marlene Bennett Jones
Triangles, 2021
Denim, corduroy and cotton, 205.7 x 157.5 cm
Souls Grown Deep Foundation, Atlanta

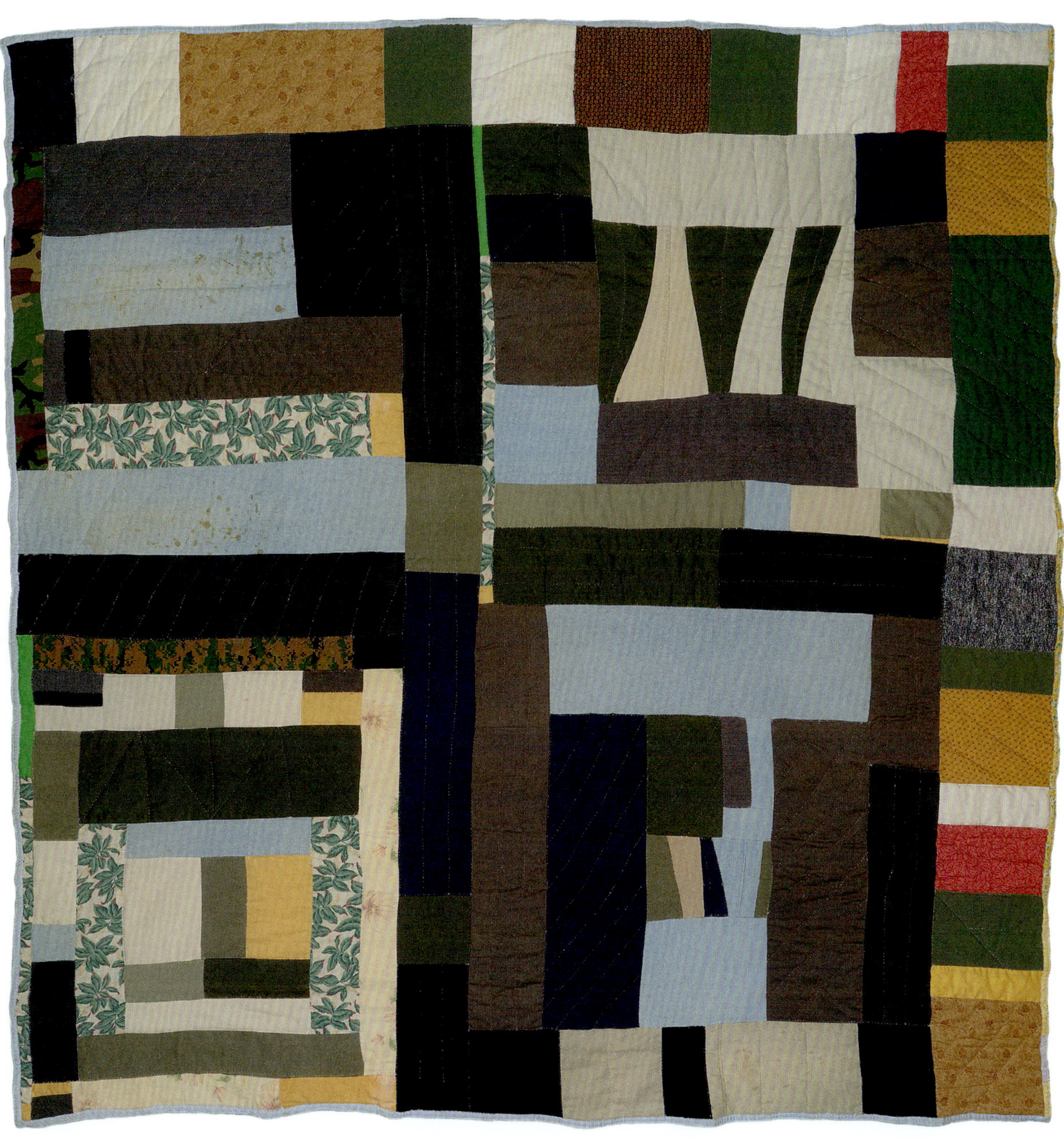

64
Essie Bendolph Pettway
Side Seams, 2018
Camouflage, denim and cotton, 203.2 x 236.2 cm
Courtesy of the artist Essie Bendolph Pettway

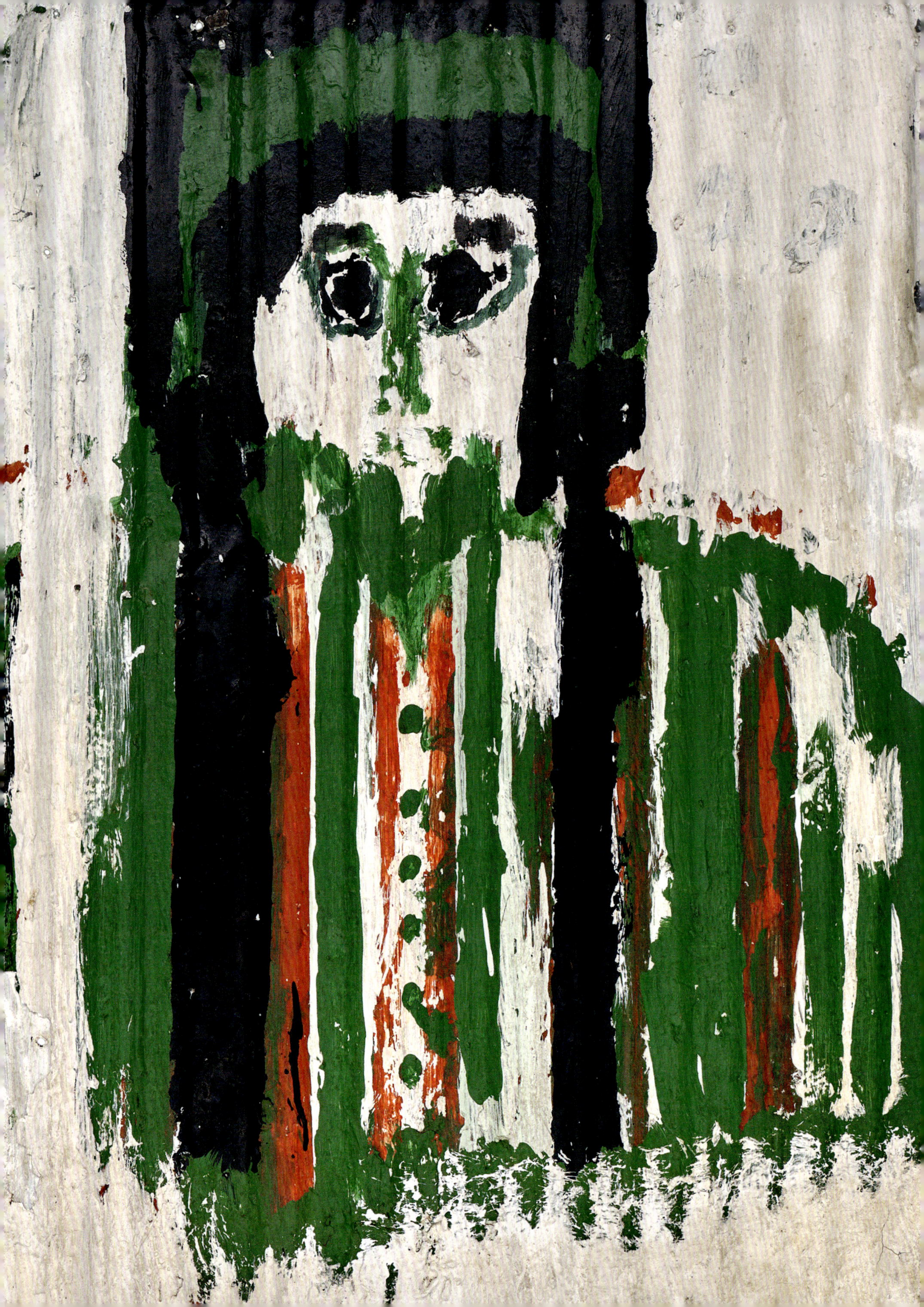

Biographies
of the Artists

Rebecca Bray | Emma Yau

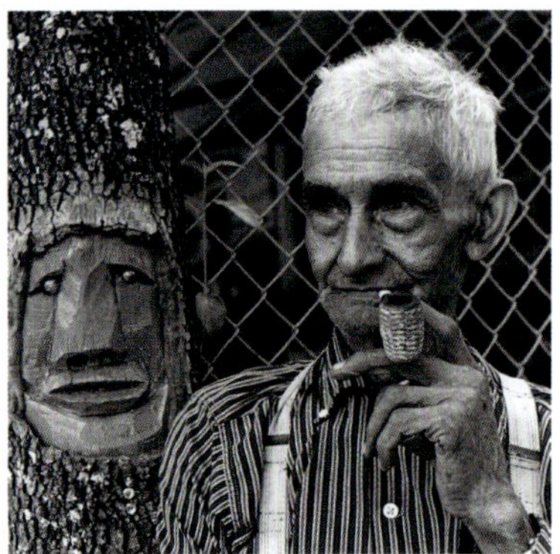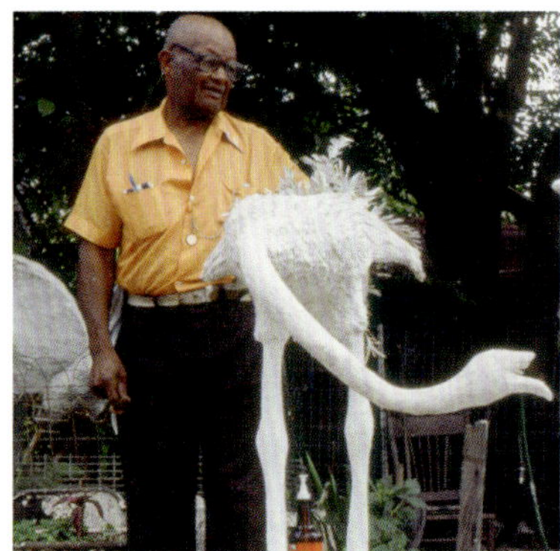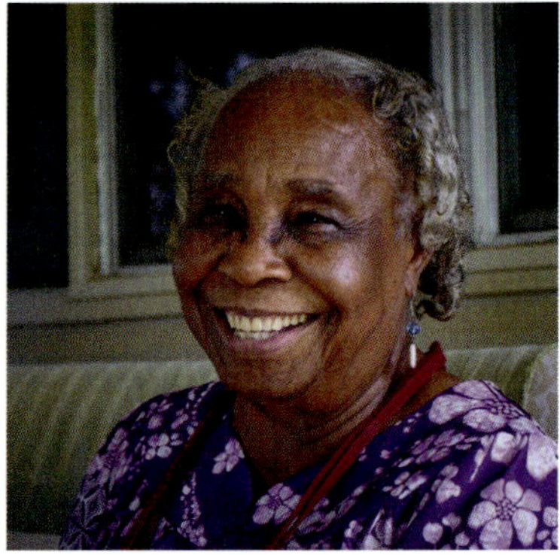

Jesse Aaron (1887–1979) was born to a farming family in Lake City, Florida. He did not attend school as a child, and instead was hired out as a field worker. At 21 he attended vocational school to become a baker, his first formal education, before working as a cook for the Seaboard Coastline Railroad. He married a teacher, and together they created a vegetable garden to feed their family, as well as growing cut flowers to sell.

Later, Aaron turned to cabinetmaking for an income, and used the woodworking skills he learnt to carve faces into trees around his property, as protective forces. In 1968, when his wife was gradually losing her sight, he recounted hearing a voice at 3am directing him to 'carve wood'. He turned his hand to creating freestanding figures from cedar, using chainsaw carving to bring out forms he saw within the wood. Within a year he had earned enough from sales of these works to pay for cataract surgery and save his wife's eyesight.

The popularity of Aaron's sculptures meant he could retire from his other jobs. He displayed and sold them from his home and yard in what he called the 'Jesse J. Aaron Museum'. In 1982 his work was included in the landmark touring exhibition 'Black Folk Art in America, 1930–80', and today is held in collections including those of the Fine Arts Museums of San Francisco and the High Museum of Art, Atlanta. **RB**

Eldren M. Bailey (1903–1987) was born in the small town of Flovilla, Georgia, the son of a railway worker. By the age of thirteen he had relocated to Atlanta, remaining there for the rest of his life. Following in his father's footsteps, he began his career on the railways, although by 1929 he had become a plasterer, gravedigger and a creator of gravestones for funeral homes across Atlanta.

His professional experience with concrete and plaster, as well as his familiarity with African-American funerary customs and symbolism, greatly informed Bailey's artistic practice, which included painting and the creation of an outdoor sculpture garden. Whereas his first concrete sculpture, a nine-foot crucifix erected in 1945, is indicative of his deep religiosity, his subsequent sculptures commemorated historical figures and events, celebrated movement and life, and evoked common symbols of death such as urns and guard dogs.

Bailey's art did not attract widespread recognition in his lifetime, but he continued to make gravestones for a living, and left the business to his two nephews on his death. His work can be found in collections such as those of the High Museum of Art, Atlanta and the Minneapolis Institute of Art. **EY**

Mary Lee Bendolph was born in 1935 in Gee's Bend, Alabama. The family moved in 1940 to one of the 'Roosevelt houses' built to improve their isolated, rural community. Bendolph learnt to quilt from an early age from her mother Aolar Mosely and her aunt Louella Pettway. They taught her the family's 'fast' style of quilting, piecing together fabric based on intuition rather than following a pattern, which Bendolph later taught to her daughter, Essie Bendolph Pettway (see page 131).

In 1965 Bendolph attended Martin Luther King Jr's speech at the Pleasant Grove Baptist Church in Gee's Bend. She became involved in the civil rights movement, including taking part in the voter registration march to the nearby white-majority town of Camden later that year. During the late 1960s she took part in the Freedom Quilting Bee, a cooperative based in the nearby community of Rehoboth that was founded to give local Black women the opportunity to earn money from their craft. In 1999 she rose to national prominence after being profiled in a *Los Angeles Times* feature on the continuing rift between Camden and Gee's Bend, in particular the refusal of Camden to reinstate the ferry that would allow Gee's Bend residents easier access to the outside world.

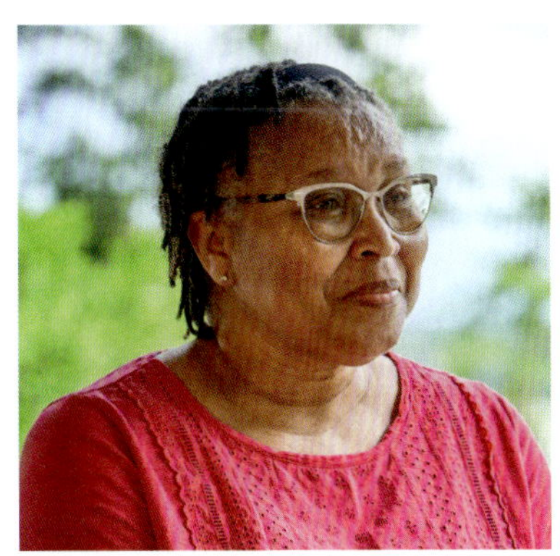

The 2002 travelling exhibition 'The Quilts of Gee's Bend', which presented the quilts as artworks beyond their practical use, inspired Bendolph to experiment with printmaking. In 2006, one of her quilts was selected to appear on US postage stamps, and in 2015 she was one of three Gee's Bend quilters awarded a National Heritage Fellowship by the National Endowment for the Arts. She continued to quilt until a stroke affected her mobility. Her quilts are now held in collections such as those of the National Gallery of Art, Washington DC and Tate Modern, London. **RB**

Loretta Pettway Bennett was born in 1960 in Gee's Bend, Alabama, the daughter of Qunnie Pettway and granddaughter of Candis Mosely Pettway, both notable quiltmakers. Raised on a farm that lacked running water and in an area without paved roads until 1975, Bennett was first introduced to sewing at the age of five or six, and she completed her first quilt in her early teens.

Bennett graduated from high school in the nearby town of Camden after the school in Gee's Bend closed, and a year later, in 1979, she married her high-school sweetheart Lovett Bennett. He soon enlisted in the army, resulting in them spending the next two decades living and raising their three sons wherever he was stationed in Germany, Texas and Alabama. When her sons were older, Bennett returned to work, training as a medical and dental assistant, and finally found time to quilt again, often collaborating with her mother.

Having been reintroduced to quilting as an adult by the older women in her family, Bennett's concern that quilting was dying out among the younger generation in Gee's Bend led to a fellowship grant from the Alabama State Council on the Arts for her to study the fine art of quilting in 2001. In 2005 she donated the 'Pine Burr' quilt that she made with her mother to the Council on the Arts, and it hangs on display in the Alabama Department of Archives and History in Montgomery.

After a two-year hiatus following her husband's death in 2018, Bennett returned to quilting now that she is 'finally ready to sew again' and to pass on her quilting skills to the next generation. Her work is held in collections including those of the Studio Museum in Harlem, New York and the Legacy Museum, Montgomery. **EY**

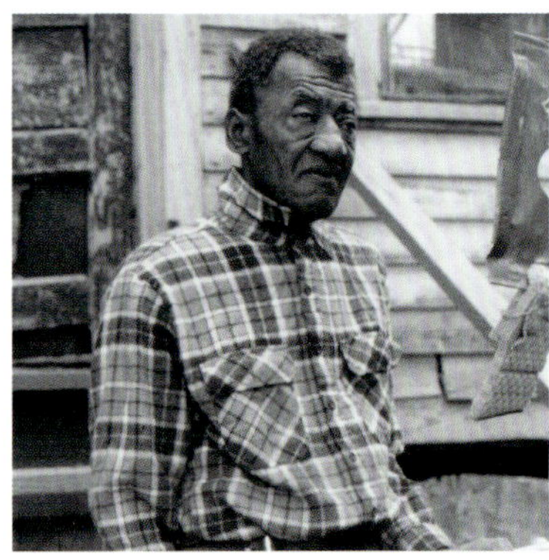 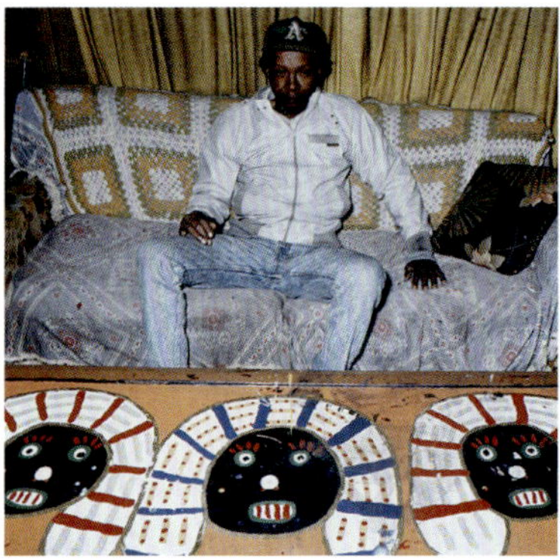 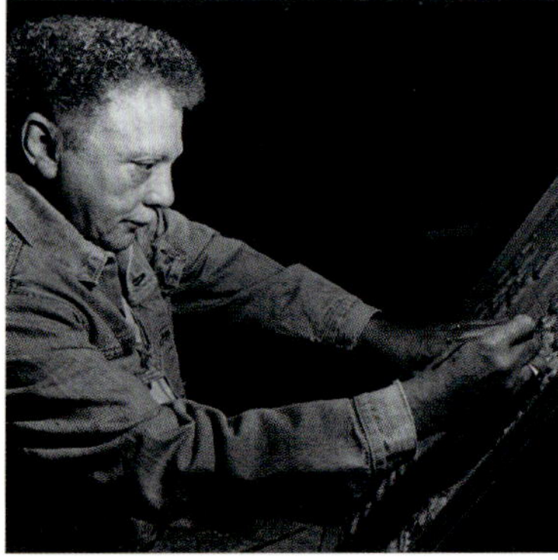

Hawkins Bolden (1914–2005) was born in Bailey's Bottom in Memphis, Tennessee. As a child he had a talent for making toys such as kites and trucks from found materials. A head injury sustained aged seven while playing baseball with his identical twin Monroe led to seizures that caused him to go blind when he was eight. He never regained his sight.

In 1930, the family moved to a small house in midtown Memphis, where Bolden would live with his sister Elizabeth for the rest of his life. When Monroe – who taught him to make radios – joined the army aged nineteen, Bolden remained in Memphis where he searched the streets, yards and vacant lots to source materials, including hoses, saucepans, extension cords and toys, which he assembled by touch to form figures: 'I don't worry about colour. I know when I can make something by how it feels.' In the 1960s, his niece suggested he arrange his sculptures in the yard to keep the birds out, so he began referring to them as 'scarecrows'.

Bolden's profile was raised in 1994 when he took part in the 'Passionate Visions of the American South' group exhibition at the New Orleans Museum of Art. Today his works can be found in collections such as those of the High Museum of Art, Atlanta and the Philadelphia Museum of Art. **RB**

Richard Burnside (1944–2020) was born in Baltimore, Maryland, although his family moved to South Carolina when he was five. He attended Sterling High School in Greenville, South Carolina, and worked as a store clerk before serving in the army between 1974 and 1978. He worked for four years as a chef in Charlotte, North Carolina, and relocated to Pendleton, South Carolina, in 1983.

A foot injury towards the end of his military career resulted in Burnside turning to art, as he discovered it to be a relief from the pain and a way to bring happiness to others. He painted on found objects such as paper bags, plywood and pieces of furniture – any material that would allow him to share his artistic talent – and often depicted kings and queens, animals and mask-like faces in a style characterised by dot patterns, heavy outlines and bright colours.

In his later years, Burnside produced art mainly for the enjoyment of his friends and family, and less for the broader art world. Despite this, his work is now held in collections such as those of the Minneapolis Institute of Art and the Smithsonian American Art Museum, Washington DC. **EY**

Archie Byron (1928–2005) was born in the Buttermilk Bottom neighbourhood of Atlanta, Georgia, the son of a music teacher and a seamstress. A childhood friend of Martin Luther King Jr, he was primarily raised by his grandmother and attended Catholic school until he was drafted into the Navy during the Second World War. After returning to Atlanta, he attended technical school on the G.I. Bill, studying architectural drawing and masonry.

In his childhood, Byron's dream was to become a policeman, but upon failing to meet the minimum height requirement when Atlanta lifted the ban on recruiting Black officers in 1945, he went into construction and masonry instead, to support his family. His lifelong fascination with law enforcement, however, never left him, and in 1961 he changed career path to co-found what he described as 'the first black-owned detective agency' in America. By the mid-1970s, he owned several small businesses, including a security-guard training school, a firing range and a gun repair shop.

Clearing sawdust from the floor of the gun repair shop one day, he realised, 'There's a beauty there that shouldn't be wasted.' He experimented in mixing the sawdust with different adhesives before finally concocting a paste made with Elmer's glue and water, the unique material he would use to create bas-relief hangings and sculptures. Such works captured the attention of collectors and curators in the early 1980s.

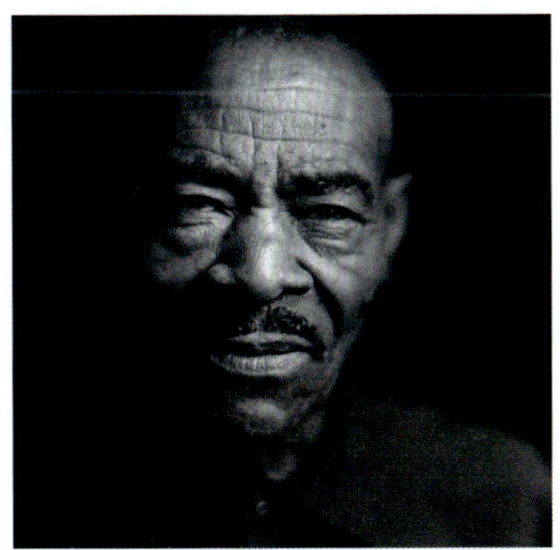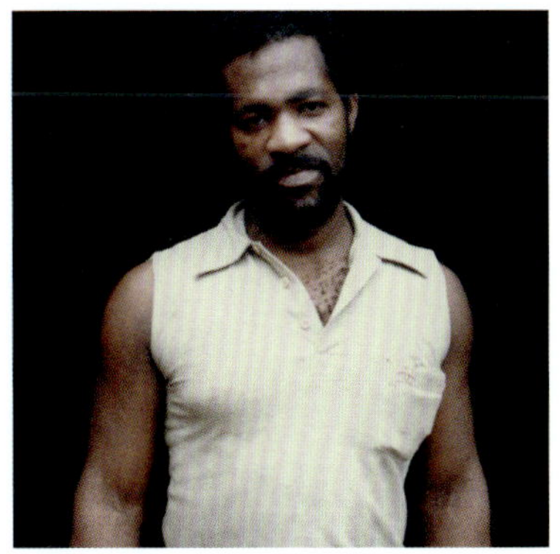

In 1981, disillusioned by the political landscape of Atlanta, Byron decided to run for Atlanta City Council himself, and won and held a seat for eight years. In addition to painting fantastical creatures and natural landscapes, his frustrations with the socio-political climate, particularly the treatment of Black people, also directly informed his artistic practice.

His work is now held in the collections of such institutions as the Smithsonian American Art Museum, Washington DC and the Fine Arts Museums of San Francisco. **EY**

Thornton Dial (1928–2016) was born in rural Alabama. He and his younger half-brother Arthur were brought up by his mother and older female relatives. By the third grade he was forced to leave school in order to work to support his family. When he was twelve the two brothers were sent to live with their great-aunt Sarah Lockett in Bessemer, a town adjacent to the city of Birmingham.

In 1950, Dial married Clara May Murrow, with whom he had five children, two of whom – Thornton Jr and Richard – would later follow in their father's artistic footsteps. He was employed for 30 years as a steelworker and later an instructor at the Pullman-Standard boxcar factory in Bessemer. When the company closed in 1981, Dial started a business with two of his sons, making metal patio furniture. They worked with found metal, which led Dial to experiment with making freestanding sculptures and assemblages. In the late 1980s he expanded his practice into drawing and painting, often including found objects within his monumental canvases. He was an astute observer and a shrewd commentator, and often took inspiration for his work from contemporary society as well as historical and current events.

Dial's art received growing critical acclaim from the early 1990s onwards. His work was featured in the Whitney Biennial 2000, and was the subject of solo exhibitions including at the American Folk Art Museum, New York in 1993, and the touring exhibition 'Hard Truths' at the Indianapolis Museum of Art, New Orleans Museum of Art, the Mint Museum, Charlotte and the High Museum of Art, Atlanta in 2011–12. Today his work can be found in collections including those of the National Gallery of Art, Washington DC and the Metropolitan Museum of Art, New York. **RB**

Thornton Dial Jr was born in 1953 in Bessemer, near Birmingham, Alabama. The eldest son of the prolific artist Thornton Dial, he shared a close bond with his father, and since childhood Dial Jr was encouraged to make things and explore his creativity.

After working in the construction business in Birmingham, Dial Jr returned to Bessemer after eight years, to work in the same Pullman-Standard boxcar factory as his father and his brother Richard (see overleaf). When that closed in the early 1980s, the three men formed Dial Metal Patterns, building furniture. Dial Jr worked part-time for the business, as well as caring for the family farm, where he lived with his wife and children. Inspired by his father, and his own experiences in construction, around this time Dial Jr began creating freestanding sculptures, and later paintings. These works often contain social and religious commentary, and frequently grapple with the dynamics of his close family of artists.

Dial Jr's works can be found in collections such as those of the National Gallery of Art, Washington DC and the Fine Arts Museums of San Francisco. **RB**

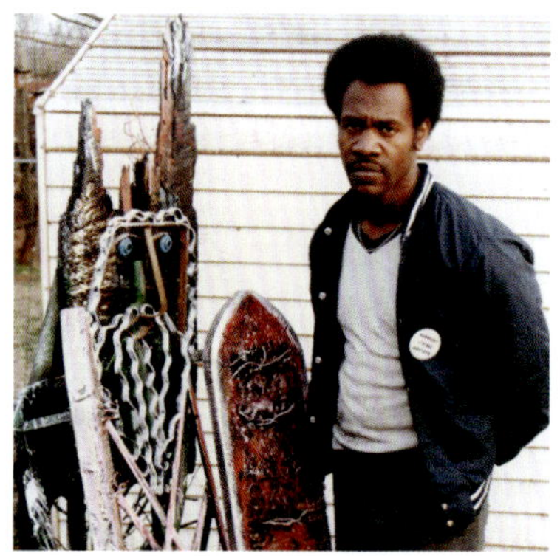 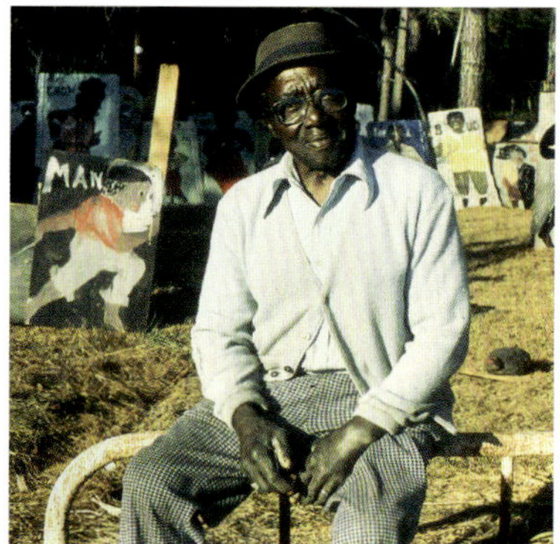

Richard Dial was born in 1955 in Bessemer, Alabama. The second son of the artist Thornton Dial, he grew up in a family atmosphere that nurtured creativity and making.

Dial worked as a machinist in the same Pullman-Standard boxcar factory as his father and brothers, but harboured hopes of setting up his own business. When the factory closed in the early 1980s, he took the opportunity to set up Dial Metal Patterns, manufacturing furniture with his father and his brother, Thornton Dial Jr. He was head of the business and employed other former workers of the Pullman factory.

Dial named his first range of furniture 'Shade Tree Comfort'. This theme of comfort became the inspiration for a series of anthropomorphic sculptures he produced from 1987. Based on the familiar form of a chair, the sculptures play with the tension between the chairs' promise of comfort and the sculptures' uncomfortable subject-matter. These works, like those of his brother Thornton Jr, often grapple with the intense bonds – and sometimes rivalries – found in a family of artists.

Today Dial's works can be found in collections such as those of the High Museum of Art, Atlanta and Toledo Museum of Art, Ohio. **RB**

Sam Doyle (1906–1985) was born on Saint Helena Island, off the South Carolina coast, the population of which was almost entirely descended from enslaved African Americans. During Doyle's youth the island remained physically and culturally isolated, which allowed the local Gullah culture to thrive. He attended the island's Penn School, founded by Quakers in the early 1860s to educate formerly enslaved people, where, as an adolescent, he was identified as showing artistic promise but left in the ninth grade. It was not until around 1944 that he began to paint, but he could only turn his attention to the practice fully after he retired in the 1970s.

Saint Helena Island's remoteness meant that information from mainland America travelled slowly. Doyle took to documenting important news, local and nationwide, on corrugated tin roofing. These paintings were displayed outside the café his estranged wife had abandoned, which became a location for neighbours to meet and learn about events. Local gossip – particularly that of a sexual nature – and history and myths were also chronicled by Doyle, coded within complex layers of meaning.

Doyle was attuned to race and completed a series called 'Black Firsts', depicting those who had been the first in their local community to join different professions. He also portrayed notable Black figures from the mainland such as Martin Luther King Jr and the boxer Joe Louis.

Three years before his death, Doyle's work had its debut in the seminal exhibition, 'Black Folk Art in America, 1930–1980' at the Corcoran Gallery of Art in Washington DC. Following this his fame grew rapidly, his work inspiring such contemporary artists as Jean-Michel Basquiat. Today it can be found in collections such as those of the Museum of Fine Arts, Houston and the High Museum of Art, Atlanta. **RB**

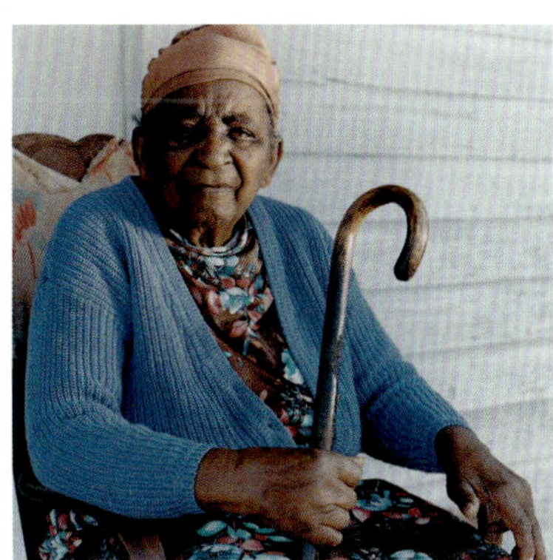

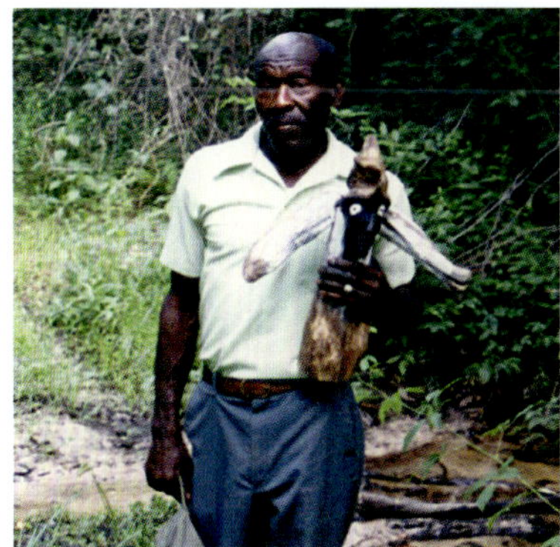

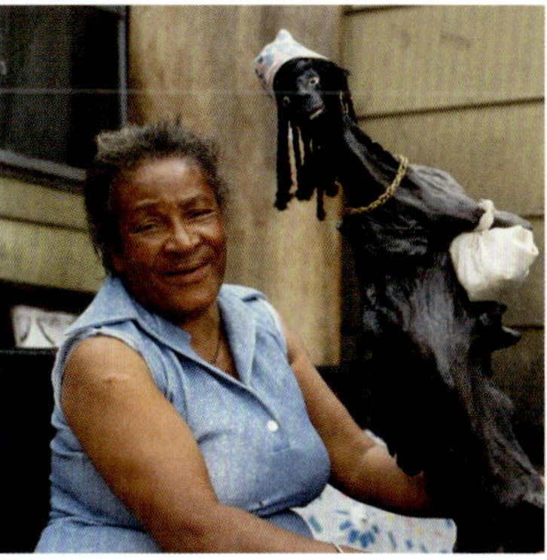

Rachel Carey George (1908–2011) was born in Mitchell Hill, Alabama. Her father was Reverend William Carey, minister of Pleasant Grove Baptist Church, the main congregation in Gee's Bend. Her aunt, Delia Bennett, was an influential quilter, and it is likely that George learnt to quilt from her and other women in the family.

As an adult, Carey lived through the Great Depression, a time in history when Gee's Bend's Wilcox County was one of the poorest in the country. Quilts she produced during this time reflect George's creative ingenuity, making use of materials including cast-off work clothes, mattress ticking and scraps from feed sacks. Later, when in the 1970s the Freedom Quilting Bee received a commission from retailer Sears Roebuck and Co., which provided the Gee's Bend community with corduroy scraps, George readily embraced this previously scarce fabric in her work.

Throughout her life, George was a prolific quilter and greatly enjoyed the process; her daughter later recalled 'she had plenty of quilts and liked to make quilts all the time'. When age eventually forced her to reduce her workload, the one activity she would not give up was quilting. Today, George's quilts are held in collections such as that of the Museum of Fine Arts, Boston. **RB**

Ralph Griffin (1925–1992) was born to a cotton-farming family in Burke County, Georgia. Financial instability led him to leave the farm when he was 30, and he worked odd jobs and travelled widely through coastal Georgia and Florida for several years. In the mid-1960s he returned to Burke County, settling near the town of Girard.

Griffin made his first sculpture in 1978, an anteater entitled *Midnight* (cat. 40). It was formed from a piece of wood found in the Poplar Root Branch creek behind his home. This creek became the source of wood and roots for all his sculptures, which he would alter minimally to create figures of people and animals. In 1987, he explained his process: 'I take a root from the water and I have a thought about it, what it looks like, then I paint it red, black and white, to put a bit of vision on the root.'

Griffin filled his yard with sculptures, reserving those he believed were imbued with positive power for inside his home. Word of his yard and talismanic figures spread, with some people taking them as signs of special powers and asking him for advice on dreams, a reputation he resisted. In 1989 he retired and was able to dedicate his time to his art, until his death from cancer three years later. Today his work can be found in collections such as those of the Baltimore Museum of Art, Maryland and the Fine Arts Museums of San Francisco. **RB**

Bessie Harvey (1929–1994) was born in Dallas, Georgia. One of ten children, her upbringing was challenging, and at the age of twenty she relocated to rural Tennessee.

Harvey recalled making dolls from roots as a child, encouraged by her mother, but did not return to making art until the 1970s. Struggling to earn a living, she reached what she described as her lowest point, and began seeing faces in the natural world around her. She realised that seeing them was a gift from God, who taught her how to bring the faces out of wood into works of art: 'I am the sculptress that God has taught me to be.'

Harvey was proud of her African heritage and studied traditional African art and techniques, incorporating them into her work. She rejected the suggestion that her artworks were related to Voodoo, at one point even burning some anthropomorphic figures to avoid this association.

In the latter decades of her life, Harvey's sculptures began to receive recognition. She travelled to New Orleans and New Jersey where she was included in group shows. In 1995, the year after her death, her work was exhibited at the Biennial of the Whitney Museum of American Art in New York, and today is held in collections including those of the National Gallery of Art, Washington DC and the Baltimore Museum of Art. **RB**

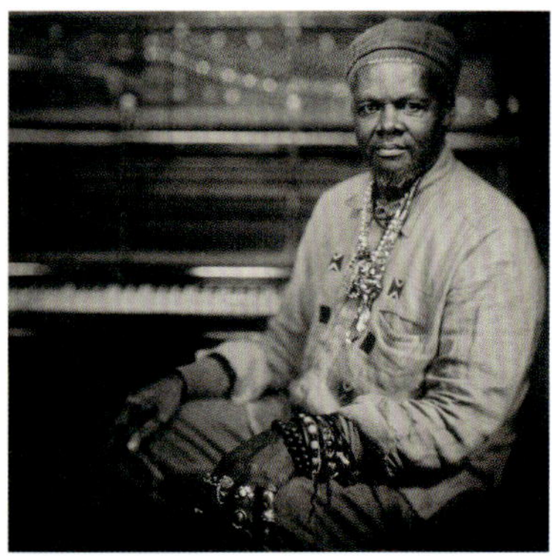

Lonnie Holley was born in 1950 in Birmingham, Alabama. He experienced a difficult childhood: he was passed through several foster homes and often ran away from them, suffered physical abuse, and served time in juvenile detention centres for petty crimes.

Holley's art was initially borne out of family tragedy when, at the age of 29, he carved two gravestones for a niece and nephew who had died in a house fire. Finding peace in the process, he continued to carve cast-off foundry stone, leading others to encourage him to share his work more widely. When he took samples of his work to the Birmingham Museum of Art in Alabama in 1981, three pieces were immediately included in an exhibition at the Smithsonian American Art Museum in Washington DC.

Following this success, Holley's artistic practice evolved from stone carving to working with collected trash and material from the Birmingham steel industries. He exhibited his collaged and sculptural creations all over his house and yard, his personal art environment, which was destroyed in 1997 after the Birmingham Airport Authority condemned the property. His oeuvre now includes drawing, photography, performance and sound, with his first album of music recorded at the age of 62.

His work has been acquired by many major collections including those of the Metropolitan Museum of Art, New York, the National Gallery of Art, Washington DC and the High Museum of Art, Atlanta, and is on permanent display in the United Nations building in New York City. **EY**

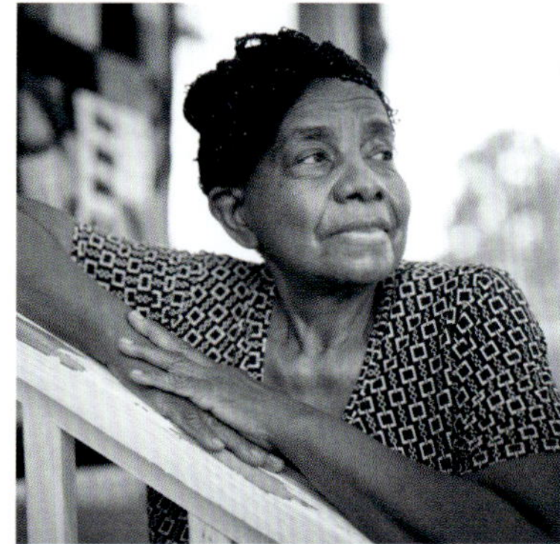

Marlene Bennett Jones was born in 1947 and raised on a farm in Gee's Bend, Alabama. She spent her childhood working in the fields with her family, and first learned how to quilt at the age of eight. After studying electronics and working as an aeronautical engineer with the aerospace and aviation companies Beechcraft and Lockheed Martin, she eventually returned to Gee's Bend in her retirement to assist her mother, Agatha Bennett who was ill with Alzheimer's.

Back in Gee's Bend, Jones returned to quilting, and would sit by her mother's bedside laying out swatches of fabric so that they could intuitively quilt together. Following her mother's passing, she continued to quilt, often using her deceased parents' clothing as material to keep their memory alive.

Her work has been featured in the Alabama Bicentennial, the Kentucky Artisan Center, Berea, and recently in a solo exhibition at the Nina Johnson Gallery in Miami, Florida. It can be found in collections such as that of the Institute of Contemporary Art, Miami. **EY**

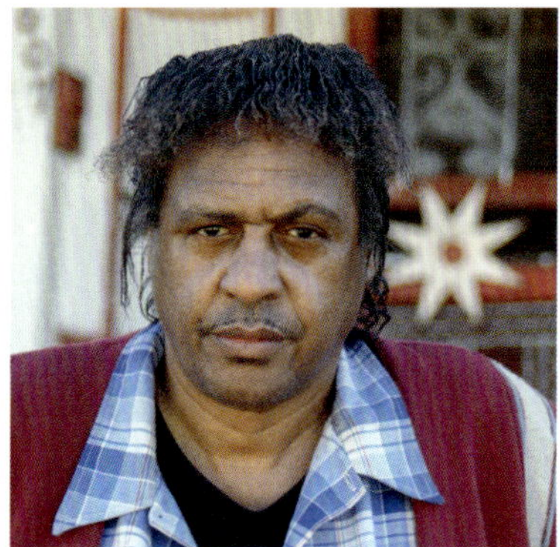

Joe Light (1934–2005) was born in Dyersburg, Tennessee, and spent his early childhood working on a farm. After enlisting in the army at the age of seventeen, he was discharged seven months later after suffering an injury. He later served two terms in prison for armed robbery; while incarcerated, he converted to Judaism after listening to a preacher read from the Old Testament.

Light's religious awakening changed the course of his life and fuelled his artistic output upon his release from prison in 1966, beginning with his writing of Old Testament verses and messages in chalk in public spaces. In the early 1970s, after settling in Memphis with his second wife Rosie Lee Cotton and their children, he translated his religious fervour into the painting of wooden or cardboard signs installed around his yard to express his opinions. These signs sought to inspire the bettering of his neighbourhood, and included lamentations against social and racial injustice among other, more controversial opinions. His practice soon evolved into making paintings and sculptures, his two biggest influences being his spirituality and the vibrant, bold aesthetics of commercialism.

Towards the end of his life, Light encountered financial difficulties that resulted in the loss of his family home, the walls of which he had painted with biblical narratives. Despite this, by the mid-1980s he had become an acclaimed artist, and his work can now be found in collections such as those of the Metropolitan Museum of Art, New York and the Smithsonian American Art Museum, Washington DC. **EY**

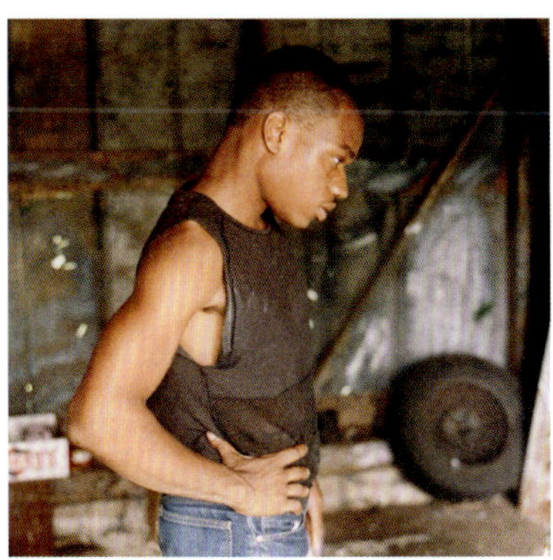

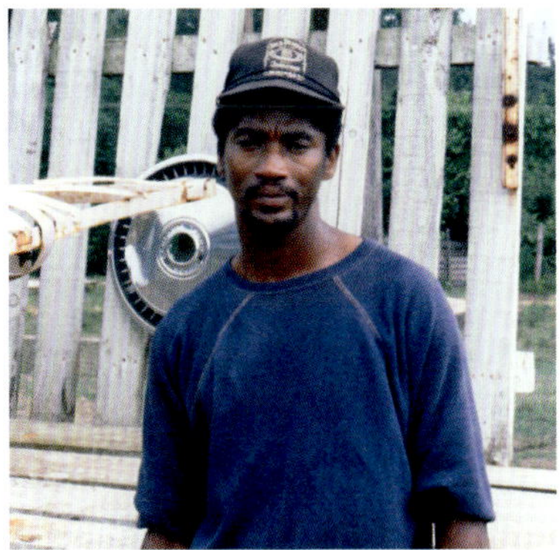

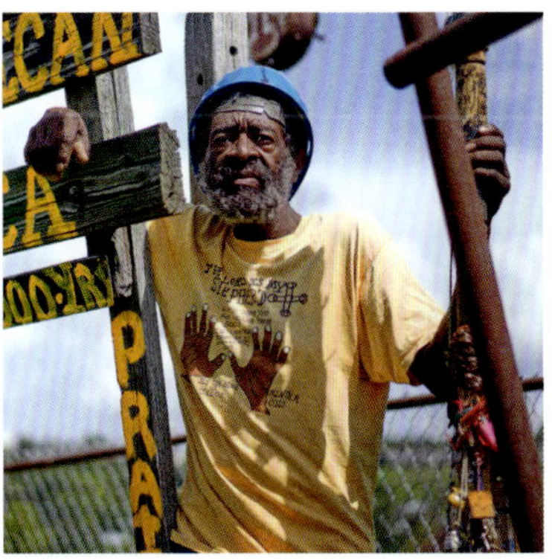

Ronald Lockett (1965–1998) was born and raised in the Pipe Shop neighbourhood of Bessemer, Alabama, where he lived his whole life. He graduated from high school but never pursued a traditional trade, having known since elementary school that he wanted to be an artist.

Although he toyed with the idea of going to art school, he was dissuaded by his older cousin and neighbour Thornton Dial Sr (see page 125), who advised that he 'had the best school of all just making artwork'. Indeed, Lockett enjoyed an invaluable art education under the close mentorship of Dial, who allowed him to watch his process and offered him endless support. His great-grandmother Sarah Lockett was also one of his earliest and deepest influences, instilling in him an appreciation of the African-American quilting tradition that he would later reference in his work.

Over the course of his decade-long career, Lockett produced around 400 works of art, primarily paintings and sculptures that grapple with both the disintegration and horrors of the twentieth century, such as those of the Holocaust and Hiroshima, and with personal matters, notably Sarah Lockett's death. Global and personal tragedy ultimately converged with his own diagnosis of HIV, which caused him to fall into a deep depression and largely shifted the themes of his work to morality, salvation and remembrance.

Lockett died from AIDS-related pneumonia at the age of 32. His work is now held in collections such as those of the High Museum of Art, Atlanta and the Metropolitan Museum of Art, New York. **EY**

Charlie Lucas was born in 1951 in the Pink Lily area of Prattville, Alabama. He grew up surrounded by family members creating things, including quilts, baskets, wood carvings and ceramics, and was taught to make toys by his blacksmith grandfather. However, at the age of eight he was told by a teacher that he could never be an artist because 'that's for white folks'. Disillusioned, he left school and worked as a water boy for a construction crew, learning building techniques over the following twenty years. After spending a short time in Florida, he returned to Pink Lily in 1971 and settled down there.

In 1984 a workplace accident left Lucas disabled and he was forced to retire at the age of 33. He saw this incident as a turning point in his life, when he could have relied on injury payments or become a farmer, but instead he dedicated himself to making art. Drawing on the practical skills taught to him by his grandfather and learnt during his earlier career, he began creating welded-metal sculptures from used automobile and machine parts. His yard became filled with these works, often autobiographical in theme, and by the late 1980s they were spilling out on to both sides of the road, drawing recognition and visitors.

Lucas now lives in Selma, Alabama, where he has established the Tin Man Studio. Continuing the family tradition of making, he passed down his skills to his children, some of whom also now work in the studio. His work can be found in collections such as those of the High Museum of Art, Atlanta and the Studio Museum in Harlem, New York. **RB**

Joe Minter was born in 1943 in Birmingham, Alabama. His father worked as a caretaker in Elmwood Cemetery; Minter recalled that 'he worked until his death to make a way for us [children]'. As an adult, Minter worked multiple jobs, including as a construction worker, and served in the army for three years. By the late 1980s health conditions, caused by exposure to chemicals including asbestos during the course of his work, forced him to retire.

In 1989, on hearing news of plans to construct a civil rights museum in Birmingham, Minter began his own response to 'that four hundred years journey of Africans in America'. Drawing on his experience in construction and welding, he created a series of sculptures formed from metal and found objects. These he displayed in the half-acre yard surrounding his home, creating a unique immersive environment titled *African Village in America*. Minter continues to work on and add to this yard show, which now stands densely packed with thousands of artworks, forming a multi-layered, continually evolving narrative of the history of Black Americans.

Outside of his work on the *African Village in America*, Minter also makes independent sculptures that reflect many of the same themes found in his yard show. Several of his sculptures were exhibited in the Whitney Biennial 2019. Today his work is held in collections including those of the Metropolitan Museum of Art, New York and the Fine Arts Museums of San Francisco. **RB**

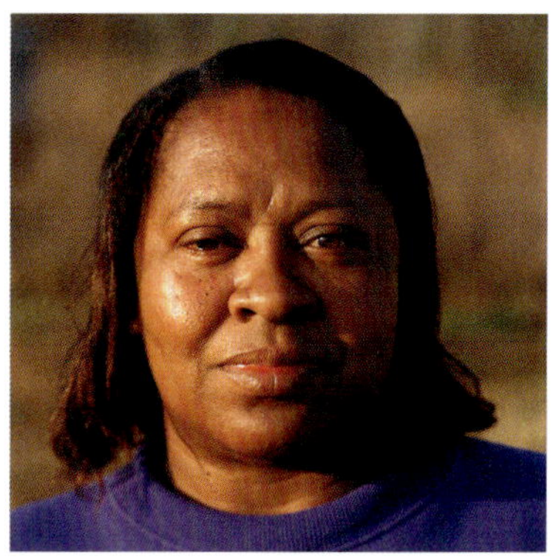 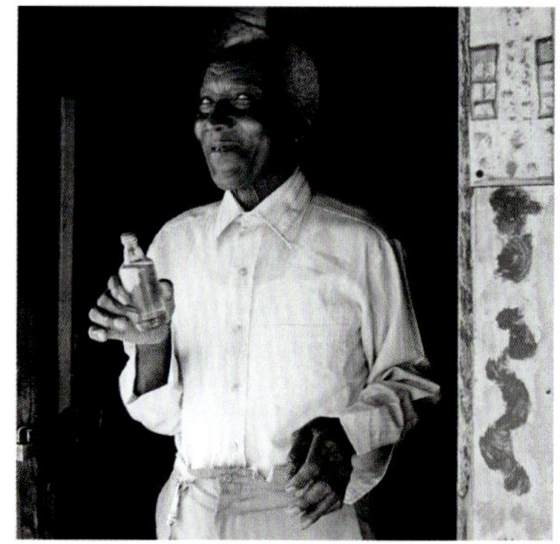

Flora Moore was born in 1951, the daughter of two farmers. She grew up in the town of Rehoboth, Alabama, a small and isolated community very close to Gee's Bend that has similarly nurtured generations of quiltmakers. As a youngster, outside of school, Moore went to work in the fields picking cotton until she 'got big enough to know what it was about'. She became inspired to start quilting as a teenager, after watching women make quilts in the home of her cousin Estelle Witherspoon, the birthplace of the Freedom Quilting Bee cooperative.

Although mentored by Witherspoon and her aunt Willie 'Ma Willie' Abrams, Moore remains determined to be guided by her own artistic voice and instincts, once noting, 'You might know how somebody else do it, but you tell yourself, I'm going to do it different.' As such, she epitomises the 'my way' tradition of quiltmaking, which favours individualism and improvisation over any reliance on an established quilt pattern.

Moore has made quilts out of old clothes donated to the quilting bee, as well as from sturdier, more challenging materials like corduroy. Her work is held in the collections of the High Museum of Art, Atlanta and the National Gallery of Art, Washington DC. **EY**

John B. Murray (1908–1988) was born in a remote community in Glascock County in rural Georgia, where he lived his entire life in near-isolation in the small house he had built for his family. He had little formal education and worked as a tenant farmer.

A hip injury in the late 1970s forced him to retire from working on his farm. In 1978 he experienced a religious vision in which God imparted divine knowledge to him about the waging of a spiritual war, which he was to convey to other believers. Unable to read or write English, he developed a calligraphic 'spirit language' which he would read out in ceremonies using 'holy water' from his property.

Around this time Murray also started creating his first artworks, beginning with assembling rocks and other natural materials, and later salvaging abandoned objects. These he covered with abstract scenes using colours that held particular meanings for him. Both artworks and 'spirit writings' were displayed around his house and yard for protection. Although Murray saw himself as devoutly Christian, some local people were troubled by his seemingly unorthodox practices.

In the early 1980s Murray was diagnosed with prostate cancer, the condition that would ultimately take his life. Doctors used medical diagrams to explain the disease to him, and motifs of human anatomy, cells and disease were subsequently integrated into his work. The news of his illness drove him to dedicate even more time to his art, as he worked to urgently convey the message divinely imparted to him. Today his work can be found in collections including those of the Metropolitan Museum of Art, New York and the Toledo Museum of Art, Ohio. **RB**

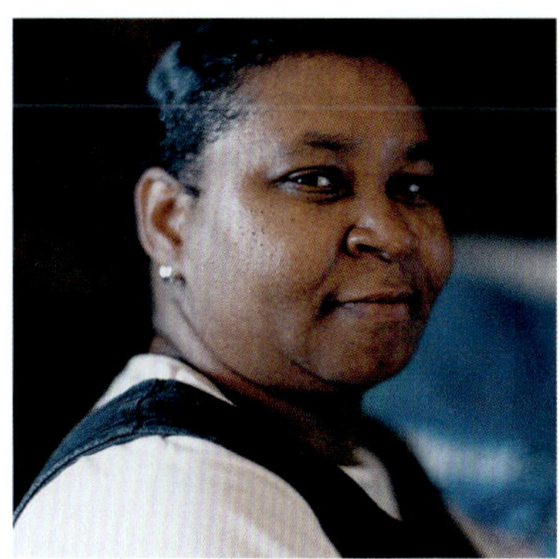 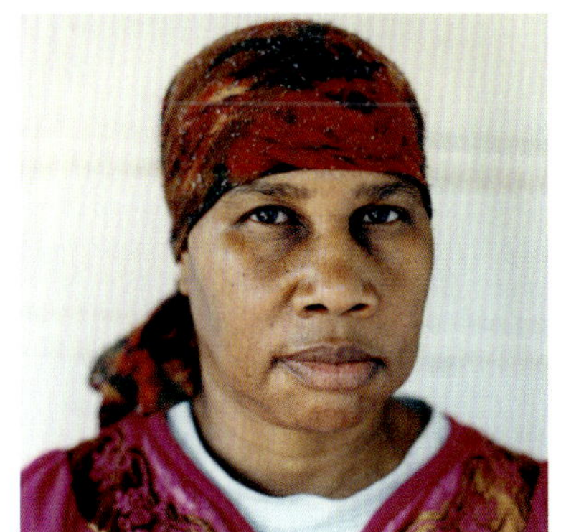 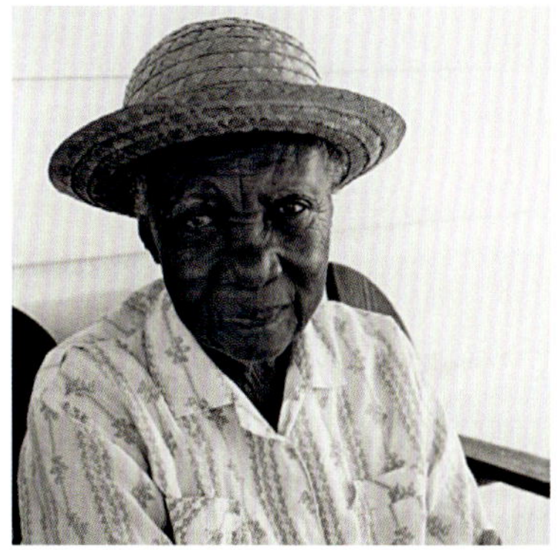

Essie Bendolph Pettway was born in Gee's Bend, Alabama, in 1956, the only daughter of Mary Lee Bendolph (see page 122) and the granddaughter of Aolar Mosely, a founding member of the Freedom Quilting Bee. From around the age of seven, after watching her mother sew, Pettway knew that she wanted to make quilts herself. Finding teachers in her mother, grandmother and aunts, she completed her first quilt at the age of twelve or thirteen, and was producing accomplished, artistically mature examples by her mid-teens.

Pettway's talent for sewing led her to make uniforms for the armed forces for many years in Selma, Alabama, but she has always been careful to separate the military precision of her day job from the creative freedom she finds in quiltmaking and sewing clothes, pillows and curtains. In the comfort of her own home, she 'can mess up like I want to'. She enjoys improvising her own patterns and takes great pleasure in seeing other people enjoying her work, once noting that she is 'happy people appreciate what I do'. Her work can be found in collections such as those of the Montgomery Museum of Fine Arts, Alabama and the Studio Museum in Harlem, New York. **EY**

Loretta Pettway was born in 1942 in Gee's Bend, Alabama. She was primarily raised by her grandmother, Prissy Pettway. Her grandmother was one of many Pettway quiltmaking teachers and mentors she had while growing up, including Missouri, Louella, Qunnie, and stepmother Plummer T., although as a child she disliked quilting, seeing it as yet another chore. However, once she moved into a house of her own, she learnt to appreciate the need for quilts: 'We only had heat in the living room, and when you go out of that room you need cover. [...] Them quilts done keep you warm.'

While drawing inspiration from her family's quiltmaking heritage, as an adult Pettway developed her own style of quilting improvisational designs. She also expressed a fondness for the Bricklayer pattern, seeing in it a nostalgic reminder of the brick house she coveted.

In 2006, two of Pettway's quilts were selected to appear on US postage stamps, and in 2015 she was one of three Gee's Bend quilters awarded a National Heritage Fellowship by the National Endowment for the Arts. Today her quilts are held in collections including those of the Metropolitan Museum of Art, New York, Baltimore Museum of Art, Maryland and the Virginia Museum of Fine Arts, Richmond. **RB**

Martha Jane Pettway (1898–2003) was born in Gee's Bend, Alabama, where she was raised working on a farm. It was not until she was about fifteen that her mother began teaching her how to quilt using standard quilting patterns.

Pettway and her husband, Little Pettway, established themselves as active members of the Gee's Bend community, liaising with federal government officials and persuading other families to participate in President Roosevelt's New Deal reform programmes, which were initiated in the wake of the Great Depression to improve the economic development of the area.

Throughout her life, quilting remained a source of solace for Pettway and a pastime that she pursued out of genuine passion: 'I don't make them to sell, I just make them and love to sew ... love to quilt.' She lived until her death in Mobile, Alabama, having proudly taught all her daughters how to quilt. Her work is now included in collections such as those of the Philadelphia Museum of Art and the Metropolitan Museum of Art, New York. **EY**

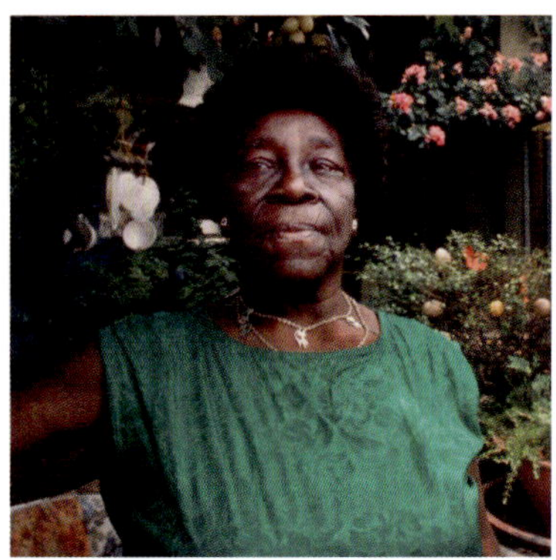 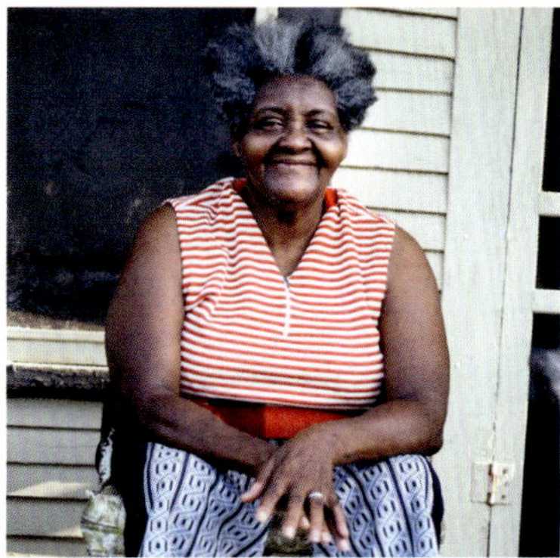 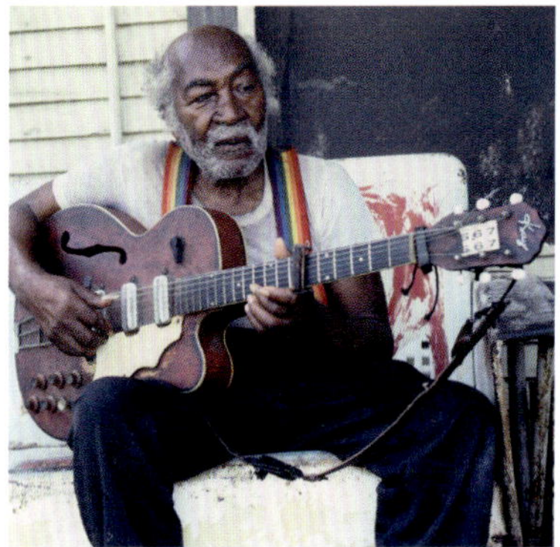

Nellie Mae Rowe (1900–1982) was born to a cotton-farming family in rural Georgia. Her father made baskets and her mother quilted, and both encouraged their children's creative pursuits. Rowe taught herself to draw 'whatever she thought of', as well as making dolls out of the family's laundry. However, after she left home to marry she started working as a domestic servant and did not have the time to continue her creative practice.

Only when her second husband Henry Rowe died in 1948 did she rededicate herself to art. Rowe decorated her yard with drawings and found objects, calling the space her 'playhouse'. Her first public exhibition took place in 1976, at the Atlanta Historical Society, and she was one of only three female artists to be included in the seminal 1982 exhibition 'Black Folk Art in America, 1930–1980' at the Corcoran Gallery of Art in Washington DC.

In 1981 Rowe was diagnosed with terminal cancer. This news increased her already prolific artistic output, as she turned to drawing for comfort and expression of her pain. The drawings she made in the final year of her life are her most well-known and complex works, filled with personal symbolism relating to her life and her deep Christian faith. Today her work is held in collections including those of the High Museum of Art, Atlanta and the Metropolitan Museum of Art, New York. **RB**

Georgia Speller (1931–1988) was born in Aberdeen, northwest Mississippi. The daughter of a blacksmith, she learned to draw at a young age, although it was not something she pursued until later in life.

In the early 1960s she met Henry Speller in Memphis, Tennessee, and the two married in 1979. Henry encouraged Speller in her drawing, and she took to displaying her and her husband's work from their house near Beale Street. The two explored similar subjects in their work, at times engaging in playful competitions to draw the same scene. Speller particularly focused her attention on erotic images, frequently depicting sexually dominant women and orgiastic scenes, which she maintained were not based on her own experience. Her work is included in collections such as those of the National Gallery of Art, Washington DC and the Studio Museum in Harlem, New York. **RB**

Henry Speller (1903–1997) was born in Rolling Fork, a small town in the Mississippi Delta. He grew up on a nearby plantation with his maternal grandmother and her husband, where they worked as sharecroppers.

Speller had to leave school at the age of twelve to help farm cotton. He remained in the Delta for several years, working on local farms to support his grandparents and two short-lived marriages, despite wishing to resume his education or move north for better opportunities. During his lunch breaks he would often draw pictures, paying for the materials he needed by selling candy to his friends and family.

In 1939 he moved to Memphis, Tennessee, where he worked a variety of odd jobs and expanded his talent as a blues musician. There he met Georgia in the early 1960s. She too loved to draw and to sing, and the two married in 1964 (or 1979; sources vary). They lived together near the now-famous Beale Street in Memphis, where Speller soon retired and spent much of his time drawing, recording life around him as well as fantasy scenes of powerful women.

Following Georgia Speller's death in 1988, Speller's health and interest in making art rapidly declined. He made thousands of drawings across his lifetime, some of which can now be found in collections such as those of the Princeton University Art Museum, New Jersey and the Metropolitan Museum of Art, New York. **RB**

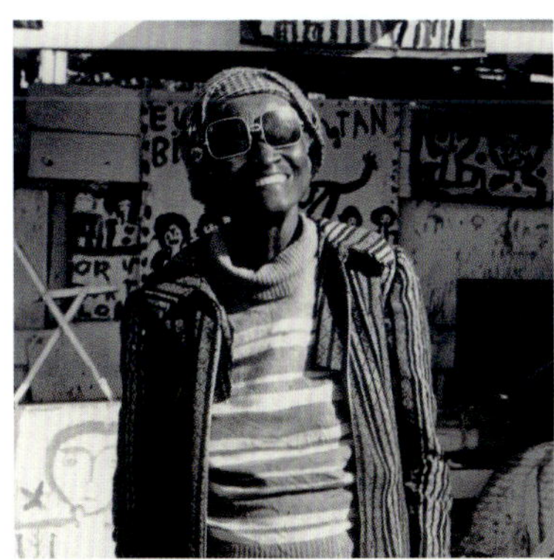

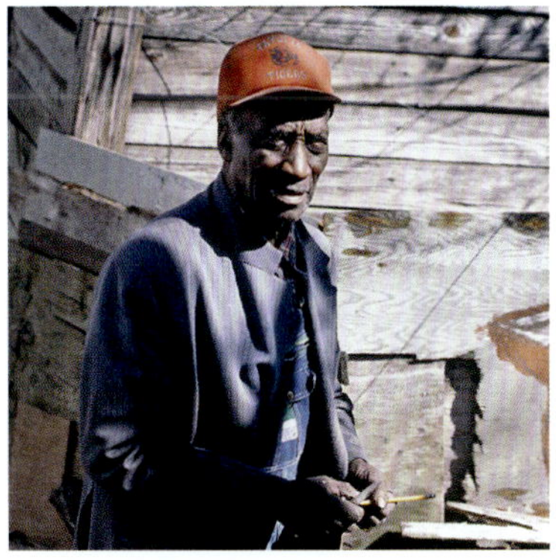

Mary T. Smith (1905–1995) was born into a sharecropping family in Copiah County, southern Mississippi. Although her family recognised her intelligence, others assumed her difficulty in communicating – the result of a congenital hearing impairment – was a sign of simple-mindedness. Often isolated, from a young age Smith turned to drawing to express herself.

By her thirties – and after two marriages – Smith was living in the town of Hazlehurst, Mississippi, working as a maid. There in 1941 she had her only child, Sheridan Major, and the child's father built her a house. Able for the first time to live independently, she began creating art using materials salvaged from a nearby rubbish dump. Through a personal vocabulary of imagery, recurring patterns and text, Smith's paintings and sculptures reveal her experience of the world, portraying friends and family as well as reflecting her strong religious beliefs.

After her retirement in 1970, Smith gradually transformed her house and yard into an immersive artistic environment. Noting the advertising billboards on a nearby highway, she constructed her own creative approach to entice passersby. She rarely left the property, stating in 1986, 'I don't go nowhere no more. I can't hear nothing. I don't need nothing. I got it all here. My church. The Lord Jesus.'

A stroke in 1985 slowed Smith's creative output, until she stopped painting around 1990. No longer receiving an income from her art, she lived in increasing poverty until her death at the age of 91. Since then, her work has received greater recognition, and is now held in collections including those of the Metropolitan Museum of Art, New York and the Smithsonian American Art Museum, Washington DC. **RB**

Jimmy Lee Sudduth (1910–2007) was born in Caines Ridge near Fayette, Alabama. His mother was of Native American descent, and he described her as a 'witch doctor' who could heal local people, a skill he learned from her. He made pictures from a very early age, recalling his frustration when the rain would wash away mud he had painted on a tree trunk. When he was nine, a local man taught him how to use sugar syrup as a binder, revealing a way he could fix natural pigments.

During the Great Depression, Sudduth had to leave his home and his art to earn a living as a manual labourer, eventually settling in the nearby town of Fayette where he worked as a gardener. He would not return to painting until the 1960s when he developed a method that involved using his fingers to apply mud, berry juice, grass stains and coffee grounds on raw plywood boards. He avoided conventional paints and tools as much as possible, although in later years he increasingly used acrylic paint.

Like his materials, Sudduth's subjects were often intensely local, depicting the nature, people and places around him. As his artistic reputation grew, he travelled to cities such as Washington DC and New York, and would often document these urban places in his paintings. Today his work can be found in collections including those of the Smithsonian American Art Museum, Washington DC and the Virginia Museum of Fine Arts, Richmond. **RB**

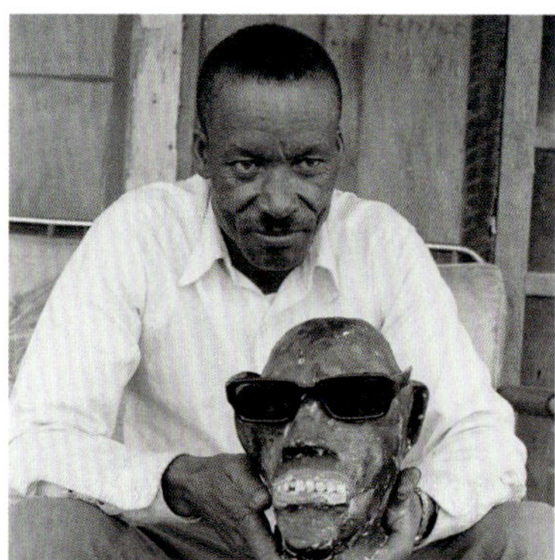

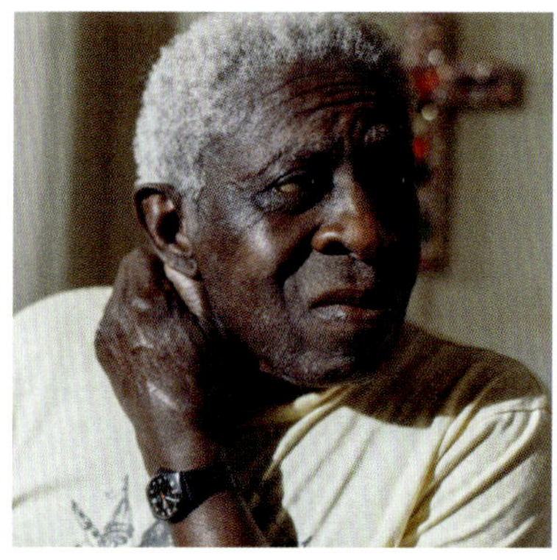

James 'Son Ford' Thomas (1926–1993) was born in Eden, a village in the Mississippi Delta. As a child he lived with his maternal grandparents. He worked with his grandfather in the cotton fields. From the age of eight, Thomas was taught to play guitar by his uncle Joe Cooper, a noted blues musician who also showed him how to use local clay to sculpt toys for himself; a favourite subject was a Ford tractor, earning Thomas his childhood nickname.

Thomas saw his artistic and musical talents as his ticket out of the cotton fields. In 1961 he moved to Leland, Mississippi, with his wife and children, where he worked as a gravedigger to supplement his income. He created funerary sculptures, skulls and portrait busts, often incorporating human hair and teeth in his works, which were intended to make viewers confront their own mortality. Some of these sculptures were included in the seminal 1982 exhibition 'Black Folk Art in America, 1930–1980' at the Corcoran Gallery of Art, Washington DC.

In the late 1960s Thomas was featured in the folklorist William R. Ferris's documentaries on African traditions in America, which led to an increased interest in his art and music. He started recording his music, adopting his childhood nickname as a stage name, and released his first studio album in 1981. He went on to record three further albums, touring across America and internationally.

By the 1980s Thomas was able to support himself purely through his creative work, until his death at the age of 66. Today his works can be found in collections such as those of the Pinault Collection, Paris and the National Gallery of Art, Washington DC. **RB**

Mose Tolliver (*c.* 1921–2006) was born to a family of tenant farmers living southeast of Montgomery, Alabama. He remembered his first home as a simple shack, lined with pictures. The impact of the Depression left the family unable to support themselves on their farm, which they left in the 1930s, moving into Montgomery. Tolliver found work as a general odd-job man and a landscape gardener. He later described this landscaping work as his first art.

Tolliver had been drawn to painting since his teenage years. He made use of the materials he found around him, painting on bones, roots, the glass of discarded television screens, and postcards. This practice dwindled when the growing pressure of providing for his family made him focus his time on paid work, including a brief stint in the army.

Tolliver was forced to retire in the late 1960s after a crate of marble in the furniture factory he worked in fell on him, crushing his legs and leaving him unable to stand without crutches. His former employer encouraged him to take up painting again, which he began to do using house paint and plywood. After first copying from books and items around him, he developed a rich iconography of subjects, including religious scenes and real and fantastical animals and people. He worked prolifically, completing up to ten works a day; he explained that he 'paint[ed] to keep his head together'.

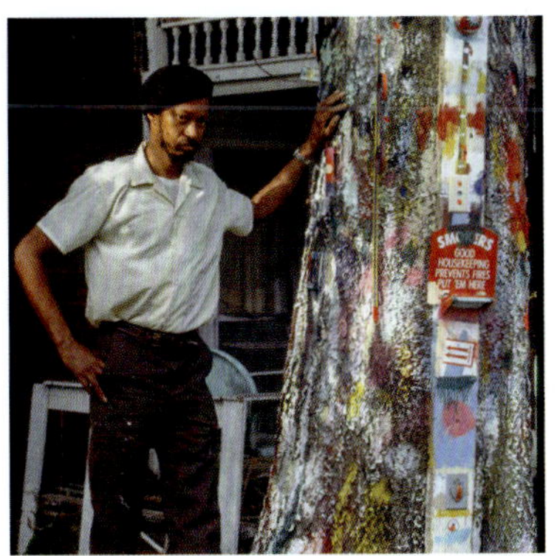 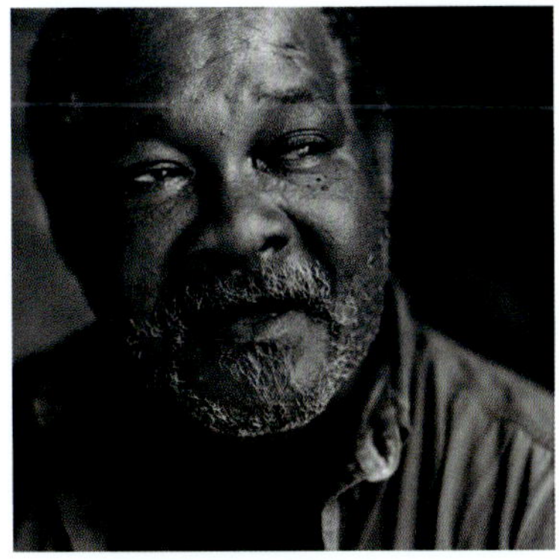

In 1981, Tolliver was given a solo show at the Montgomery Museum of Fine Arts, and took part in the landmark 1982 exhibition 'Black Folk Art in America, 1930–1980' at the Corcoran Gallery of Art in Washington DC. These shows raised his profile and attracted the attention of collectors. Today his paintings are to be found in many American galleries, including the Metropolitan Museum of Art, New York and the Fine Arts Museums of San Francisco. **RB**

Charles Williams (1942–1999) was born in Blue Diamond, a small coal-mining settlement near Hazard, Kentucky. He was raised by his maternal grandparents, a family of miners who lived among the town's other Black residents in the hills outside the main settlement. He attended the local one-roomed school for Black children, which also doubled up as the community's church on Sundays.

Williams began making art as a child, copying figures from his comic books. He also 'accidentally figured out ceramics' while making mud pies, drying out his creations in his grandparents' stove when it was left unattended. In the early 1960s he enrolled at the government-run Jobs Corps centre to learn vocational skills, during which he created a regular comic strip for the local paper.

He worked prolifically throughout his life, continuously expanding his art practice. As well as creating further comic strips, he made sculptures with everyday items found around his home, transforming them into fantasy objects that he then displayed in his yard. His work can be found in collections such as that of the High Museum of Art, Atlanta. **RB**

Purvis Young (1943–2010) was born in the Liberty City neighbourhood of Miami, and introduced to drawing and painting from a young age by his uncle, Irvin Young, a local sign painter. During his incarceration for three years as a young adult for breaking and entering, his interest in art was reignited, and he began drawing again and studied art books in the prison library. After his release in 1964, he produced thousands of small drawings and continued to consult books on Western art history from public libraries, finding particular influence in artists like Rembrandt, Van Gogh and Picasso.

In 1971, Young moved to Miami's Overtown neighbourhood and settled on Good Bread Alley, a vacant alley of former Jamaican bakeries that were to serve as his empty canvas. Inspired by protest art and the mural movements of Chicago and Detroit, he began painting on scrap lumber and plywood salvaged from his urban environment, nailing his creations to the boarded-up storefronts of the alley. Within two years his artwork, which reflected urban street life and often served as a call to action for social and racial justice, had caught the attention of tourists, the media and collectors.

The subsequent acclaim Young received from the art world allowed him to continue to pursue art professionally, although he was troubled by health problems and financial disputes in later life. He died at the age of 67. His work can be found in collections such as those of the Smithsonian American Art Museum, Washington DC and the Metropolitan Museum of Art, New York. **EY**

Endnotes

1   Many Jim Crow laws were overruled by the Civil Rights Act of 1964 and the Voting Rights Act of 1965. However, in 2013 the Supreme Court of the United States ruled by a 5 to 4 vote that critical protections against voter discrimination within the Voting Rights Act were unconstitutional. Since the landmark Shelby County vs Holder decision, several states and jurisdictions have enacted laws restricting voting access without requiring the federal government to determine whether those laws discriminate against ethnic minorities.

2   Thornton Dial, 'Mr Dial Is a Man Looking for Something', in Arnett 2001, p. 196.

3   Binelli 2014.

4   Thornton Dial, 'Mr Dial Is a Man Looking for Something', p. 201.

5   *Ibid.*, p. 221.

6   With his brothers, Richard Dial established Dial Metal Patterns in 1984 in Bessemer, Alabama, a fabrication shop that designs and creates metal patio furniture inspired by furniture made by their father, Thornton Dial Sr, in the 1980s.

7   Ronald Lockett, *Once Something Has Lived It Can Never Really Die*, 1996. Wood, enamel, graphite, tin, found materials and industrial sealing compound on wood, 144.8 x 128.3 x 10.2 cm. Collection of the High Museum of Art, Atlanta. Museum purchase and gift of the Souls Grown Deep Foundation from the William S. Arnett Collection.

8   Videotape 15: Ronald Lockett interview raw footage, 1997, by David Seehausen. Series 2. Video Recordings, c. 1982–2001, in the Souls Grown Deep Foundation Collection #20491, Southern Folklife Collection, The Wilson Library, University of North Carolina at Chapel Hill.

9   When Thornton Dial was thirteen years old, he was sent to stay with his great-aunt Sarah Lockett and her husband Dave in Bessemer.

10   Elujoba 2021.

11   'Lonnie Holley: The Growth of Communication', Edel Assanti Press Release, 2022, https://edelassanti.com/usr/documents/exhibitions/press_release_url/95/lonnie-holley-pr.pdf.

12   Alexander 2020.

13   Gundaker and McWillie 2005.

14   'Souls Grown Deep: African-American Vernacular Art of the South', exhibition at the Michael C. Carlos Museum at City Hall East, Atlanta, 29 June–3 November 1996. See Jones 1996.

15   Robert Rauschenberg Foundation, 'Neapolitan Gluts', https://www.rauschenbergfoundation.org/art/archive/neapolitan-gluts.

16   Joe Minter, 'Peacemaker', in Arnett 2001, p. 504.

17   Tortorello 2013.

18   'Middle Passage', *Encyclopedia Britannica*, consulted 29 August 2022, https://www.britannica.com/topic/Middle-Passage-slave-trade.

19   William Arnett. 'Her Name Is Someone', in Arnett 2001, p. 114.

20   *Purvis Young of Overtown*, 2006, directed by David Raccuglia and Shaun Conrad, Rural Studios.

21   *Purvis Young of Overtown*.

22   Purvis Young, 'This is the Life I See', in Arnett 2001, p. 414.

23   *Ibid.*, p. 392.

24   Loretta Pettway Bennett, 'Dinah, Sally, Tank, Mother, and Me', in Houston 2006, p. 163.

25   *Montgomery Advertiser* 1968.

Further Reading

ABOREDEN 2021
Ashley-Anna Aboreden, 'Quilt Maker Marlene Bennett Jones Connects with Her Past Through Pieces of Fabric', *Miami New Times*, 22 October 2021, https://www.miaminewtimes.com/arts/things-to-do-in-miami-marlene-bennett-jones-at-nina-johnson-gallery-13174307

ALAGIAH 2021
Matt Alagiah, 'How a Small Alabama Community Stitched Itself into the History of American Art', *It's Nice That*, 13 October 2021, https://www.itsnicethat.com/features/loretta-pettway-bennett-gees-bend-quilt-makers-exhibition-art-131021

ALEXANDER 2020
Aleesa Pitchamarn Alexander, 'Magically Lodern: A Short History of the Birmingham–Bessemer School', *Panorama, Journal of the Association of Historians of American Art*, 6, 1, Spring 2020

ARNETT 2000
Paul Arnett and William Arnett (eds), *Souls Grown Deep: African American Vernacular Art of the South*, vol. 1, Atlanta, 2000

ARNETT 2001
Paul Arnett and William Arnett (eds), *Souls Grown Deep: African American Vernacular Art of the South*, vol. 2, Atlanta, 2001

ASPDEN 2022
Peter Aspden, 'Artist Lonnie Holley, "I didn't know that what I was doing was art"', *Financial Times*, 19 May 2022, https://www.ft.com/content/a31fdfb5-db7d-49da-bb35-4cfb193cfc1e

ATLANTA 2021
Katherine Jentleson, *Really Free: The Radical Art of Nellie Mae Rowe*, exh. cat., High Museum of Art, Atlanta, 2021

AUSTIN 2006
Dana Friis-Hansen, Joanne Cubbs and Matt Arnett, *Mary Lee Bendolph, Gee's Bend Quilts, and Beyond*, exh. cat., Austin Museum of Art, Texas, 2006

BERNIER 2019
Celeste-Marie Bernier, *Stick to the Skin: African American and Black British Art, 1965–2015*, Oakland, 2019

BINELLI 2014
Mark Binelli, 'Lonnie Holley, The Insider's Outsider', *New York Times*, 23 January 2014, https://www.nytimes.com/2014/01/26/magazine/lonnie-holley-the-insiders-outsider.html.

BIRMINGHAM 1995
Pictured in My Mind: Contemporary American Self-taught Art from the Collection of Kurt Gitter and Alice Rae Yelen, exh. cat., Birmingham Museum of Art, Alabama, 1995

BIRMINGHAM 2004
Do We Think Too Much? I Don't Think We Can Ever Stop: Lonnie Holley, A Twenty-five Year Survey, exh. cat., Ikon Gallery, Birmingham, UK, 2004

BRAMLETT 2021
Andrew Bramlett, 'Eldren Bailey: The Story of a Cemetery Artist', Historic Oakland Foundation, 15 July 2021, https://oaklandcemetery.com/eldren-bailey-the-story-of-a-cemetery-artist/

ELLIS 2020
Mike Ellis, 'The Little-known Life of a Well-known "Outsider" Artist from Upstate SC Has Ended', *Independent Mail*, 28 October 2020, https://eu.independentmail.com/story/news/2020/10/28/upstate-sc-artist-richard-burnside-has-died/3719829001/

ELUJOBA 2021
Yinka Elujoba, 'Lonnie Holley's Life of Perseverance, and Art of Transformation', *New York Times*, 6 May 2021, https://www.nytimes.com/2021/05/06/arts/design/lonnie-holley.html

FULLER 2021
Daniel Fuller, 'Like Pulling Teeth: The Mythology of James "Son Ford" Thomas', *Burnaway*, 28 July 2021, https://burnaway.org/magazine/james-son-ford-thomas/

GOODWIN 2021
Paul Goodwin, 'Yard art: Fugitive Encounters and the Aesthetics of Fugitivity', *Blackout Magazine*, Issue 2: T/Here, 2021, pp. 51–67

GUNDAKER AND McWILLIE 2005
Grey Gundaker and Judith McWillie, *No Space Hidden: The Spirit of African American Yard Work*, Knoxville, 2005

HOUSTON 2002
The Quilts of Gee's Bend, exh. cat., Museum of Fine Arts, Houston, 2002

HOUSTON 2005
Thornton Dial in the 21st Century, exh. cat., Museum of Fine Arts, Houston, 2005

HOUSTON 2006
Gee's Bend: The Architecture of the Quilt, exh. cat., Museum of Fine Arts, Houston, 2006

INDIANAPOLIS 2011
Hard Truths: The Art of Thornton Dial, exh. cat., Indianapolis Museum of Art, 2011

JONES 1996
Malcolm Jones Jr, 'The Art Games', *Newsweek*, 20 July 1996, https://archive.org/details/sim_newsweek_1996-07-29_ 128_5/.

KALAMAZOO 2001
Kinshasha H. Conwill, *Testimony: Vernacular Art of the African-American South. The Ronald and June Shelp Collection*, exh. cat., Kalamazoo Institute of Arts, Michigan, 2001

LEXINGTON 2022
The Life and Death of Charles Williams, exhibition guide, University of Kentucky Art Museum, Lexington, Kentucky, 2022, https://issuu.com/ukfinearts/docs/charles_williams_exhibition_ guide

MOEHRINGER 1999
J. R. Moehringer, 'Crossing Over', *Los Angeles Times*, 22 August 1999, https://www.latimes.com/archives/la-xpm-1999-aug-22-mn-21385-story.html

MONTGOMERY 2005
Susan Mitchell Crawley, *The Life and Art of Jimmy Lee Sudduth*, exh. cat., Montgomery Museum of Fine Arts, Alabama, 2005

MONTGOMERY ADVERTISER 1968
'Judge Denies Town of King Incorporation', *Montgomery Advertiser*, Montgomery, Alabama, 15 May 1968, p. 5.

NASHVILLE 2012
Creation Story: Gee's Bend Quilts and the Art of Thornton Dial, exh. cat., Frist Center for the Visual Arts, Nashville, 2012

NEW ORLEANS 1993
Passionate Visions of the American South: Self-taught Artists from 1940 to the Present, exh. cat., New Orleans Museum of Art, 1993

NEW YORK 2016A
Fever Within: The Art of Ronald Lockett, exh. cat., American Folk Art Museum, New York, 2016

NEW YORK 2016B
William R. Ferris, *James 'Son Ford' Thomas: The Devil and His Blues*, exh. cat., 80WSE Gallery, New York, 2016

NEW YORK 2018
My Soul Has Grown Deep: Black Art from the American South, exh. cat., The Metropolitan Museum of Art, New York, 2018

RICHMOND 2019
Cosmologies from the Tree of Life: Art from the African American South, exh. cat., Virginia Museum of Fine Arts, Richmond, Virginia, 2019

SAN FRANCISCO 2017
Revelations: Art from the African American South, exh. cat., Fine Arts Museums of San Francisco, 2017

SLOMINSKI 2022
Lisa Slominski, *Nonconformers: A New History of Self-taught Artists*, New Haven and London, 2022

TORTORELLO 2013
Michael Tortorello, 'Scrap-Iron Elegy', *New York Times*, 24 April 2013, https://www.nytimes.com/2013/04/25/garden/ joe-minters-african-village-in-america.html.

WALHMAN 2001
Maude Wahlman, *Signs and Symbols: African Images in African-American Quilts*, Atlanta, 2001

WASHINGTON 1982
Jane Livingstone, *Black Folk Art in America, 1930–1980*, exh. cat., Corcoran Gallery of Art, Washington DC, 1982

WERTKIN 2004
Gerard C. Wertkin, *Encyclopaedia of American Folk Art*, New York, 2004

Photographic Acknowledgements

All works of art are reproduced by kind permission of the owners. Every attempt has been made to trace copyright holders. We apologise for any inadvertent infringement and invite appropriate rights holders to contact us. Specific acknowledgements are as follows:

Photo credits
© Matt Arnett: p. 130 (left). Birmingham, Ala. Public Library Archives: p. 131 (right). Marie Catalano: cats 43, 45, 46. Chapel Hill, Southern Folklife Collection at Wilson Special Collections Library, University of North Carolina: figs 3, 10–12 (photo: © William S. Arnett), 7 (photo: William R. Ferris); pp. 125 (right), 126 (left), 127 (centre, right), 129 (centre), 132 (centre, right), 133 (right) (photo: © William S. Arnett); p. 134 (left) (photo: William R. Ferris); p. 135 (left) (photo: Robert Arnett). © Roy Craven: p. 122 (left). © Ted Degener: p. 124 (centre). © Timothy Duffy: p. 128 (left). © Larry Hilton: p. 129 (left). © Gerald Jones: pp. 124 (right), 128 (right), 134 (right). London, Zabludowicz Collection: cat. 20 (photo: Will Amlot). Roger Manley: pp. 126 (right), 130 (right). Miami Herald: fig. 13. Colby Rabon: fig. 1. Richmond, © Virginia Museum of Fine Arts: cat. 6 (photo: Travis Fullerton). © Scala/Dig. Image MoMA, New York: fig. 9. © James Smith Pierce: p. 122 (centre). Ron Lee/The Silver Factory: cat. 32. © George Snyder: p. 133 (left). Stephen Pitkin/Pitkin Studio: figs 2, 4–6, 8, 14; cats 1–5, 7–19, 21–31, 33–42, 44, 47–52, 54, 58–64; pp. 122 (right), 123, 128 (centre), 129 (right). © David Raccuglia: pp. 125 (left), 127 (left), 131 (left, centre), 135 (right). Maciej Urbanek: cats 53, 55–57

Additional copyright
Jesse Aaron © The estate of Jesse Aaron: cat. 42. Eldren M. Bailey © The estate of Eldren M. Bailey: cat. 49. Mary Lee Bendolph © ARS, NY and DACS, London 2023: fig. 4; cat 12. Loretta Pettway Bennett © ARS, NY and DACS, London 2023: cat. 62. Hawkins Bolden © ARS, NY and DACS, London 2023: cat. 37. Richard Burnside © The estate of Richard Burnside: cat. 28. Archie Byron © ARS, NY and DACS, London 2023: cat. 38. Richard Dial © ARS, NY and DACS, London 2023: cat. 11. Thornton Dial © 2023 Estate of Thornton Dial / Artists Rights Society (ARS), New York / DACS, London 2023: fig. 2; cats 1–9. Thornton Dial, Jr. © ARS, NY and DACS, London 2023: cat. 10. Sam Doyle © The estate of Sam Doyle: cat. 29. Rachel Carey George © Estate of Rachel Carey George / DACS 2023: cat. 58. Ralph Griffin © ARS, NY and DACS, London 2023: cats 40, 41. Bessie Harvey © The estate of Bessie Harvey: cat. 39. Lonnie Holley © 2023 Lonnie Holley / Artists Rights Society (ARS), New York / DACS, London: fig. 5; cats 15–20. Marlene Bennett Jones © 2023 Marlene Bennett Jones / Artists Rights Society (ARS), New York / DACS, London: fig. 14; cat. 63. Joe Light © ARS, NY and DACS, London 2023: cats 30, 31. Ronald Lockett © ARS, NY and DACS, London 2023: fig. 3; cats 13, 14. Charlie Lucas © Charlie Lucas: cat. 50. Joe Minter © ARS, NY and DACS, London 2023: figs 1, 11; cats 51, 52. Flora Moore © Flora Moore / ARS, NY and DACS, London 2023: cat. 61. John B. Murray © ARS, NY and DACS, London 2023: cat. 33. Essie Bendolph Pettway © ARS, NY and DACS, London 2023: cat. 64. Loretta Pettway © 2023 Loretta Pettway / Artists Rights Society (ARS), New York / DACS, Lon-don: cat. 60. Martha Jane Pettway © Estate of Martha Jane Pettway / ARS, NY and DACS, London 2023: cat. 59. Robert Rauschenberg © Robert Rauschenberg Foundation/VAGA at ARS, NY and DACS, London 2023: fig. 9. Nellie Mae Rowe © ARS, NY and DACS, London 2023: cats 47, 48. Georgia Speller © The estate of Georgia Speller: cat. 26. Henry Speller © The estate of Henry Speller: cat. 27. Mary T. Smith © ARS, NY and DACS, London 2023: fig. 12; cats 21–23. Jimmy Lee Sudduth © The estate of Jimmy Lee Sudduth: cats 34–36. James 'Son Ford' Thomas © The estate of James 'Son Ford' Thomas: fig. 7; cats 43–46; p. 134 (left). Mose Tolliver © Estate of Mose Tolliver / DACS 2023: cats 24, 25. Charles Williams © The estate of Charles Williams: cat. 32. Purvis Young © 2023 The Larry T. Clemons Collection / Artists Rights Society (ARS), New York: fig. 13; cats 53–57

Index

Supporters of the Royal Academy

THE PRESIDENT'S CIRCLE
Blavatnik Family Foundation
Bloomberg Philanthropies
Mrs Linda Brownrigg
The Clore Duffield Foundation
Mervyn and Jeanne Davies
The Dorfman Foundation
Dunard Fund
Mrs Drue Heinz Hon DBE
Mr and Mrs Jungels-Winkler
Mrs Gabrielle Jungels-Winkler
Ronald and Rita McAulay
The McLennan Family
Sir John Madejski OBE DL
The Mead Family Foundation
Mr and Mrs Robert Miller
The Monument Trust
National Lottery Heritage Fund
Julia and Hans Rausing
The Rothschild Foundation
Dame Jillian Sackler DBE
The Garfield Weston Foundation
The Maurice Wohl Charitable Foundation
The Wolfson Foundation

MAJOR BENEFACTORS
The Band Trust
Ambassador Matthew Barzun and Brooke Brown Barzun
Aryeh and Elana Bourkoff, LionTree
Sir Francis and the Hon Lady Brooke
Mrs Linda Brownrigg
The Cadogan Charity
Sir Richard and Lady Carew Pole
Chenevière Travel Award
Adrian Cheng
Jeremy Coller Foundation
John and Gail Coombe
Sir Roger de Grey Memorial Fund
Lady Alison Deighton
Sir Harry Djanogly
The Eranda Rothschild Foundation
The Fidelity UK Foundation
The Foyle Foundation
J Paul Getty Jr Charitable Trust
Glenbevan Trust
Mrs Grete Goldhill
Horace W Goldsmith Foundation
Mr and Mrs Gounaris-Milner
Peter Greenham Fund
Mr and Mrs Jim Grover
The Alexis and Anne-Marie Habib Foundation
Charles and Kaaren Hale
E Vincent Harris Fund
The Kirby Laing Foundation
Nicolette and Frederick Kwok
Lord Leverhulme's Charitable Trust
Christian Levett and Mougins Museum of Classical Art
The Linbury Trust
Miss Rosemary Lomax Simpson
Mr William Loschert
Molly Lowell and David Borthwick Maintenance Fund
Philip and Valerie Marsden
The 29th May 1961 Charitable Trust
The Lord Mayor's Appeal
The Paul Mellon Estate
Milner Educational Trust
The Batia and Idan Ofer Family Foundation
Christina Ong
Mr and Mrs James Paradise
The Estate of the late Miss Constance-Anne Parker
J Heritage Peters
P F Charitable Trust
The late Mr John Porter
Ivor Rey Scholarship Fund
Sir Simon and Lady Robertson
Schools Portfolio Fund
The Schroder Foundation
Mr Sean Scully RA
Jake and Hélène Marie Shafran
Mr Richard S Sharp
Dasha Shenkman
William and Maureen Shenkman
The Estate of the late Mrs Pauline Sitwell Starr Fund
David and Deborah Stileman
The Swire Charitable Trust
The late Sir Anthony Tennant and Lady Tennant
The Thompson Family Charitable Trust
Patricia Turner Award
Vandaleur
Sir Siegmund Warburg's Voluntary Settlement
The Welton Foundation
Mr W Galen Weston and the Hon Mrs Hilary Weston

BENEFACTORS
Aldama Foundation
Lord and Lady Aldington
Mrs Allen-Huxley
Joan and Robin Alvarez
The Anson Charitable Trust
Artists Collecting Society
The Band Trust
Veronica and Lars Bane
Ms Linda Bennett and Mr Philip Harley
Sir Win Bischoff
Charlotte Bonham-Carter Charitable Trust
The William Brake Charitable Trust

The Deborah Loeb Brice Foundation
The Consuelo and Anthony Brooke Charitable Trust
Garvin and Steffanie Brown
Mr and Mrs John Burns
Ilaria Bulgari
Peter and Sally Cadbury
Carew Pole Charitable Trust
Dr Edmund Carter
Mr Richard Chang
Sir Trevor and Lady Susan Chinn
CHK Foundation
Mr and Mrs Jonathan Clarke
Mr Andrés Clase
The John S Cohen Foundation
Ms Elizabeth Crain
Crankstart
Mr Michael Cowper
The Manny and Brigitta Davidson Charitable Trust
Ina De and James Spicer
The Roger De Haan Charitable Trust
Ron Dennis
The Gilbert and Eileen Edgar Foundation
The John Ellerman Foundation
Mr Richard Elman
Epson
The Lord Faringdon Charitable Trust
Mr and Mrs Stephen Fitzgerald
Mrs Jill Garcia
Mr and Mrs M Gee
Genesis Foundation
The Golden Bottle Trust
Nicholas and Judith Goodison's Charitable Settlement
Antony Gormley and Vicken Parsons
Mr Stephen Gosztony
The late Sir Ronald Grierson
Sir Nicholas Grimshaw CBE PPRA
Fiona and Peter Hare
Hauser & Wirth
Ms Katrin Henkel
Mr and Mrs Julian Heslop
Holbeck Charitable Trust
The Charles Michael Holloway Charitable Trust
Mr and Mrs Jeremy Hosking
Huo Family Foundation (UK)
Harry Hyman and family
The Inchcape Foundation
Japanese Committee of Honour of the
    Royal Academy of Arts
Chantal Joffe RA
Alistair D K Johnston CMG FCA
Mr Ivan Katzen
Mr Lagrange and Mr Burnough
Christopher Le Brun PPRA and Charlotte Verity
The David Lean Foundation
Mr Nelson Leong
Mr and Mrs Mark Loveday
The Maccabaeans
Dr Lee MacCormick Edwards Charitable Foundation
Mrs McAlpine
HRH Princess Marie-Chantal of Greece
J P Marland Charitable Trust
The Rt Hon the Lord and Lady Marland
The David Ellis Marlow Trust
The late Mr Minoru Mori Hon KBE and Mrs Mori
Sir Michael Moritz
The Murray Family
Lady Alison Myners
Normanby Charitable Trust
Dr and Mrs Orentreich
Mr Charles Outhwaite
PF Charitable Trust
Stanley Picker Charitable Trust
The Pilgrim Trust
Mr and Mrs Maurice Pinto
The Earl and Countess of Plymouth
The Polonsky Foundation
Mrs Tineke Pugh
Red Butterfly Foundation
The Estate of the late Mr Ivor Rey
Peter Rippon
Sir Simon and Victoria, Lady Robey OBE
Richard and Ruth Rogers
The Rose Foundation
Sir Paul and Lady Ruddock
The Basil Samuel Charitable Trust
Mrs Coral Samuel CBE
Edwina Sassoon
Guy Senior, in memory of Brian and Mary Senior,
    Friends of the RA
Louisa Service OBE
David and Sophie Shalit
Archie Sherman Charitable Trust
Mr Brian Smith
Mr Christopher Smith
Sir Paul and Lady Smith
The South Square Trust
Mr and Mrs Roger Staton
Sir Hugh and Lady Stevenson
The Nina and Roger Stewart Charitable Trust
Mr John Studzinski
The late Sir David Tang KBE
Tavolozza Foundation
Tileyard London
Julian and Louisa Treger
Tresidor Investment Management
Celia Walker Art Foundation

Martin and Anja Weiss
Sian and Matthew Westerman
Chris Wilkinson OBE RA and Diana Edmunds
Mr Peter Williams
Ivor and Caroline Windsor
The Harold Hyam Wingate Foundation
Manuela and Iwan Wirth
The Lennox and Wyfold Foundation
Mr Yuzo Yagi
and those who wish to remain anonymous

**MAJOR BENEFACTORS TOWARDS REDEVELOPING
THE RA SCHOOLS**
The Band Trust
Adrian Cheng
Lady Alison Deighton
Dunard Fund
Mrs Gabrielle Jungels-Winkler
Nicolette and Frederick Kwok
The Mead Family Foundation
Milner Educational Trust
The Estate of the late Miss Constance-Anne Parker
Julia and Hans Rausing
Jake and Hélène Marie Shafran
Sir Siegmund Warburg's Voluntary Settlement
The Garfield Weston Foundation

**MAJOR BENEFACTORS OF THE RA SCHOOLS
ENDOWMENT FUND**
Chenevière Travel Award
Sir Roger de Grey Memorial Fund
Dunard Fund
The Eranda Rothschild Foundation
Peter Greenham Fund
E Vincent Harris Fund
J Heritage Peters Maintenance Fund
Ronald and Rita McAulay
Ivor Rey Scholarship Fund
Schools Portfolio Fund
The Estate of the late Mrs Pauline Sitwell
Starr Fund
Patricia Turner Award
Vandaleur

BENEFACTORS OF THE RA SCHOOLS
Artists Collecting Society
Charlotte Bonham-Carter Charitable Trust
John S Cohen Foundation
Ron Dennis
Dreamchasing
Dunard Fund
The Gilbert and Eileen Edgar Foundation
Epson
The Eranda Rothschild Foundation
Peter Greenham Fund
The Charles Michael Holloway Charitable Trust
Mr Nelson Leong
Leverhulme Trust
Mr and Mrs Mark Loveday
The Maccabaeans
Dr Lee MacCormick Edwards Charitable Foundation
The Machin Foundation
The Normanby Charitable Trust
The Batia and Idan Ofer Family Foundation
Andrés Olow Clase
Christina Ong
Mr and Mrs James Paradise
Stanley Picker Charitable Trust
Red Butterfly Foundation
The Estate of the late Mr Ivor Rey
Peter Rippon
Bianca Roden
The Rose Foundation
Archie Sherman Charitable Trust
The South Square Trust
Sir Paul and Lady Smith
The Stewarts Foundation
David and Deborah Stileman
The Adrian Swire Charitable Trust
The Swire Charitable Trust
Tileyard London
Celia Walker Art Foundation
and those who wish to remain anonymous

PATRONS

CHAIR OF RA PATRONS
Mr Matthew Langton

INTERNATIONAL CIRCLE
Mrs Niloufar Bakhtiar-Bakhtiar Mr Lars Bane
Mr Alexander Green
Ms Bella Kesovan
Ms Ida Levine
Mr Nick Loup
Mr Sebastien Mazella di Bosco
Gaukhar Nurgalieva
Mr Thaddaeus Ropac
Yukiko and Anders U Schroeder
Antigone Theodorou & Stefan Bollinger Ms Chizuko
    Yashiro
Mr and Mrs Basil Zirinis
Ms Mercedes Zobel
and those who wish to remain anonymous

PLATINUM PATRONS
Tim Ashley
Celia and Edward Atkin CBE
Paul Baines
Mr Christopher Bake
Alex Beard and Emma Vernetti
The Deborah Loeb Brice Foundation
Mrs Sophie Diedrichs-Cox
Mrs Willemien Downes
Hugo Eddis
Mr Stephen Gosztony
Mr and Mrs Jim Grover
Mrs Margaret Guitar
Charles and Kaaren Hale
Mr Yan Huo
Mrs Elizabeth Lenz
Mr Nick Loup
Lady Alison Myners
Mrs Bianca Roden
Jake and Hélène Marie Shafran
Mr Howard Shore
Mr Peter Williams
and those who wish to remain anonymous

GOLD PATRONS
Mr Stephen Allcock
Mrs Spindrift Al Swaidi
Joan and Robin Alvarez
Ms Vanessa Aubry
Sam and Rosie Berwick
Richard Bram and Monika Machon
Molly Lowell Brothwick
Sir Francis Brooke Bt
Mr Thomas E Cantwell
Ms Lisa Carrodus
Margherita Castellani
Varun and Emma Chandra
Ms Natasha Cheung
Mr Andrés Clase
The Lady Renwick of Clifton
Maria Cristina Codognato
Christopher and Alex Courage
Dr Juli Crocombe
Kate de Rothschild Agius and Marcus Agius CBE
Susan Elliott
Swag and Nupur Ganguly
Mrs Carol Gibson Jackson
Mr Stephen Griggs
Mr Jim Grover
Mr Joshua Harris
Rosalyn and Hugo Henderson
Dame Vivian Hunt
Mr Kevin Kane
Sir and Lady Khalili
Ms Maxine Kohn
Sir Sydney Lipworth KC and Lady Lipworth CBE
Ms Olena Lutsenko
Mr Nicholas Maclean
Scott and Laura Malkin
Mr Stephen Marquardt
Louise Nathanson
Simon and Sabi North
Asta Paulauskaite
Paulo and Caroline Pereira
Mr Stuart Piercy
Mrs Ivetta Rabinovich
Ms Melanie Rademacher
Lady Rayne Lacey
Dianne Roberts
Mr Richard Simmons CBE
Tim and Lynda Smith
Jane Spack
Mrs Raksha Sriram
Mr Michael Stiff
David and Deborah Stileman
Mr Robert Suss
Kathryn Uhde
Miss M L Ulfane
Countess Cornelia Von Rittberg
Erica Wax
Mr Neil Westreich
Mr Peter Williams
Mrs Janet Winslow
Manuela and Iwan Wirth
David Yates and Yvonne Walcott Yates
Mr Robert John Yerbury
Mr Riccardo Zacconi
and those who wish to remain anonymous

SILVER PATRONS
Ms Ruth Anderson
Mr John Attree
Mrs Leslie Bacon
Mrs Ginny Battcock
Catherine Baxendale
Mr and Mrs Jonathan and Sarah Bayliss
Mrs J K M Bentley, Liveinart
Ms Sara Bianchi
Mr Bollinger
Ms Miel de Botton
Eleanor E Brass
Viscountess Bridgeman
Mrs Basia Briggs
Mrs Marcia Brocklebank
Mrs Charles Brown
Mr Jack Burgess

Ms Debra Burt
Mrs Ann Chapman-Daniel
Sir Trevor and Lady Chinn
Damian and Anastasia Chunilal
Mr John Clappier
Mrs Jane Clark
Rosalind Clayton
Denise Cohen Charitable Trust
Sir Ronald and Lady Cohen
Andrew M Coppel, CBE and June V Coppel
Cathy Corbett
Edmund Coulthard
Mrs Caroline Cullinan
Monica and Knut Dahl
Mrs Georgina David
Mr Daniel Davies
Mrs Dominic Dowley
Mr and Mrs Jim Downing
Ms Noreen Doyle
Mrs Maurice Dwek
Mrs Marianna E Simpson
Mrs Samira Govers-El Hachioui
Mr and Mrs Jeff Eldredge
Susan Elliott
Mr David Fawkes
S Isern-Feliu
Mrs Stroma Finston
James Freedman
Virginia Gabbertas
Mr Stephen Garrett
Jacqueline and Jonathan Gestetner
The Hon Piers and Mrs Gibson
Caroline and Alan Gillespie
Mr Mark Glatman
David Godwin
Peter and Elizabeth Goulds, L.A. Louvre
Lady Amanda Gowing
John Gruzelier, Professor Emeritus
Ms Kim Habraken
Alex Haidas and Thalia Chryssikou
Mr Christopher Harrison
Mrs Sarah Harvey-Collicott
Sir John and Lady Hegarty
Sir Michael and Lady Heller
Mrs Katrin Henkel
Mrs Pat Heslop
Mr and Mrs Jonathan Hindle
Mrs Susan Hitchin
Anne Holmes-Drewry
Mr Philip Hudson
Mr and Mrs Jon Hunt
Mrs Caroline Jackson
Sir Martin and Lady Jacomb
Mr Tom Jacomb
Mrs Raymonde Jay
Fiona Johnstone
Mrs Marcelle Joseph
Mrs Ghislaine Kane
Dr Elisabeth Kehoe
Mrs Kit Kemp MBE
Paul and Susie Kempe
Miss Rebecca Kemsley
Simon and Emma Keswick
Mr Gerald Kidd
Mr and Mrs James Kirkman
Mrs Anna Kirrage
Mrs Aboudi Kosta
Mrs Alkistis Koukouliou
Mr and Mrs Herbert Kretzmer
Mr Matthew Langton
Ms Isabella Lauder-Frost
Jessica Lavooy
Ms Patricia Lawrie
Mrs Anna Lee
Lady Lever of Manchester
Richard Burger and Rachel Lipson
Mr Jeremy and Dr Julie Llewelyn
Miss R Lomax-Simpson
Mr and Mrs Robin Lough
Mr George Maher
Olivier and Priscilla Malingue
Mr Richard Mansell-Jones
Mrs Janet Martin
Gillian McIntosh
Andrew and Judith McKinna
Itxaso Mediavilla-Murray
Victoria Miro
Shalini Misra
Simon Morris and Annalisa Burello
Mr Alan Morton
Mr Blair Morton
Mrs Alexandra Nash
Mrs Tessa Nicholson
Patrick and Bénédicte de Nonneville
Thomas de Noronha e Silva
Emma O'Donoghue
Flavia Ormond
Mrs Harriet O'Rourke
Neil Osborn and Holly Smith
Sir Michael Palin
Maria N Peacock
Mr and Mrs D J Peacock
The Hon Julian Phillimore
Mr Adam and Mrs Michelle Plainer
Mary Pollock
Lady Purves

Mr William Ramsay
Ms Mouna Rebeiz
Peter Rice Esq
Erica Roberts
Miss Elaine Rowley
Sir Paul and Lady Ruddock
Sarah Ryan
Mrs Janice Sacher
Ms Kim Samuel
Mrs Sirkka Sanderson
Mr Paul Sandilands
Mr Adrian Sassoon
Christina, Countess of Shaftesbury
Mr Robert N Shapiro
Mr David Shaw
Ms Elena Shchukina
Dr Shirley Sherwood OBE
Skarstedt Gallery
Mrs Jane Smith
Lady Henrietta St George
Mr Marc St John
Miss Sarah Straight
Mrs Ziona Strelitz
Ms Catherine Sutton
Mr Matt Symonds
Anne Elizabeth Tasca
Mr Anthony J Todd
Mrs Kirsten Tofte Jensen
Maria Toxavidi
Mrs Narmali Utley
Ms Roxane Vacca
Mrs Madhavi Vadera
Petri & Jolana Vainio
Tamara Varga
Mr Waqas Wajahat
Mrs Charlotte Warshaw
John and Carol Wates
The Duke and Duchess of Wellington
Ms Christine Westwood-Davis
Mrs Adriana Winters
Marek and Penny Wojciechowski
Mr and Mrs Maurice Wolridge
David Zwirner
and those who wish to remain anonymous

YOUNG PATRONS
Kalita Al Swaidi
Mr Eduardo Alves
Daniel Boehm
Mr Nicholas Bonsall
The Breathe Project
Ariana Brighenti
Mr Matthew Charlton
XiaoMeng Cheng
Sophie Dickson
Dr Brian Fu
Rebecca Glenapp
Miss Lucy von Goetz
Adam Gordon
Miss Lemara Grant
Miss Amelia Hunton
Mr Phoebus Istavrioglu
Peter Jones
Miss Min Kemp
Mr Callum Kempe
Sergey Kozlov
Miss Matilda Liu
Mrs Louisa Macmillan
Christina Makris
Mr Jean-David Malat
Patrick McCrae
Miss Yekaterina Munk
Mr Thomas Mustier
Miss Mimi Nguyen
Mr Gaudenz Probst
Ms Julie Scotto
Fazilet Seçgin
Irene Sieberger
Lily Stone
Gigi Surel
The Honourable Clarence Tan
Mr Milan Tomic
Miss Ayse Unluturk
and those who wish to remain anonymous

PATRON DONORS
Geoffrey Ainsworth and Johanna Featherstone
The William Brake Foundation
The Breathe Project
Dr Bruce Horten
Mr D H Killick
The de Laszlo Foundation
The Michael and Nicola Sacher Charitable Trust
Jake and Hélène Marie Shafran
Melanie and Michael Sherwood Charitable Foundation
Mr and Mrs Anthony Williams
Ms Cynthia Wu
and those who wish to remain anonymous